Studies in Rhetorics and Feminisms

Series Editors, Cheryl Glenn and Shirley Wilson Logan

Regendering Delivery

REGENDERING DELIVERY

The Fifth Canon and Antebellum Women Rhetors

Lindal Buchanan

Southern Illinois University Press
Carbondale

Library of Congress Cataloging-in-Publication Data
   Buchanan, Lindal, date.
   Regendering delivery : the fifth canon and antebellum
women rhetors / Lindal Buchanan.
      p. cm. — (Studies in rhetorics and feminisms)
   Includes bibliographical references and index.
      1. Oratory—United States—History—19th century.
2. Women orators—United States—Biography.
3. Elocution. I. Title. II. Series.
PN4055.U53W663 2005
808.5'1'0820973—dc22
ISBN 0-8093-2657-4 (cloth : alk. paper)
ISBN 0-8093-2658-2 (pbk. : alk. paper)   2005006771

For my daughter, Fairfax

Contents

Illustrations

Acknowledgments

I owe thanks to many people for their help and support over the course of this project. First and foremost, my appreciation goes to Carol Mattingly, who has from this work's inception responded to my drafts and ideas, shared her insights into nineteenth-century women's rhetoric, inspired me with her own research, and provided encouragement every step of the way. She is a jewel. I am also grateful for E. Jennifer Monaghan's great kindness. She, too, has graciously shared her expertise in the history of literacy, her impeccable research and writing abilities, and her teaching and publication experiences with me to my great benefit. Carol and Jennifer are stellar role models, and I am indebted to them both.

Others contributed along the way as well. Nan Johnson—in an impromptu discussion one year at CCCC about the intersections of feminism, the body, and delivery—helped me to identify key issues early on. Many individuals provided guidance or feedback on early drafts of this material: Nicole Pepinster Greene, John Greene, Janet Richards, Keith Dorwick, Mary Ann Wilson, and Mary Farmer Kaiser. Cheryl Glenn and Shirley Wilson Logan, editors of the Studies in Rhetorics and Feminisms Series, kept the revision suggestions coming and thus advanced the manuscript's development. Catherine Hobbs, reader for Southern Illinois University Press, likewise offered very useful advice. I also appreciate the assistance of Karl Kageff, Kristine Priddy, Carol Burns, and Barb Martin at the press and the sharp eyes of copyeditor Mary Lou Kowaleski. Finally, my thanks go to Greg Clark, editor of *Rhetoric Society Quarterly*, for permission to revise and reprint two articles: "Forging and Firing Thunderbolts: Collaboration and Women's Rhetoric," 33 (2003): 43–63 and "Regendering Delivery: The Fifth Canon and the Maternal Rhetor," 32 (2002): 51–73.

Throughout this project, I have benefited from institutional assistance. Kettering University's generous support of junior faculty has been invaluable as has interlibrary-loan wizard Bruce Deitz's help, which makes my research so much easier. The University of Louisiana's fellowship and award monies during this work's inception as a dissertation are appreciated as well.

On a personal level, I owe thanks to a great many friends and family members. My parents Buck and Rochelle Buchanan, sister Colleen, and brothers Bruce and Brett provided rest and relaxation, encouragement and laughter along the way. In addition to sharing meals and conversation, my dear friends Carolyn Pastel Anderson, Paul Butler, Diane Dewolley, Fairfax Ewing, Leslie Moise, Sue Patton, and Denise Stodola listened, empathized, advised, and, occasionally, collaborated in order to help me juggle maternal and professional obligations. Finally, I acknowledge my daughter Fairfax, whose presence has motivated, patience sustained, and understanding upheld me throughout this long process. I hope that the remarkable women I describe within will motivate, sustain, and inspire her in return.

Regendering Delivery

Introduction
Gender and Rhetorical Delivery

When Lucy Stone began lecturing for the American Anti-Slavery Society in 1848, she plunged into a hectic touring schedule that often required her to make "six speeches in five different towns" within a single week (Kerr 50). In the course of these talks, Stone and other antislavery agents routinely confronted rowdy and hostile crowds, whose antics ranged from throwing hymn books, eggs, pepper, and tobacco plugs at speakers to tarring and feathering them. Therefore, for the sake of survival, antislavery agents learned to read and handle audiences adeptly, an ability at which Stone excelled as an incident from one of her early speaking tours suggests.

Stone was participating in an open-air antislavery meeting in Cape Cod, Massachusetts, when an angry mob gathered, "looking so black and ugly, and so evidently meaning mischief, that the speakers one by one got down from the platform and quietly slipped away," all, that is, but Stone and fellow agent Stephen Foster (Blackwell 80). As the throng grew increasingly antagonistic, petite, one-hundred-pound Stone urged Foster to run and save himself, assuring him that she would be fine:

> At that moment, the mob made a rush, and one of the ringleaders, a big man with a club in his hand, sprang up on the platform. Lucy turned to him and said, without hesitation, "This gentleman will take care of me." It touched his feelings, and he declared that he would. Taking her upon one arm, and holding his club in the other hand, he started to march her out through the mob, who were roughly handling Mr. Foster, and such of the other speakers as they had been able to catch. On the way, she talked to him; and presently he mounted her on a stump, and stood by her with his club while she addressed the mob. She made them so ashamed of themselves that they not only desisted from further violence, but took up a collection of twenty dollars on the spot, to pay

1

Mr. Foster for his coat, which they had torn in two from top to bottom, half of them hauling him one way and half the other. (Blackwell 80–81)

Stone wields the rhetoric of gender to defuse a dangerous situation. She uses the term *gentleman* and thereby elicits chivalrous behavior, places her hand on her assailant's elbow and thereby invites protection, converses steadily with the mobster-turned-bodyguard, and thereby creates connection. Then, with his assistance, she repositions the speaker's platform and addresses the crowd from a tree stump. This incident includes a remarkable series of negotiations involving gender and discursive performance, but if we try to analyze it via the fifth rhetorical canon, the most interesting aspects of the event—namely, Stone's strategic use of gender norms and deployment of space—must go unaddressed because they are not conventionally recognized as components of delivery.

The traditional fifth canon—variously described as *hypokrisis*, elocution, and delivery over the centuries—examines how orators convey their messages in terms of volume and tone, rhythm and speed, gesture, movement, and expression. In particular, the fifth canon focuses on two distinct facets of rhetorical presentation: *pronuntiatio*, the vocal elements of delivery, and *actio*, the gestural. Vocal considerations might include the proper pronunciation of vowels and consonants, the correct accentuation of syllables, the appropriate emphasis of words and phrases, the effective use of pauses or stops, the distinction between vocal tone and key, and the proper management of the voice. Gestural considerations, on the other hand, might address how facial expression, physical positioning, posture, and movement convey emotion or construct ethos. Although *pronuntiatio* and *actio* are certainly central to any study of delivery, rhetorical performance involves additional issues and concerns as well that the traditional fifth canon simply does not acknowledge.

For example, although the physical and vocal concerns of delivery initially appear relevant to all public speakers, closer scrutiny of the canon soon reveals masculinist biases and assumptions. Delivery has not pertained equally to both men and women because, for millennia, women were culturally prohibited from standing and speaking in public, their voices and forms acceptable only in the spectator role (if at all). Thus, women were systematically discouraged from the very actions that constitute delivery, a matter unrecognized in the traditional fifth canon. Because of women's exclusion from the public sphere, the canon only needed to address masculine issues of rhetorical performance. Once seventeenth-, eighteenth-, and nineteenth-century women began to defy convention and address audiences in religious, theatrical, and civic settings, female speakers discovered powerful undercurrents at play in public spaces. Women rhetors, for instance, automatically incurred suspicions of sexual and moral impropriety, suspicions that did *not* routinely plague male speakers; however, the social and ideological forces that shaped women's rhetorical performances are, again, not recognized in the traditional fifth canon. Indeed, I would argue that when researchers' attention is focused too narrowly on the voice, gesture, and expression of the good woman speaking well, much that is germane to her delivery is overlooked. Clearly, the traditional fifth canon is in need of renovation.

I suggest we begin the task by recognizing that rhetorical delivery is a socially situated act and that the surrounding context exerts enormous pressure on the speaker, imposing constraints, affording compensating strategies, and establishing audience expectations. Change the speaker, change the space, change the time period, and the surrounding constraints, strategies, and expectations change, too. Delivery involves far more than a speaker's use of voice, gesture, and expression on a public platform; it involves complex interplay among a speaker, an audience, and a plethora of social and ideological factors. Roxanne Mountford reaches a similar conclusion in *The Gendered Pulpit: Preaching in American Protestant Spaces* (2003), her study of three contemporary women ministers:

> Delivery involves space, the body, and the place of both in the social imaginary. Delivery involves historical concepts of the public and private spheres. As an art, delivery is creative, progressive, active, mobile; it promotes and reflects relationships. . . . Delivery is based in and on cultural norms and the breaking of those norms. (152)

It follows, then, that since a speaker's delivery unfolds in social surroundings, her performance should be read in relation to them.

Positioning delivery in a particular social and historical context dramatically alters the scope of the fifth canon, which continues to address the speaker's use of voice and body, of course, but also interprets that performance in relation to the larger cultural currents that envelop and affect it. Such analysis necessitates expanding one's focus from the speaker's performance onstage to include offstage elements not normally associated with delivery. Thus, a socially situated fifth canon might examine who is permitted or denied access to the public platform as well as how rhetors obtain an education to prepare for public speaking. It might identify the types of rhetorical constraints imposed upon particular groups in particular contexts as well as the strategies devised by groups to honor, circumvent, or revise those constraints. Additionally, in order to understand the many variables that inform (and are reflected in) an orator's delivery, it might review earlier stages of the rhetorical process, addressing the speaker's strategies of invention, research, drafting, and revision. Finally, it might consider such unconventional rhetorical factors as the behind-the-scenes arrangements needed for nonprivileged groups to reach public platforms in the first place.

Envisioning delivery as socially situated public performance affords scholars a useful site for investigating how a variable like gender (or sexuality, race, religion, nationality, ethnicity, age, class, disability, and so on) affects rhetoric. It also offers them a window for viewing the speaker's performance of gender and rhetoric in relation to a particular social context, which ultimately, of course, involves issues of power. A socially situated fifth canon requires a broader analytical framework, one that encompasses the speaker onstage as well as the setting that surrounds her. Indeed, extending the fifth canon's scope is absolutely essential if scholars hope to understand how gender affects delivery and, consequently, how delivery differs for women and men. Therefore, my analysis will enlarge conventional boundaries around the speaker in order to consider how cultural context, gender conventions, elocutionary education, sexuality, maternity, feminine ethos, rhetorical process, and collaboration inform women's delivery. Although this exploration is wide ranging, I am not suggesting that delivery should be erased as a viable canon or key aspect of public address. A fifth canon grounded in context may at times stray far from the public platform, but it always returns to the speaker as its central interest, interpreting her public performance in relation to surrounding social, cultural, and ideological forces.

My interest in the intersection of gender and delivery was initially piqued by scholarship that uncovered gender biases within the overarching discipline of rhetoric itself, which, until recently, was the undisputed "property of men, particularly men of property" (Connors, *Composition* 24). Feminist scholars first challenged male-centered rhetorical histories by recovering long-neglected women rhetors. Lillian O'Connor's *Pioneer Women Orators: Rhetoric in the Ante-Bellum Reform Movement* (1954), for example, identifies the unique rhetorical obstacles confronting early women rhetors as well as their strategic uses of ethical, logical, and pathetic appeals. Similarly, Karlyn Kohrs Campbell's *Man Cannot Speak for Her: A Critical Study of Early Feminist Rhetoric* (1989) reclaims the primary texts and details the distinctive rhetorical style of American women rhetors.

These landmark studies launched an avalanche of research aimed at recuperating the texts and accomplishments of women speakers. Cheryl Glenn's

Rhetoric Retold: Regendering the Tradition from Antiquity Through the Renaissance (1997) theorizes the need for and demonstrates the potential of regendered rhetorical history through its examination of overlooked figures, from Aspasia and Diotima to Julian of Norwich and Margery Kempe. Particularly germane to my study is the rich and diverse body of work produced by scholars in communication studies, rhetoric, and history examining the public discourse of nineteenth-century American women. A number of important essays highlighting the ingenuity of ante- and postbellum women rhetors have appeared in such edited collections as Catherine Hobbs's *Nineteenth-Century Women Learn to Write* (1995), Andrea Lunsford's *Reclaiming Rhetorica: Women in the Rhetorical Tradition* (1995), Molly Wertheimer's *Listening to Their Voices: The Rhetorical Activities of Historical Women* (1997), and Christine Sutherland and Rebecca Sutcliffe's *Changing Tradition: Women in the History of Rhetoric* (1999). Significant books in this area include Carol Mattingly's *Well-Tempered Women: Nineteenth-Century Temperance Rhetoric* (1998), which details the rhetorical acumen of temperance reformers, including Amelia Bloomer, Frances Willard, and the Woman's Christian Temperance Union. Carla Peterson's *"Doers of the Word": African American Women Speakers and Writers in the North (1830–1880)* (1995), Shirley Wilson Logan's *"We Are Coming": The Persuasive Discourse of Nineteenth-Century Black Women* (1999), and Jacqueline Royster's *Traces of a Stream: Literacy and Social Change among African-American Women* (2000) recover the legacy of African-American women orators and writers and explore how gender intersects with race and class to create a multiplicity of women's rhetorics. Stephen Browne's *Angelina Grimké: Rhetoric, Identity, and the Radical Imagination* (1999) analyzes how the pioneering antebellum lecturer crafted a prophetic identity in order to advance abolition and woman's rights. Feminist historiographers have also begun to challenge conventional definitions of what counts as rhetorical evidence. Nan Johnson's *Gender and Rhetorical Space in American Life, 1866–1910* (2002) studies parlor rhetorics, Carol Mattingly's *Appropriate[ing] Dress: Women's Rhetorical Style in Nineteenth-Century America* (2002) explores women's fashions, and Susan Zaeske's *Signatures of Citizenship: Petitioning, Antislavery, and Women's Political Identity* (2003) details reform women's use of petitioning.[1]

In addition to revising the discipline's historical narratives, feminist scholars have also scrutinized rhetorical precepts through the lens of gender and, whenever necessary, have developed "alternate critical and theoretical frameworks" to reconceptualize them (Campbell, "Consciousness" 51). These feminist revisions of rhetoric have taken a variety of forms. Sonja Foss, Cindy

Griffin, and Karen Foss, for example, have sought to redefine rhetoric, moving away from an agonistic, Aristotelian concentration on discovering available means of persuasion and moving toward an invitational approach that values "feminist principles of equality, immanent value, and self-determination" (31). Another tactic for revising rhetoric consists of identifying the ways in which a universalized or prototypical male speaker inhabits rhetorical precepts and then challenging the resulting assumptions and exclusions. Lisa Ede, Cheryl Glenn, and Andrea Lunsford undertake precisely this project in "Border Crossings: Intersections of Rhetoric and Feminism" (1995). They argue the importance of recasting the five-part classical canon (consisting of invention, arrangement, style, memory, and delivery) by situating a gendered rhetor within a "larger context of personal, social, economic, cultural, and ideological forces," noting whom that context includes and supports as well as whom it excludes and silences (412). Collectively, these fine works provide the foundation upon which mine is built.

Regendering Delivery: The Fifth Canon and Antebellum Women Rhetors contributes to ongoing feminist efforts to revise the history and conceptual groundings of rhetoric by focusing on the changes that occur when a particularly situated woman, rather than a man, delivers public discourse. Nineteenth-century America provides a rich locus for regendering the fifth canon, first, because of the period's deep resistance to women's delivery and, second, because of the large numbers of women who, nevertheless, elected to speak publicly in order to advance social justice and improvement. Although a rhetor can address an audience or deliver a message through oral, textual, or visual means, I concentrate primarily on the first, examining how women used voice, gesture, movement, and expression on public platforms in an antebellum social context.

To trace the contours of a regendered and retheorized fifth canon, I ground my analysis in the rhetorical practices of pioneering American women rhetors, identifying the gender constructs promoted in the surrounding context and examining how speakers honored or modified those constructs in their public performances.[2] In the process, I address a series of questions concerning late-eighteenth- and early-nineteenth-century women. Where, for instance, and when did American women typically learn about elocution? How and where did they hone the skills needed for public speaking? What distinctive styles of delivery did women develop and employ once they began to address civic matters? What unique audience considerations arose when women, rather than men, spoke publicly? How did the body, especially pregnancy, affect women's rhetorical delivery? What kinds of offstage assistance did antebellum women require in order to stand and deliver discourse on public platforms? In a quest for answers to these questions, *Regendering Delivery: The Fifth Canon and Antebellum Women Rhetors* moves chronologically through the life cycle, beginning with schoolgirls in the academy and progressing to mature women rhetors in public and private spaces. Furthermore, it examines the rhetorical practices of a wide variety of American women, including former slaves and social aristocrats, northerners and southerners, religious and secular women.

Chapter 1, "Readers and Rhetors: Schoolgirls' Formal Elocutionary Instruction," challenges conventional wisdom holding that late-eighteenth- and early-nineteenth-century women received no formal elocutionary training because of their exclusion from higher education and the public sphere. Schoolbooks tell a different story. Reading was one of the few nongendered school subjects, and it served as a staple of the curriculum throughout the colonial, early national, and antebellum periods. Therefore, when eighteenth-century reading textbooks began to incorporate elocutionary instruction as well as reading selections, both girls and boys learned formal precepts of delivery. Furthermore, reading selections typically included orations, debates, and declamations, thereby providing schoolgirls with models of civic discourse for imitation, adaptation, and appropriation. Eighteenth-century school readers thus contributed to women's rhetorical education in important ways. In the nineteenth century, however, school readers began to adjust coverage and content according to gender. Readers targeting a male audience continued to cover the full range of elocutionary matter, addressing both *actio* and *pronuntiatio*, while those directed toward female or mixed-sex audiences limited coverage chiefly to *pronuntiatio*. I suggest that gender differences apparent in textbooks' coverage of elocution reflect an educational backlash that developed in response to antebellum women's heightened presence in public forums, a result stemming, in part, from the elocutionary knowledge they had obtained through reading instruction. As the connection between education and women's rhetorical delivery became apparent, institutions and educators modified instructional materials to make full elocutionary knowledge less accessible to schoolgirls.

Chapter 2, "Practicing Delivery: Young Ladies on the Academic Platform," addresses another significant but little studied site of women's rhetorical education. Beginning in the late eighteenth century, schools regularly provided girls and boys opportunities for oral display both in the classroom and at public exhibitions, forums I describe as academic platforms. Typical student exercises included reading compositions, performing dialogues or skits, debating, declaiming, or orating to mixed-sex audiences, and schoolgirls often used these occasions to examine such gender issues as women's education and social roles. Carrying forward the notion of educational backlash examined in chapter 1, I argue that once antebellum women adapted the rhetorical abilities acquired in sanctioned school settings to previously prohibited public venues, controversy increased concerning schoolgirls' performances on academic platforms as well. As women petitioned political bodies for legislative changes, asked the powerful to fund educational and philanthropic projects, organized and directed benevolent and reform associations, lectured to mixed-sex audiences on political topics, and preached in churches and camp meetings, young women's access to academic platforms became more tightly policed. Common school educators debated whether schoolgirls' public displays damaged feminine character while coeducational colleges vacillated over women's participation in mixed-sex rhetoric classes, literary societies, and public exhibitions. Despite widespread institutional resistance, many female students fought for access to academic platforms and, when unsuccessful, created extracurricular venues in which to obtain the elocutionary training and practice they desired.

Chapter 3, "Performing Gender and Rhetoric: 'Feminine' and 'Masculine' Delivery Styles," turns from schoolgirls' acquisition to women's application of elocutionary abilities. As antebellum women emerged as civic rhetors during the 1820s and 1830s, two distinct manners of delivery became apparent. The feminine delivery style was unlikely to challenge or alienate audiences, succeeding through a number of strategies that complemented conventional gender ideals. Women rhetors who employed this style might read their addresses from a seated position or, when addressing large or mixed-sex audiences, sit silently onstage while men delivered their speeches for them. The masculine delivery style, on the other hand, was initially more shocking to spectators. Its practitioners unapologetically stood and spoke directly to listeners of both sexes, thereby embracing a delivery style typically used by men. After contrasting the rhetorical strategies and gender ideals associated with these two manners of delivery, I examine why the feminine style, despite its undeniable success and effectiveness, has been forgotten while the masculine style has been celebrated in historical and canonical treatments of nineteenth-century rhetors. I conclude that the feminine delivery style, although highly unconventional in terms of the traditional fifth canon, merits recognition and acknowledgment within the discipline.

Chapter 4, "Delivering Discourse and Children: The Maternal Difficulty," explores the challenges that public performance posed for women who delivered discourse *and* children, in other words, for those who were both speakers and mothers. Although maternity's shaping force in the lives of nineteenth-century women is well-traveled terrain in history and literary studies, it has largely been ignored in rhetoric. The antebellum maternal rhetor's particular constraints and compensating strategies, however, highlight the ways in which gender affects rhetorical delivery. For example, maternal speakers not only had to negotiate the visual rhetoric of pregnancy on the public platform but also had to reassure the audience that their public appearance did not entail the neglect of either their homes or families, justifications *not* required of paternal speakers. Furthermore, maternal obligations often determined the arc of women's rhetorical careers, sometimes interrupting or delaying them for years or decades. Thus, antebellum women's tandem delivery of children and discourse intersected in complicated ways, and its study can provide insights into gender's impact on rhetorical performance.

Chapter 5, "Forging and Firing Thunderbolts: Collaboration and Women's Delivery," examines the network of behind-the-scenes relationships that surrounded and supported antebellum women rhetors. Although such a framework is unorthodox in studies of the fifth canon, which traditionally focus upon the solitary public speaker, it is necessary if scholars are to do justice to the complexities of women's rhetorical production and delivery in hostile surroundings. Antebellum women collaborated with families, friends, and hired help in order to negotiate conflicting private and public obligations, accommodate gender norms, construct feminine ethos, and create and present public discourse. However, despite collaboration's central importance to women's rhetoric, scholars currently lack a model that can account fully for its many forms, multiple functions, and impressive versatility. This chapter introduces a new model of rhetorical collaboration capable of explaining how and why this cooperative method offers marginalized groups an indispensable means for coming to public voice in resistant settings.

When delivery is reconsidered in the light of antebellum women's experiences, its concerns and contours shift in surprising ways. Traditionally perceived as the most physical, sensory, and material of the classical canons, delivery begins to reveal its social and ideological grounding, which determines masculine and feminine gender ideals and thus shapes public performance. Once we acknowledge that the fifth canon is socially situated, the need to broaden conventional analytical frameworks surrounding the public speaker becomes apparent as well. The book's conclusion outlines the regendered fifth canon and identifies six topoi useful for analyzing socially situated delivery: education for public speaking, access to public platforms, the connotations of delivery in public spaces, the available genres of rhetorical presentation, the challenges and opportunities posed by the body, and typical patterns of oratorical careers. Finally, I suggest how interested scholars might adapt these topoi to study the delivery of differently located women or other disenfranchised groups.

Ultimately, by considering delivery from the vantage point of marginalized rhetors, researchers recognize new dimensions to the canon and thus begin to reconceptualize it, a project that provides a powerful site for feminist analysis and theorizing. A regendered fifth canon addresses who is and is not entitled to stand and speak in public spaces, examines how women educate themselves (formally and informally) for public speaking, identifies the rhetorical strategies developed by women determined to deliver civic discourse despite social prohibitions, and recognizes that gender ideology influences the forms of public expression available to women rhetors. Furthermore, a regendered fifth canon permits feminist scholars to examine the immediate temporal and material issues confronting the rhetor as well as the overarching social and ideological forces enacted, resisted, or revised by her in the act of public speaking.

My efforts to regender delivery and thus incorporate women's experiences into the fifth rhetorical canon represent "a feminist performative act, a commitment to the future of women, a promise that rhetorical histories and theories will eventually and naturally include women" (Glenn, "Regendering" 29). This endeavor, however, is more broadly relevant. By proposing frameworks and theories that can account fully for women's rhetorical experiences, feminist historiographers develop methods adaptable to the study of other nonprivileged groups as well, those who have likewise been excluded because they deviated from rhetoric's rational, masculine, elitist standards. Collectively, our examinations of heretofore unquestioned concepts and traditions can renovate the discipline and create a more comprehensive, complex, and compelling understanding of the history and practice of rhetoric.

1

Readers and Rhetors
Schoolgirls' Formal Elocutionary Instruction

Rhetorical scholars have long assumed that as long as women were prohibited from civic participation, they received little to no formal training
in the arts of public expression. Lillian O'Connor, for example, speculating
on the educational backgrounds of pioneering American women rhetors,
states that "formal training in schools, with few exceptions, was lacking, and
. . . practice in public speaking was for women *anathema*" (230). Such sup-
positions have led scholars to overlook evidence indicating that late-eigh-
teenth- and early-nineteenth-century schoolgirls actually learned about delivery in reading classes and textbooks, which introduced them to basic
principles of elocution as well as models of civic discourse.

The relevance of this instruction is apparent at the outset of Ebenezer
Porter's popular textbook *The Rhetorical Reader* (1831). Porter observes that
the "art of reading well" is of value not only to future orators but also to those
debarred by class or gender from public address:

> The art of reading well is indispensable to one who expects to be a public
> speaker; because the principles on which it depends are the same as those
> which belong to rhetorical delivery in general, and because nearly all bad
> speakers were prepared to be so, by early mismanagement of the voice in
> reading. . . . Of the multitudes who are not called to speak in public, including
> the whole of one sex, and all but comparatively a few of the other, there is no
> one to whom the ability to read in a graceful and impressive manner, may not
> be of great value. In this country, then, where the advantages of education are
> open to all, and where it is a primary object with parents of all classes, to have
> their children well instructed, it would seem reasonable to presume that nearly
> all our youth, of both sexes, must be good readers. (2)

If the same principles of rhetorical delivery apply whether one reads or orates, then it stands to reason that when "youth of both sexes" learn these principles in the course of reading instruction, they are prepared to adapt their elocutionary abilities from reading to public speaking whether they are encouraged to do so or not. Antebellum women did precisely this with the elocutionary education they obtained through reading classes and textbooks like Porter's.

To understand how and why young women learned about delivery, it is important to remember that reading was taught and practiced as an oral rather than a silent skill until nearly the end of the nineteenth century. In fact, Nila Smith's extensive survey of American reading textbooks did not uncover a single reference to silent reading prior to *Webb's Normal Reader, No. 3*, published in 1856 (91). It is also essential to recall that from the colonial period on, reading was one of the few nongendered subjects in the educational curriculum, so children of both sexes were taught to read. Girls' reading instruction proved especially significant as elocutionary material worked its way into American school readers during the eighteenth century, a sign of the growing influence of the British elocutionary movement. Elocutionists like Thomas Sheridan, James Burgh, and John Walker considered effective oral reading to be the first step toward effective oratory, and they recommended teaching children the proper use of voice, gesture, and expression as they learned to read. Thus, eighteenth-century girls and boys studied delivery and civic discourse in their reading classes, a crucial but generally disregarded source of rhetorical education for American women.

School readers provide a rich, if underexamined, site for exploring women's formal elocutionary training. From the genre's beginnings in the late eighteenth century, schoolgirls were recognized as consumers of school readers, which typically consisted of two parts, an introductory section detailing principles of elocution followed by a collection of reading selections for memorization and recitation. This chapter begins by examining three popular eighteenth-century school readers, demonstrating that their reading selections acknowledge a female audience and that their elocutionary chapters introduced that audience to precepts of delivery. It then analyzes three nineteenth-century textbooks directed to male, female, and mixed-sex audiences and uncovers significant differences in the books' contents and coverage of elocution, differences that reflect an educational backlash developing in tandem with antebellum women's increasing rhetorical competence and public presence. As the unanticipated consequences of schoolgirls' reading instruction became apparent—in particular, as women used their academically acquired elocutionary abilities to address civic issues in public spaces—educational materials changed in response. I argue that backlash led to the truncation of the elocutionary coverage and oratorical contents of school readers likely to be consumed by a female audience, an attempt to restrict women's eloquence to the private sphere by limiting their knowledge of the arts of oral expression.

Elocution and Reading Instruction

Gender has always had an enormous impact on education, determining women's access to formal schooling and to the curriculum itself. Therefore, the status of women's education and its correlation to changing gender ideology are interwoven throughout this chapter's discussion of reading instruction and textbooks. In this section, I review the typical course of literacy instruction in the Northeast during the colonial period.

Children between the ages of three and seven generally obtained their early education either at home or at dame schools, nursery schools run by neighborhood women who taught reading for a small fee. Children who ended their formal education after dame school usually embarked on some form of work training, boys entering apprenticeships to acquire a trade and girls learning from other women the household arts of producing cloth and sewing clothes; growing, cooking, and preserving food; raising livestock; creating medicines and treating illnesses; cleaning; and child care (McMelland 54–55).

Children who continued their formal education following dame school entered what was essentially a two-tiered school system, the first tier consisting of district schools, the second tier of Latin grammar schools. Both first- and second-tier schools usually received support from surrounding towns, districts, or churches and were attended by children between the ages of six and twelve (Perlmann, Siddali, Whitescarver 124–25). Class as well as gender determined which type of school children attended. Only boys, and for the most part only boys from privileged or ambitious families, attended second-tier grammar schools, where they studied the classical curriculum, consisting of Greek, Latin, advanced mathematics, philosophy, and classical literature. After all, a thorough knowledge of the classical languages was necessary for boys who would go on to college, for Latin remained the language of instruction until the late eighteenth century. First-tier district schools, on the other hand, were reserved for boys destined for the trades or crafts and for girls fortunate enough to pursue additional education. The district school curriculum typically focused on basic English literacy and numeracy skills rather than on the classical languages.[1]

Gender not only influenced the extent of children's education but also determined which subjects they learned. Historically, as Averil McMelland observes, women have always had difficulty accessing and exercising society's most prized forms of knowledge:

> No matter how well they succeeded in acquiring formal education, *women have generally been excluded from whatever education was perceived to be of the most value at any particular time and place.* Education for women has historically been used to separate the spheres in which the sexes operated. One way in which this has been expressed is through the practice of providing women certain kinds of education but denying them the particular kind of education that has been thought to be the special province of men and thus automatically of higher status or value. (13; original emphasis)

Privileged realms of knowledge, including the classical languages and oratory, were culturally coded as masculine and reserved exclusively for boys. During the colonial period, this was also the case with writing instruction, which typically consisted of teaching penmanship and various scripts needed in the workplace. In "Literacy Instruction and Gender in Colonial New England," E. Jennifer Monaghan observes that the "gender bias implicit in the term 'penmanship' was not fortuitous: writing was largely a male domain." This gender bias resulted, in part, from the expense of learning to write. Writing textbooks were imported and, therefore, costly and difficult to obtain, all of which promoted a perception of writing as a special and specialized skill. Because girls were expected to run households rather than conduct business, penmanship was considered an "irrelevant acquisition" for them, and they were taught to sew instead (E. J. Monaghan, "Literacy" 60–64). These gender assumptions regarding the curriculum are reflected in court decisions of the period. In 1655, a Hartford court required administrators of an estate to "educate the children, learning the sons to read and write, and the daughters to read and sew well." Similarly, it ruled in another estate case that "the sons shall have learning to write plainly and read distinctly in the Bible, and the daughters to read and sew sufficiently for the making of their ordinary linen" (qtd. in Woody 1: 144). Thus, gender determined the extent of children's schooling as well as their access to socially valuable forms of knowledge like Latin and composition.

Unlike writing, Protestant theology promoted reading as a necessary skill for all Christians: "The message of Protestantism was that men [and women] could find in Scripture the means to salvation, the keys to good and evil, the rules by which to live, and the standards against which to measure the conduct of prince and pastor" (Cremin 40). Reading instruction was, therefore, suitable for children of both sexes. In 1642, the Massachusetts Bay Colony passed a law mandating that all children be taught to read, a precedent soon followed by neighboring colonies; not until 1771, however, did Massachusetts require that girls as well as boys learn to write (E. J. Monaghan, "Literacy" 62–63). Secular pressures also encouraged both boys and girls to become competent readers. It was common practice for one person to read aloud to others, enabling "those who could not read . . . to participate as listeners to and discussants of texts. Whether the text was a newspaper or a sermon, contact with texts was a collective process rather than the solitary, silent reading we know today" (Keller-Cohen 161). Cultural perceptions of reading as an oral and communal rather than a silent and solitary skill persisted until the dawn of the twentieth century. Because colonial society encouraged effective oral reading for secular and religious reasons, it became a regular feature of the school curriculum and one of the few subjects taught to both girls and boys.[2]

Elocution became a regular component of reading instruction in the late eighteenth century due to the influence of the British elocutionary movement, which had originally developed in response to widespread alarm over poor pulpit oratory and plummeting church attendance. Journalist Richard Steele, for example, who devoted an entire issue of the *Spectator* (18 August 1711, no. 147) to lambasting the sorry state of British oratory, assigned blame for the clergy's inability to read or speak well to schools' misguided emphasis on Latin and neglect of English. The classical curriculum's focus on ancient languages left schoolboys (and, ultimately, clergymen) ignorant of how accent, emphasis, and pronunciation affected oral expression in their native tongue (Howell 154–55). In addition to demonstrating vocal ineptitude, the clergy's poor physical delivery came under fire as well. Jonathan Swift complained of sermons delivered by ministers

> with their heads held down from the beginning to the end within an inch of the cushion to read what is hardly legible; which, beside the untoward manner, hinders them from making the best advantage of their voice: others again have a trick of popping up and down every moment from their paper to the audience, like an idle schoolboy on a repetition day. (qtd. in Guthrie 20)

Again, faulty delivery was due to inadequate schooling, in this case, to poor habits tolerated in the recitation room. Criticisms such as Steele's and Swift's stimulated public interest in elocution.

The first notable spokesman of the British elocutionary movement was Thomas Sheridan, who likewise traced speakers' problems back to the schoolroom:

> Here then is to be found the true source of the bad manner of reading and speaking in public, that so generally prevails: which is, that we are taught to

read in a different way, with different tones and cadences, from those which we use in speaking; and this artificial manner, is used instead of the natural one, in all recitals and repetitions at school, as well as in reading. (4)

Upon graduation, pupils carried this "artificial manner" from school to the pulpit or public platform, the educational system thus propagating generation after generation of poor readers and speakers. However, if the problem's cause was in the schoolroom, so was the cure. Sheridan argued that university students needed to study English and elocution as well as the classical languages. Adding English to the curriculum would produce well-trained schoolmasters prepared not only to teach schoolboys "their native tongue grammatically" but also to model and encourage new standards of eloquence, which Sheridan defined as "the just and graceful management of the voice, countenance, and gesture in speaking" (98, 19). Poor reading instruction might have produced a nation of ineffective orators, but proper training promised to create competent public speakers who would regenerate the nation through moving pulpit and political oratory.[3]

Virtually all of the eighteenth-century elocutionists—including Sheridan, Walker, and Burgh—believed that the ability to read well would ultimately translate into the ability to speak well (Bahn and Bahn 117). This stance was due to the slippery dividing line between reading and speaking and their equal importance in professional life. The clergyman, for example, was undeniably an orator, yet his public tasks consisted of reading the church service and speaking the sermon, which, if written down rather than memorized, might require reading after all. Therefore, the elocutionists' pedagogical methods promoted using oral reading as a stepping stone to oratory and concentrated "more upon the practice of reading aloud, than on the delivery of original speeches" (Haberman 108–9). These educational strategies would eventually afford women access to the fifth canon, for as elocutionary material worked its way into reading textbooks, girls as well as boys learned principles of effective delivery applicable to both reading and public speaking.

Eighteenth-Century School Readers

As the tenets of the British elocutionary movement crossed the Atlantic, they influenced how American educators taught reading and the types of books used to teach it. By the late eighteenth century, students moved through an established sequence of reading textbooks. They began with spellers, books that concentrated upon the proper pronunciation of letters, syllables, and words. After mastering this material, students progressed to readers, which introduced basic principles of elocution and included reading selections for practice. Finally, boys might eventually advance to speakers, texts containing more sophisticated elocutionary matter and practice selections focusing chiefly upon oratory and public performance (Venezky 249–52). In this section, I analyze early examples of the second type of textbook, school readers.

From the first, American school readers acknowledged both male *and* female students, evidence of reading's status as a nongendered subject and of eighteenth-century women's increased access to schooling. Prior to 1750, formal education beyond the dame school level was limited primarily to boys, who often attended classes during the winter months when their services in farm and field were less essential. By the 1760s, however, townships began to hire women teachers to conduct summer sessions for girls in otherwise unused schoolhouses or, alternatively, to allow girls to attend school before or after boys' regular school hours. Young women thus gained entry into some first-tier district schools although second-tier Latin grammar schools remained off limits, their more advanced curriculum deemed irrelevant or too taxing for the female sex (Woody 1: 144).[4] In addition to improved access to district schools, late-eighteenth-century schoolgirls soon had the options of attending venture schools or ladies' academies as well, private institutions that offered instruction in ornamental and academic subjects, ranging from French, German, music, dancing, singing, drawing, painting, sewing, and needlework to history, geography, natural science, English grammar, spelling, and writing (Tolley, "Rise" 231). Regardless of school or subject choices, however, reading remained a staple of the curriculum.

School reading textbooks usually followed a two-part structure, the first section introducing rules of elocution, the second section presenting selections for oral reading and recitation. The elocutionary segments of the first American readers and speakers generally addressed both *pronuntiatio* (the vocal aspects of delivery, including pronunciation, accentuation, emphasis, pauses, vocal tone and key, and management of the voice) and *actio* (the gestural aspects, including the rhetor's use of stance, movement, gesture, and expression). School readers typically contained more reading than elocutionary matter and incorporated excerpts from multiple genres, including essays, drama, verse, letters, lectures, and orations.

To demonstrate that textbooks recognized young women as audience members and introduced them to principles of elocution, I examine three of the most popular readers of the early national period: Noah Webster's *An American Selection of Lessons in Reading and Speaking* (1789), Caleb Bingham's *American Preceptor* (1794), and Lindley Murray's *English Reader* (1799). All three writers had ties to women's education. Webster worked to improve girls' educational opportunities when he assumed charge of a coeducational academy in Sharon, Connecticut, in 1781, and he is reported to have been "deeply impressed" by a 1787 visit to Andrew Brown's female academy in Philadelphia (Brickley 44). Bingham opened the first full-time private girls' school in Boston in 1784 (E. J. Monaghan, *Common* 102), and Murray taught grammar at a young ladies' academy following the Revolutionary War (C. Monaghan 93–94). The three men's landmark readers not only reflected schoolgirls' increasing presence in the classroom but also influenced the elocutionary training they received there.

Noah Webster: *An American Selection*

Between 1783 and 1785, Noah Webster published *A Grammatical Institute of the English Language*, a three-part series consisting of a speller, a grammar, and a reader. Of the three, Webster's speller proved most popular, selling seventy million copies over the course of a century (E. J. Monaghan, *Common* 219). The speller disseminated Webster's views on pronunciation and orthography and eventually helped to distinguish British from American English. Although his reader did not enjoy the enduring popularity of the speller, it was, nevertheless, an important schoolbook in its day, printed in numerous cities and undergoing six editions in its first year of publication alone (Nietz 65). Webster's reader was the first to be produced in America, and it was later revised and reissued as *An American Selection of Lessons in Reading and Speaking* (1789). Like the speller and grammar, the reader promoted American language, literature, and citizenship and signaled Webster's patriotic agenda in its opening epigraph: "Begin with the infant in his cradle: Let the first word he lisps be WASHINGTON" (1).

As soon became standard in the developing school-reader genre, *An American Selection* opens with eleven pages of "Rules for Reading and Speaking." Webster covers *pronuntiatio* (or vocal considerations) in two pages, detailing "clear and distinct" articulation, the proper accentuation of stressed syllables, pauses and word emphasis according to sense rather than punctuation, and rising or falling cadence, again, as required by sense. The bulk of the elocutionary section, however, concerns *actio*, the gestural aspect of delivery. Some nine pages detail the look of various emotions, much of the material drawn from Burgh's *Art of Speaking* (1761). Burgh (and hence Webster) emphasizes the speaker's ability to convey emotion through the manipulation of gesture and expression. Fear, for example, has its own appearance:

[It] opens the eyes and mouth, shortens the nose, draws down the eye-brows, gives the countenance an air of wildness; the face becomes pale, the elbows are drawn back parallel with the sides, one foot is drawn back, the heart beats violently, the breath is quick, the voice weak and trembling. Sometimes it produces shrieks and fainting. (Webster 6)

Webster details the full range of emotions, from shame, malice, and envy to wonder, courage, and joy, each description followed by a short reading passage for practice. Despite the prescriptiveness of the *actio* section, Webster recommends a "natural" style, advising that both voice and gesture should be "the same which we use in common conversation" (5). Furthermore, the reader's or speaker's ability to experience and convey passion is presented as the key to good elocution: "The whole art of reading and speaking . . . may be comprised in this concise direction: *Let a reader or speaker express every word as if the sentiment were his own*" (5–6; original emphasis). The elocutionary section is followed by 190 pages of selections for reading and speaking, including essays, orations, petitions, dialogues, poetry, and sketches.

In terms of difficulty, the book's reading selections indicate that Webster targeted what would today be considered a secondary- rather than a primary-school student. Excerpts cover a range of subjects—social conduct, history, geography, and civic rhetoric—all the while emphasizing American writers, content, and values. The section entitled "Lessons in Speaking," for example, contains both American and Roman civic rhetoric, setting "The First Petition of [the American] Congress to the King, in 1774" beside "Cicero's Orations Against Verres." Twenty-five pages are devoted to American oratory culled from the period just preceding or following the Revolutionary War and only ten pages to classical selections, a sign of Webster's patriotic fervor.

The reader's acknowledgment of schoolgirls becomes apparent in its selections concerning proper conduct. Although Webster instructs both young men and women about appropriate social habits and behavior—"Never put your fingers in your nose or ears—it is a nasty vulgar rudeness, and an affront to company" (63)—conduct selections dwell primarily upon the qualities and concerns of American women, idealized though the characters may be. Rather than focusing on historical or biblical exemplary women, such sketches as "Character of a Young Lady," "Juliana, a Real Character," and "Emelia, or the Happiness of Retirement" introduce contemporary women who display solid sense, filial piety, and domestic virtue. Emelia, for example, prefers retirement to the social whirlwind with its attendant dangers of "dissipation and folly" due to "the flattery and admiration of men," but she is too level-headed to reject all forms of social interaction: "It is in company only that [women] can acquaint themselves with mankind, acquire an easy address, and learn numberless little decorums, which are essential and cannot be taught by precept" (56–57). The hearth, however, is their particular province:

> Women are destined by nature to preside over domestic affairs. Whatever parade they make abroad, their *real* merit and *real* characters are known only at home. The behavior of servants, the neatness of furniture, the order of a table, and the regularity of domestic business, are decisive evidences of female worth. Perhaps sweetness of temper does not contribute more to the happiness of their partners and their families, than a proper attention to these articles. (55)

Such passages explicitly make the case that duty and domesticity constitute women's destiny, a refrain calculated to restrain young women should the liberty of education prove too exhilarating. As eighteenth-century women began to receive fuller and more substantial schooling, they were constantly reminded that their educational labors should never interfere with their domestic obligations.

An American Selection also includes courtship tales, some conventional and others surprisingly racy. "Modesty, Doubt, and Tender Affection: Agothocles and Calista" traces the attraction, courtship, and marriage of the "brave and prudent" Agothocles and the "young and beautiful" Calista, its advocacy of young love and early marriage discreetly encouraging the legal propagation of American children (30). A more interesting entry is "Innocent Simplicity Betrayed: Story of Sir Edward and Louisa." The tale advances Webster's patriotic project by contrasting aristocratic and democratic values, but it is simultaneously a sophisticated and somewhat jaded romantic narrative, relating the seduction and eventual redemption of a passionate Italian commoner by a proud English nobleman. After a near fatal fall in the Italian Alps, Sir Edward is saved by a simple Italian farmer (who fortunately possesses keen surgical abilities) and nursed back to health by the farmer's lovely and erudite daughter Louisa. Edward soon falls in love with her, but pride in his noble lineage prevents him from proposing marriage. Instead, he persuades her to run away to England and become mistress of his heart and estate. Louisa's shame and Edward's snobbishness threaten to wreck the couple's happiness, but, eventually, Edward recognizes Louisa as his spiritual equal:

> [F]orgive me, my Louisa, for rating your excellence at a price so mean. I have seen those high-born females to which my rank might have allied me; I am

ashamed of their vices, and sick of their follies. Profligate in their hearts amidst affected purity, they are slaves to pleasure, without the sincerity of passion; and with the name of honor, are insensible to the feelings of virtue. You, my Louisa! ... Continue to love your Edward but a few hours and you shall add the title to the affections of a wife. (52)

Sir Edward's rejection of dissipated aristocratic beauties for Louisa and her pure passion could not help but appeal to titleless American girls. Furthermore, the tale's affinity with sentimental novels suggests that the market-savvy Webster may have been appealing to popular taste. Nevertheless, the story's cosmopolitan examination of love, sex, and marriage makes it an odd choice for a school reader, validating as it does passion over convention, reason, and restraint.

How did Webster envision young women employing the elocutionary ability they developed courtesy of his reader? The exemplary woman in "Juliana, a Real Character" suggests an answer. Juliana, we are told, is "lively and sentimental" in conversation and free of "false wit, frivolous minuteness, and affectations of learning." She shows feminine restraint and does not "lead the conversation," "stun the ears of company with perpetual chat," or "interrupt the discourse of others. But when occasion offers, she acquits herself with ease and grace; without the airs of pertness or the confusion of bashfulness" (58–59). Juliana is articulate but also feminine and modest, socially adept but disdainful of the limelight for its own sake. She uses voice, gesture, and expression to forge interpersonal connections and to gain respect and influence within private spaces, speaking, for instance, to company rather than an audience.

In many ways, Juliana exemplifies the new ideal of womanhood that emerged following the Revolutionary War, an evolution in gender ideology that recast American women's social and family roles. Jill Conway argues that the fledgling nation's decision to maintain no standing army or national church—the traditional means of instilling discipline and moral values in the populace—shifted the task of inculcating republican virtues onto the family (4). Linda Kerber notes that this burden fell chiefly to middle- and upper-class women, who came to be seen as "custodian[s] of civic morality" responsible for developing the character and patriotism of American children (11). With the construct of republican motherhood, the domestic (or feminine private realm) gained significance because of its connection to the polis (or masculine public realm). In order to fulfill both their private and public duties, American women need to be educated and eloquent. How else could they raise knowledgeable, virtuous, patriotic sons who would in turn ensure the continuing vitality of the nation?

Webster's character sketches illuminate the qualities of the new republican woman, and his courtship tales indicate that schoolgirls were recognized reading students. In all, ten of the reader's forty-five selections (or approximately 22%) appeal specifically to young women.

Caleb Bingham: The *American Preceptor*

Another popular reader of the day, Caleb Bingham's *American Preceptor; Being a New Selection of Lessons for Reading and Speaking* (1794), also acknowledges young women as readers. The book was one of the best-selling textbooks of the late eighteenth and early nineteenth centuries, going through sixty-four editions and selling 640,000 copies by 1832 (Smith 51). Bingham's reader, like Webster's, begins with a treatment of elocution (in Bingham's case, three pages' worth). It is followed by 220 pages of assorted reading and speaking selections. Regarding *pronuntiatio*, Bingham briefly examines articulation, emphasis, and tone:

> [The]first object of a reader or speaker, is, to be clearly understood by his hearers. In order for this, it is necessary that he should pronounce his words distinctly, and deliberately; that he should carefully avoid the two extremes of uttering either too fast or too slow; and that his tone of voice should be perfectly natural. (A2)

Regarding *actio*, Bingham addresses gesture and countenance, the chief rule here being "that [facial expression] should correspond with the nature of the discourse and when no particular emotion is expressed, a serious and manly look is always the best," advice indicating that, while school readers might address both boys and girls, a male figure still functioned as the presumed speaker (7).

Bingham's textbook is, nevertheless, keenly aware of its female readership. Bingham initially compiled the *American Preceptor* because he felt strongly that certain sections of Webster's reader were "indelicate & improper to be read, especially by young Misses," likely referring to risqué selections like "Sir Edward and Louisa" (qtd. in E. J. Monaghan, *Common* 102). The *American Preceptor*'s preface announces that it omits "romantic fiction" and "tales of love" and opts instead for moral essays and stories "exemplifying moral virtues ... calculated to engage the attention and improve the heart." No tales of seduction appear here. Instead, the selections directed toward female students—in all, ten of ninety-nine excerpts—consist chiefly of character studies and biographies of women exemplars, orations and dialogues on women's schooling, and advice on feminine comportment.

A number of pieces examine women's education, an extremely popular topic during the early national period. "Dialogue Between Mrs. Careless and Mrs. Friendly, upon Female Education," for example, presents two mothers' views on the preferred curriculum for young women, one advocating ornamental accomplishments, the other more substantial studies. Mrs. Careless remarks that learning "dancing, music, and drawing" are the primary objectives of her daughters' schooling: "They shall indeed know something of reading, writing, and needle work; but to give them a *polite* education and make them accomplished is my aim" (91). Mrs. Friendly, on the other hand, argues the importance of a thorough and useful education that develops girls' morality and self-discipline; promotes knowledge of "reading, writing, arithmetic, and English grammar"; and instills a love of "domestic employments" (92). She clarifies her position on the relative merits of polite and useful learning:

> I have no objection to dancing, dress and company, when they form not the chief object of solicitude and attention, and are cultivated merely as the recreation and ornaments of life, and not as the business and end of it. Be assured, a well furnished mind, a well governed temper, love of domestic pleasures, and an inclination and capacity to pursue domestic employments are the first requisites in a woman, and the foundation of her respectability and enjoyment. (92)

The exchange between Mrs. Careless and Mrs. Friendly reflects a national preoccupation with the proper extent of women's schooling. Mrs. Friendly counters the argument that education masculinizes women by insisting that it instills both a love of the domestic and of learning. She warns of the dire consequences of limiting women to polite or ornamental subjects, describing one of its products as a woman so vain and selfish that she "disgusts her husband; neglects her children, and order, peace and industry are strangers in her house" (93). Mrs. Friendly thus uses the centrality of the mother's role to her family and society, a fundamental tenet of republican motherhood, to urge a weightier and more practical curriculum for women. Through such selections, Bingham introduces schoolgirls to current issues in women's education and provides them with justifications for their own endeavors.

In addition to learning elocution from school readers, young women were also exposed to civic rhetoric. Almost a fifth of Bingham's reading selections (twenty of ninety-nine passages) consists of oratory, a potpourri of ancient and contemporary speeches. Schoolgirls read Demosthenes and Cicero, William Pitt and John Adams and thus familiarized themselves with models of persuasion, argument, and style. As Shevaun Watson observes, students learned about the uses of public speaking from Bingham's excerpts, which "illustrate the variety of political exigencies for rhetoric in the ancient world. Bingham leads his readers to conclude that analogous exigencies exist in America of the 1790s, and further, that classical rhetoric offers Americans viable ways to address sociopolitical needs" (59). The *Preceptor's* selections thus demonstrated the power of oratory in the polis and shaped young women's understanding of its uses even as they were admonished to restrict their own eloquence to school and home.

Lindley Murray: The *English Reader*

Suspected of loyalist sympathies and activities, Lindley Murray fled to England following the Revolutionary War and, as an American expatriate, produced the most popular and influential readers of the early nineteenth century: The *English Reader* (1799), *Sequel to the English Reader* (1800), and *Introduction to the English Reader* (1801). Unlike Webster's and Bingham's patriotic schoolbooks packed with American readings and subject matter, Murray chose only British and classical writers for the *English Reader*, and his selections promoted morality rather than patriotism. The approach apparently worked because, from its publication in 1799, Americans embraced Murray's reader enthusiastically. By 1805, its sales "crushed" Webster's reader and, by 1812, regularly exceeded Bingham's totals for both the *American Preceptor* and *Columbian Orator* (C. Monaghan 137). The *English Reader* reached its apex between 1815 and 1836, during which time it went through 259 American editions and made Murray the "best-selling producer of books in the world during the first four decades of the nineteenth century" (C. Monaghan 96). Furthermore, Murray's *English Reader* was popular in ladies' academies, where it was used to teach the fine points of reading and elocution to two generations of American schoolgirls (Woody 1: 561).

Murray was a Quaker, a religious sect that supported women's education, and after his move to England, he taught grammar at Esther Tuke's Quaker school for young women, an experience that likely inspired him to begin writing schoolbooks (C. Monaghan 93–94). However, contrary to what one might expect, the selections in Murray's *English Reader* show less awareness of a female audience than Webster's or Bingham's texts. A few historical pieces do indeed concern women (for example, those on Lady Jane Grey and Queen Elizabeth), and a few letters and poems promote conventional feminine qualities like modesty, retirement, and faith. Although there is a smattering of oratory addressing civic concerns, most excerpts consist of prose or poetry examining issues of morality, religion, and proper conduct. Therefore, as regards women's rhetorical education, the reader is more noteworthy for its treatment of elocution than for its reading selections.

The *English Reader* opens with the twelve-page "Introduction: Observations on the Principles of Good Reading," which acknowledges indebtedness to Hugh Blair's *Lectures on Rhetoric and Belles Lettres* (1783). Murray confines himself to *pronuntiatio*, and its treatment is more thorough than that offered by either Bingham or Webster, covering a number of vocal issues: "Proper loudness of voice; distinctness; slowness; propriety of pronunciation; emphasis; tones; pauses; and mode of reading verse" (v). Murray distinguishes between reading and speaking, defining a reader as one who conveys an author's thoughts and a speaker as one who conveys his own thoughts to others. Effective reading and speaking require different methods of delivery, with readers typically performing in a more muted physical, vocal, and emotional style than the "vivid and animated" manner required of speakers (xii). Nevertheless, many of Murray's suggestions for improving oral reading apply equally to oratorical delivery. For example, while discussing loudness, he explains that the "first attention of every person who reads to others, doubtless, must be, to make himself be heard by all those to whom he reads." One means of accomplishing this is

> to cast our eye on some of the most distant persons in the company, and to consider ourselves as reading to them. We naturally and mechanically utter our words with such a degree of strength, as to make ourselves be heard by the person whom we address, provided he is within the reach of our voice. (vi)

Although young women had relatively few opportunities to read or speak publicly, they learned important elocutionary techniques and strategies from school readers that they later adapted from the parlor to the platform. Furthermore, schoolgirls might be encouraged to be readers rather than speakers, but once they mastered the arts of elocution, they were free to apply their abilities to whatever ends they chose, even that of communicating their own thoughts and emotions to an audience.

Webster's, Bingham's, and Murray's textbooks provide three important insights into American schoolgirls' rhetorical education. First, school readers acknowledged young women as students and consumers and, second, offered them instruction in elocution. Third, school readers not only provided young women with rationales for their education and with representations of learned women but also introduced them to models of oratory and civic rhetoric for imitation and appropriation. According to Janet Carey Eldred and Peter Mortensen, early American textbooks like these gave schoolgirls "real and significant, if not revolutionary" opportunities for rhetorical education. However, as the infant genre evolved and refined itself, school readers

> moved thematically from independence-building lessons that "assisted" young pilgrims to lessons that assisted only young male patriots while they "monitored" young girls of middling status. As textbooks became more conspicuously national, then, they also became more conspicuously gendered, often focusing less on women's rhetorical abilities and reasoning and more on their external conduct and piety. (16)

To explore this trend, my examination turns next to the impact of gender on the elocutionary coverage and contents of nineteenth-century schoolbooks designed specifically for male, female, and mixed-sex audiences.

Nineteenth-Century Schoolbooks: Gendered Reading and Speaking

During the first half of the nineteenth century, changes in economics, gender ideology, public speaking, and education had a pronounced impact on women's lives. I review these developments briefly before refocusing on gender and the textbook.

Advances in northern economic production in the early decades of the century radically altered middle-class women's domestic roles. Prior to this point, households had been predominantly rural, and the housewife assumed primary responsibility for "the processing and preserving of food, candle-making, soapmaking, spinning, weaving, shoemaking, quilting, rugmaking," producing cloth and sewing clothes, tending a garden and livestock, and raising children (Douglas 50). By 1830, however, her economic function changed due to the increased industrialization and urbanization of the American landscape and consequent movement of production from the home to the public sphere. The middle-class housewife became a consumer rather than a producer and her relative freedom from mundane tasks an indication of her husband's financial prowess.

Concurrently with these economic changes, a new feminine gender ideal began to emerge, one designed to reconcile women to their enforced leisure and endow them with a new sense of purpose. Barbara Welter identifies this construct as the cult of true womanhood and its "four cardinal virtues [as] piety, purity, submissiveness and domesticity," qualities that increasingly came to be associated with the feminine (152). As the interconnections between the private and public spheres earlier promoted by republican motherhood gradually eroded, antebellum women were instead encouraged to concentrate their energies on their homes, husbands, and children.

Domestic ideology, however, did not affect all women equally. Privatization of the domestic realm and the cult of true womanhood pertained chiefly to white women of the middle and upper classes. Patricia Hill Collins has urged scholars to avoid universalizing white, middle-class experience and to recognize the "alternative family structures . . . [and] different political economies" of women of color and the working class. For them, "work and family . . . rarely functioned as dichotomous spheres," and the public and private spaces remained fluid and "interwoven" (58). During the nineteenth century, as Evelyn Glenn observes, the restriction of women to the home applied to a narrow segment of the population, "namely the European and American bourgeoisie":

> For the majority of working-class families and women—native whites, immigrants, African-American and other racial ethnic minorities, the separation between private and public spheres, between love and labor, and between full-time motherhood for women and full-time employment for men, even if desired, could not be maintained. . . . Women had to combine income earning in and out of the home with child care and domestic labor. (14)

It follows, then, that antebellum women who worked outside the home, whether due to economics or enslavement, confronted markedly different gender norms and constraints than those encountered by more privileged women. The cult of true womanhood, therefore, chiefly affected the latter group's efforts to obtain an elocutionary education and speak in public.

Alongside these economic and ideological developments, a preoccupation with public performance swept the nation, resulting in expanded opportunities for and heightened scrutiny of rhetorical display:

> It was commonplace for nineteenth-century literary journals and local newspapers to publish reviews of the addresses of well-known speakers such as Daniel Webster and Henry Clay and of the lectures and sermons of distinguished pulpit and platform speakers. . . . Local newspapers gave similar coverage to orations and dramatic readings presented at community events, church occasions and college and school ceremonies. Such reviews offered summaries of the speaker's arguments and typically evaluated the speaker's ideas, style, and elocutionary technique . . . such as the modulated voice, timing and emphasis in reading, and control over gesture. (N. Johnson, "Popularization" 142-43)

The educational curriculum also reflected the public's fascination with delivery. Elocution became a more significant component of reading instruction at the elementary- and secondary-school levels, a required course at most colleges, and a popular subject of study with the general public.

Finally, antebellum women's educational options took a quantum leap forward with female admission into American colleges (discussed more fully in chapter 2) and with the growth of the common-school movement in the 1820s and 1830s. Alarmed by the cost, inaccessibility, and irregularity of private education, reformers like Horace Mann and Henry Barnard instituted a push to provide children with

> universal, public, and free education; to reform the harsh, even abusive, manner in which children were sometimes treated in independent schools; to improve the quality of instruction children received; and to regularize the curriculum in some way, that is, to make certain elements of learning "common" to all children. (Schultz 16)

Lucille Schultz notes that the movement's ambitions would not be achieved for some time because students remained predominantly white and middle class until the turn of the century. Nevertheless, common schools made learning more widely available for a great many children and marked an important development in women's education.

Burgeoning student populations at the elementary, secondary, and college levels conjoined with widespread interest in public performance to create new markets for elocutionary textbooks. A great many were published during the antebellum period, and they varied the mix of elocutionary theory and practice selections to suit their targeted audiences. Typically, elocutionary manuals for college students and professionals presented detailed discussions of elocution while manuals for academy students and private learners contained less substantial treatments of elocution and more extensive reading selections (N. Johnson, "Popularization" 143). Despite such variation, the amount of textbook space devoted to elocution increased markedly between the late eighteenth and mid-nineteenth century, as becomes apparent when we compare three pages of coverage in Bingham's *American Preceptor* (1794) with seventy-three pages in Porter's *Rhetorical Reader* (1835).[5]

Although many elocutionary textbooks assumed that their readers were young men with interests in or opportunities for public speaking, some acknowledged young women as well. Merritt Caldwell's *A Practical Manual of Elocution* (1845), for example, notes the critical advantages afforded the female student of elocution:

> [I]s it a matter of no interest to her to be able to speak intelligibly of the excellences and defects of those whom from time to time she hears speak?—to give names to the qualities of the voice and of the action which they employ?

It is not, perhaps, too much to say, that the time will come, when the power to criticize a *speech* shall be considered as essential to the scholar as is now the ability to criticize a *written composition*. (x)

Caldwell represents the female student as a critic and consumer who can savor and analyze the addresses of other (presumably male) speakers more completely thanks to her education. The possibility that she herself might enact the elocutionary principles she has learned is not acknowledged.

C. P. Bronson's *Elocution; or, Mental and Vocal Philosophy* (1845) touches upon women's health and fashion in the course of its exploration of elocution and human physiology. Noting that no one can read, speak, or sing with a compressed thorax, Bronson rails against women's corsets, admonishing, "What is the difference between killing one's self in five minutes with a razor, and doing it in five years by tight lacing?" (ix). Women's testimonials endorse Bronson's system, a Mrs. G relating that it helped her recover from spinal injuries resulting from poor posture and rigorous lacing and a "distinguished lady in Boston" telling how she once regularly lost her voice after reading or speaking but can now "with perfect ease, converse, or read aloud, *hour after hour* without the least fatigue" (3). Both women use elocutionary knowledge to recover physical and vocal abilities, but their study does not challenge dominant gender conventions or extend the boundaries of women's speech, which remains securely situated in private spaces.

Finally, Ebenezer Porter's popular *Rhetorical Reader*, written for advanced secondary schools, nominally recognizes both male and female students. Porter begins by announcing that his textbook is designed principally for those "called to read the Bible as heads of families, or still more publicly, as preachers of the gospel" (in other words, for men) and then, following directly in the footsteps of the British elocutionists, observes that reading well is preliminary to speaking well (v). Furthermore, as was noted previously, Porter argues that reading well also confers benefits on those who will never address the public, "including the whole of one sex, and all but comparatively a few of the other":

> Every intelligent father, who would have his son or daughter qualified to hold a respectable rank in well-bred society, will regard it as among the very first of polite accomplishments, that they should be able to read well. But beyond this, the talent may be applied to many important purposes of business, of rational entertainment, and of religious duty. (2)

Within his first few pages, Porter effectively debars women from public speaking while encouraging them to read well in the interests of social respectability.

The relevance of elocution to women's lives receives no further elaboration. The textbook's illustrations consist entirely of male speakers, and its reading selections focus on masculine experiences like war, military life, and shipwreck. Thus, after cursory acknowledgment, women are conspicuous only for their absence in Porter's *Rhetorical Reader*. Indeed, this kind of glancing recognition and subsequent oversight characterizes many of the most popular and influential elocutionary textbooks of the antebellum period.

Some writers and publishers, however, recognized young women as a bona fide segment of the textbook market and created readers especially for them, for instance, Ebenezer Bailey's *Young Ladies' Class Book* (1837), William Russell and Anna Russell's *Introduction to the Young Ladies' Elocutionary Reader* (1845) and *Young Ladies' Elocutionary Reader* (1846), T. S. Pinneo's *Hemans Reader for Female Schools* (1847), and Charles Sanders's *Sanders' Young Ladies' Reader* (1855). The next section discusses how readers designed for young ladies differed from those addressing mixed-sex or male audiences. My analysis focuses, in particular, on three advanced textbooks by Sanders and explores three interrelated questions:

1. How does gender influence the genres and themes of the textbooks' practice selections?

2. How do the textbooks portray the purposes and applications of women's eloquence?

3. How does gender influence the textbooks' presentation of *pronuntiatio* and *actio*?

Charles Sanders's Readers and Speakers

Charles Sanders was a successful writer of primary- and secondary-level schoolbooks during the antebellum period.[6] His reading series, consisting of a primer and five graded readers, outsold the famed McGuffey series in the East during the 1840s and 1850s (Nietz 80).[6] *The School Reader, Fifth Book* (1848) is the penultimate book in the series and is designed for "the use of academies and the highest classes in common and select schools," which I interpret to mean that it addresses a mixed audience of boys and girls (title page). Sanders also published two specialized textbooks relevant to this study. *Sanders' Young Ladies' Reader: Embracing a Comprehensive Course of Instruction in the Principles of Rhetorical Reading* (1855), which obviously targets a female audience, is "for the use of the higher female seminaries" and "the higher classes in female schools generally" (title page). *Sanders' School Speaker: A Comprehensive Course of Instruction in the Principles of Oratory;*

with Numerous Exercises for Practice in Declamation (1857), on the other hand, does not specify its intended audience, its title page announcing only that the book provides "a comprehensive course of instruction in the Principles of Oratory." However, given oratory's strong masculine connotations at this time, it is reasonable to assume that the speaker targets young men exclusively. Thus, the textbooks' title pages state or suggest that *The School Reader, Fifth Book* addresses a mixed-sex audience, *Sanders' Young Ladies' Reader* a female audience, and *Sanders' School Speaker* a male audience.[7]

How does gender affect the types of practice selections in Sanders's textbooks? The selections included in the books diverge sharply in terms of genre. As table 1 indicates, *Sanders' School Speaker* offers far more oratory and drama than the two readers, an unsurprising finding given the speaker's focus on public performance.[8] The most intriguing gender difference concerns oratory. Both *The School Reader, Fifth Book* and *Sanders' School Speaker* contain political, legal, pulpit, ceremonial, and popular addresses, such as Daniel Webster's "The Federal Union," Patrick Henry's "An Appeal to Arms," George Washington's "Address to the American Troops Before the Battle of Long Island," and John Quincy Adams's "The Sword of Washington and the Staff of Franklin," selections that introduce students to the style and substance of public discourse. As expected, *Sanders' School Speaker* contains more oratory than *The School Reader, Fifth Book*, 19% versus 6% of the selections respectively. However, oratory is entirely absent in the female reader. Granted, one address does appear among the selections in *Sanders' Young Ladies' Reader*, "An Address to an Arm-chair Newly Clad," but the soliloquy's narrator is an old man confiding the pleasures of retirement to an armchair rather than an audience. Thus, oratory is completely missing in the female reader, effectively eliminating young women's access to this genre of public discourse.

Gender influences the themes of reading selections as well. As table 2 indicates, *Sanders' Young Ladies' Reader* emphasizes religious and moral themes, which make up 41% of the excerpts. Similarly, 36% of the selections in *The School Reader, Fifth Book* center around religion or morality—for example, "The Christian's Hope," "Discoveries of Geology Consistent with the Spirit of Religion," "The Pure in Heart Shall Meet Again," and "Omnipresence of God"—the dominance of these "feminine" themes an indication that the textbook addresses girls as well as boys. However, only 10% of the selections in *Sanders' School Speaker* concern these topics. Overall, the speaker's tone is lighter and more secular than that of the two readers, chiefly stressing such patriotic concerns as the nation, valor, military might, and proper government (which constitute 25% of its selections). Although patriotism is rarely

Table 1. Distribution of genres in Sanders's school readers and speakers

Genres	*The School Reader, Fifth Book*		*Sanders' Young Ladies' Reader*		*Sanders' School Speaker*	
Oratory (assembly, bar, pulpit, public address, epideictic)	12	(6%)	0	(0%)	59	(19%)
Drama (plays, soliloquies, dialogues)	8	(4%)	6	(3%)	40	(13%)
Prose (essays)	87	(41%)	86	(44%)	46	(15%)
Poetry	104	(49%)	104	(53%)	166	(53%)
Total reading selections	211	(100%)	196	(100%)	311	(100%)

mentioned in *Sanders' Young Ladies' Reader*, it appears in 21% of the selections in *The School Reader, Fifth Book*, additional confirmation that the latter addresses a mixed-sex audience.

Sanders' Young Ladies' Reader offers fifty selections featuring women, the majority examining women's conduct in relation to the home and their roles as daughters, wives, and mothers. For instance, "Angelo and Claudia" presents a daughter torn between a beau and a disapproving father; "A Mother's Love" lauds boundless, eternal maternal affection; and "Social Enjoyment—Where Found" examines the sources of marital happiness, concluding "would the wife be happy and beloved, she must be in subjection to her own husband. He may not always be reasonable, but she can not 'usurp authority,' without at once warring against Heaven and her own peace and respectability" (399).

One unexpected finding is that *Sanders' School Speaker* has a higher number of selections featuring women than *The School Reader, Fifth Book* (8% versus 1%). The large number of selections featuring female characters in the speaker initially seems puzzling given the book's male audience, but closer scrutiny reveals a pageant of derisive and stereotypical depictions of women, including shrews, spinsters, mad wives, callous widows, heartless coquettes, demure Indian maidens, and vacuous virgins. One of the least offensive examples, "The Bachelor Sale," plays upon the conventions of the slave trade. Forty ancient bachelors step onto the auction block and immediately attract a gaggle of desperate "old maidens." The women contend for the privilege of paying "highly extravagant" prices for the aging merchandise, and when their purchases are completed, each victor lugs "an old bachelor home on her

Table 2. Prevalence of themes in Sanders's school readers and speakers

Themes	*The School Reader, Fifth Book*		*Sanders' Young Ladies' Reader*		*Sanders' School Speaker*	
Religion/morality	76	(36%)	81	(41%)	32	(10%)
Patriotism (America government, war, military)	43	(21%)	6	(3%)	76	(25%)
Women (character, education, court-ship, domesticity)	3	(1%)	50	(26%)	24	(8%)
Humor	0	(0%)	4	(2%)	32	(10%)
Death/Old Age	24	(0%)	38	(19%)	25	(8%)
Other	65	(31%)	17	(9%)	122	(39%)
Total reading selections	211	(100%)	196	(100%)	311	(100%)

shoulder!" (383). The masculinized "old maids" are thus associated with slaveholders, their desire for passive, powerless, feminized men serving as the joke. Although misogyny likely accounts for the inclusion of such sketches, the speaker's consistently unflattering portraits of women may also have been intended to offend female students and thus discourage their use of the book.

How do Sanders's textbooks portray women rhetors, whose successes and failures taught antebellum students about the [im]proper uses of female eloquence? A negative exemplar appears in "Extract from Madame Roland's Defense Before the French Tribunal," a selection from *Sanders' School Speaker* concerning Marie-Jeanne Roland, who was condemned to the guillotine during the French Revolution. Prior to her arrest, she collaborated closely with her husband Jean-Marie Roland, a political representative from Lyons and minister of the interior. In addition to coauthoring books, governmental reports, and letters, Madame Roland helped her husband run governmental departments, where her contributions were an "open secret" (Winegarten).

The "Extract" presents Madame Roland after her husband's fall from grace and her own imprisonment. She appears before a tribunal and boldly defends herself and her beliefs:

> I have neither concealed my sentiments nor my opinions. . . . I know that in times of delusion and party rage, he who dares avow himself the friend of the proscribed, exposes himself to their fate. . . . May I be the last victim sacrificed

to the furious spirit of party! I shall quit with joy this unfortunate earth which swallows up the friends of virtue, and drinks the blood of the just. Truth! Friendship! my Country! sacred objects, sentiments dear to my heart, accept my last sacrifice. (484–85)

Madame Roland is political, outspoken, articulate, patriotic, and brave, certainly an admirable portrait. However, the direct and confrontational discourse presented here runs counter to the actual practices of the woman herself, who typically communicated her views indirectly through collaboration with her husband and did not speak at all during her trial on 8 November 1793 (Winegarten). The speech is an imaginative rendering of what Madame Roland *might* have said, but, significantly, her eloquence fails to save her, and her venture into the public, political realm ultimately leads to death. Thus, the fictionalized Roland serves as a cautionary figure, warning of the inadequacy of women's intellectual and oratorical skills within the masculine, political domain and of the dire consequences befalling those who fail to restrict their sentiments and opinions to private spaces.

A more auspicious example of female eloquence appears in "Female Patriotism," a piece from *Sanders' Young Ladies' Reader* inspired by Shakespeare's *Coriolanus*. As the selection opens, Coriolanus—an exiled Roman general now employed by Rome's enemies—has marched the Volscian army to within five miles of the city. Rome is thrown into an uproar as it prepares for battle, and its women, "terrified by . . . the impending danger, into a neglect of their wonted decorum, [run] tumultuously from their houses to the temples" (234). There, Valeria assembles the frightened women and declares that the republic's preservation depends upon its women's "performance of the duty they [owe] their country":

> It is not by the sword, nor by strength of arms . . . that we are to prevail; these belong not to our sex. Soft moving words must be our weapons and our force. Let us all, in our mourning attire, and accompanied by our children, go and entreat Veturia, the mother of Coriolanus, to intercede with her son for our common country. Veturia's prayers will bend his soul to pity. Haughty and implacable as he has hitherto appeared, he has not a heart so cruel and obdurate as not to relent, when he shall see his mother, his revered, his beloved mother, a weeping suppliant at his feet. (235)

Coriolanus's mother and a retinue of Roman women and children dressed in mourning proceed to the Volscian camp where Veturia utters "soft moving words" to her son before throwing herself at his feet and begging for mercy on

Rome. Coriolanus orders the Volscian army to break camp and return home, and Veturia has sacrificed her son in order to save the republic, as duty demands.

Through the figures of Valeria and Veturia, "Female Patriotism" promotes feminine eloquence as a private art capable of influencing male public actors. Roman women use their discursive powers only under duress, and they employ both the verbal and visual means of persuasion at their disposal (the donning of mourning, the procession of Roman mothers and children, the mother begging at her son's feet). Although women may address other women (Valeria admonishing women in the temple), they address men individually (Veturia pleads with Coriolanus rather than his army). Women may justifiably discuss affairs of state in order to protect their homes and families; indeed, their patriotic duty requires them to overcome hesitation and reluctance in times of crisis. However, though they may talk and act in hopes of swaying men's decisions, women themselves are not public actors or speakers. Sanders's successful female rhetors consistently promote women's private eloquence and discourage their public speech, values fully compatible with antebellum gender ideals situating women firmly within domestic boundaries.

Finally, how does gender shape the textbooks' coverage of elocution? Typically, schoolbooks' elocutionary instruction covered two aspects of delivery, *pronuntiatio* (the study of vocal production and manipulation) and *actio* (the study of expression, gesture, and movement). Although *Sanders' School Speaker* (directed to male students) examines both *pronuntiatio* and *actio, Sanders' Young Ladies' Reader* and *The School Reader, Fifth Book* (which address female and mixed-sex audiences) focus exclusively on *pronuntiatio* and ignore *actio*, a curious finding at first glance.

All three textbooks begin with elocutionary sections of varying lengths. *The School Reader, Fifth Book* devotes fifty-seven pages to *pronuntiatio*, covering articulation, emphasis, inflection, modulation, expression, personation, rhetorical pauses, and poetical elocution. The treatment of *pronuntiatio* in *Sanders' Young Ladies' Reader* is shorter, only thirty-four pages, but it is more advanced than that offered in *The School Reader, Fifth Book*, assuming previous knowledge on the part of the student and condensing a great deal of information into table form. Somewhat unexpectedly, the treatment of *pronuntiatio* in the male speaker is identical to that in the female reader, indicating that both textbooks address advanced (if differently gendered) secondary students. Although their handling of *pronuntiatio* is the same, only *Sanders' School Speaker* contains a ten-page treatment of *actio*, including four illustrated pages showing a male speaker conveying such emotions as "joyful surprise," admiration, aversion, and sudden terror (see fig. 1.1). It also addresses common physical failings in delivery—for example, stooping and bad posture—and advises the student to hold his body erect with the chest fully expanded when reading or speaking (48). Although good posture would appear to be relevant to all students, information pertaining to *actio* is absent in both *Sanders' Young Ladies' Reader* and *The School Reader, Fifth Book*.

Fig. 1.1. *Actio* in *Sanders' School Speaker*, 1857

The elision of *actio* in Sanders's female and mixed-sex school readers made me wonder how gender affected other textbooks' coverage of elocution. I analyzed twenty-three reading and speaking manuals in all, twenty nineteenth-century textbooks and three eighteenth-century textbooks that continued to enjoy brisk sales into the antebellum period (those by Bingham, Murray, and Scott). As table 3 indicates, it was common practice to cover *pronuntiatio* and omit *actio* in textbooks likely to be read by young women. Of the six readers clearly targeting a female audience, two contain no coverage of elocution at all, and four address *pronuntiatio* but neglect *actio* completely. Readers targeting mixed-sex audiences display more variation in their treatment of delivery's two branches. Of the nine examined in this study, one contains no coverage of elocution, six cover *pronuntiatio* but ignore *actio*, and two cover *pronuntiatio* extensively while also addressing *actio*, albeit very briefly. Samuel Goodrich's *Third Reader* (1839) allocates two of twenty-eight elocutionary rules to gesture; William McGuffey's *McGuffey's New Sixth Eclectic Reader* (1857) allots three of forty-five pages on elocution to gesture. Of the eight specialized readers, speakers, or manuals primarily targeting a male audience, all cover both *pronuntiatio* and *actio*. These findings suggest that gender had a decisive impact on elocution's coverage in antebellum textbooks and that schoolgirls' access to *actio* was severely restricted. Next, I examine the implications of and reasons for withholding a knowledge of gesture from young women.

Voice, Body, and Backlash

The systematic elimination of *actio* in school readers targeting young women calls into question disciplinary assumptions concerning the obstacles that confronted pioneering female rhetors. Rhetorical scholars have favored metaphors of voice when discussing women's challenges, speaking in terms of their struggles to "express" their views publicly, to "address" mixed-sex audiences, to obtain a "hearing" from legislators or authorities. However, the widespread inclusion of *pronuntiatio* and exclusion of *actio* in schoolgirls' or mixed-sex readers suggests that women's disembodied or domestically bound voices became acceptable long before their public bodies did. In *Appropriate[ing] Dress: Women's Rhetorical Style in Nineteenth-Century America*, Carol Mattingly observes that the "place of the gendered body has historically been peripheral to the study of rhetoric" and that the automatic cultural association of oratory with the masculine body may well have represented the "greatest barrier women speakers faced" (135). If that is indeed the case, how does our understanding of women's rhetoric change once we substitute metaphors of the body for those of voice? I believe that we begin to uncover a series of

Table 3. Gender and textbooks' coverage of elocution

Female Audience	No Elocution	*Pronuntiatio*	*Actio* and *Pronuntiatio*
Bailey, *The Young Ladies' Class Book* (1837)	x		
Sigourney, *The Girl's Reading-Book* (1838)	x		
Russell and Russell, *The Young Ladies' Elocutionary Reader* (1845)		x	
Russell and Russell, *Introduction to the Young Ladies' Elocutionary Reader* (1845)		x	
Pinneo, *Hemans Reader for Female Schools* (1847)		x	
Sanders, *Sanders' Young Ladies' Reader* (1855)		x	

Mixed-sex Audience	No Elocution	*Pronuntiatio*	*Actio* and *Pronuntiatio*
Pierpont, *American First Class Book, or, Exercises in Reading and Recitation* (1836)	x		
Murray, *English Reader* (1827)		x	
Osgood, *Osgood's Progressive Fifth Reader* (1858)		x	
Town and Holbrook, *The Progressive Third Reader* (1857)		x	
Sanders and Sanders, *School Reader, Fourth Book* (1852)		x	
Sanders and Sanders, *School Reader, Fifth Book* (1855)		x	
McGuffey, *McGuffey's New Fifth Eclectic Reader* (1857)		x	
McGuffey, *McGuffey's New Sixth Eclectic Reader* (1857)			x
Goodrich, *The Third Reader* (1839)			x

Male Audience	No Elocution	*Pronuntiatio*	*Actio* and *Pronuntiatio*
Bingham, *Columbian Orator* (1832)			x
Bronson, *Elocution* (1845)			x
Caldwell, *Practical Manual of Elocution* (1856)			x
Porter, *Analysis of the Principles of Rhetorical Delivery* (1827)			x
Porter, *The Rhetorical Reader* (1835)			x
Russell, *American Elocutionist* (1851)			x
Sanders, *Sanders' School Speaker* (1857)			x
Scott, *Lessons in Elocution* (1820)			x

new questions concerned chiefly with space and physical form. Where, for example, does the woman rhetor discover a public location in which to stand and then speak? What corporeal stances, movements, gestures, postures, and expressions are available or off limits to her? Which bodily states and appearances can or cannot be acknowledged by her or her audience? How does she employ the visual rhetoric of physical form and fashion to complement the discursive act?

The dissimilar coverage of elocution in gender-specific textbooks also raises questions about the antebellum context, the chief one being why would information about the physical aspects of delivery be withheld from school-girls? I would suggest that *actio*'s absence in female and mixed-sex readers is related to the increasing numbers of women who began to address public issues in public spaces during this period. As is detailed more fully in chapter 3, women evangelists preached in churches, camp meetings, and even the U.S. Congress. In 1827, for example, Harriet Livermore delivered a ninety-minute sermon from the speaker's chair in the House of Representatives, where she "admonished, instructed, and beseeched her listeners until many of them began to weep" (Brekus 2). Furthermore, women educators asked legislators and citizens to fund ladies' academies, women benevolents implored the powerful and wealthy to back moral improvement projects, and women activists circulated petitions on behalf of Native Americans and the enslaved and then flooded state and national assemblies with their documents (see Goodsell; Ginzberg's *Women and the Work of Benevolence*; Zaeske's *Signatures of Citizenship*). Finally, women reformers began to address mixed-sex audiences and advocate abolition, temperance, and woman's rights (see Ginzberg's *Women in Antebellum Reform*).

Cumulatively, these efforts aroused enormous anxiety among conservatives, who viewed women's rhetorical activities as a potentially "contagious disease" threatening to spread out of control if not rigorously contained (Brekus 277). Antebellum ministers repeatedly discouraged women's public discourse: In 1831, the General Synod of the Dutch Reformed Church pronounced women's preaching to be "against the word of God"; in 1832, the General Assembly of Presbyterians warned that the Bible clearly forbade women's teaching or exhortations to mixed-sex audiences; and in 1837, the General Association of Congregational Ministers denounced women's preaching and lecturing in response to their heightened profile in the abolition movement (Brekus 281–82).

Might educators, like ministers, have participated in a general backlash response to antebellum women's heightened public profile? Offering school-girls a truncated version of elocution may well represent educators' attempt to control the dissemination of rhetorical knowledge, particularly knowledge of public speaking. Indeed, the consistent elimination of *actio* and oratory from schoolgirls' readers suggests a reciprocal relationship between women's education and their public address. Eighteenth-century school readers' elocutionary content taught students to read, stand, and speak effectively while their oratorical selections introduced students to models of persuasive discourse. When American women appropriated the elocutionary knowledge acquired in the classroom and adapted it from private to public forums, their physical and vocal delivery threatened established gender norms and hierarchies. I argue that antebellum educators responded by curtailing the instruction provided female students in an effort to restrict their access to the full arts of elocution and thus discourage their public appearances. The elimination of *actio* and oratory from female and mixed-sex readers meant that antebellum schoolgirls focused more upon enunciation than gesture and more upon the muted reading than the expressive speaking style. Nevertheless, despite these limitations, young women used their elocutionary abilities to access another important public venue, the academic platform, and challenge restrictive gender and discursive conventions, topics that are the focus of the next chapter.

2

Practicing Delivery
Young Ladies on the Academic Platform

Late in life, the suffragist and Universalist minister Olympia Brown reminisced about her childhood education in frontier Michigan during the 1850s and recalled that her first struggle for equal rights occurred on a school stage:

> We had a "Literary Society" in the school, of which teachers as well as pupils were members. The teachers made our program, and I soon noticed that only boys had been given recitations and debates, while the girls were restricted to reading. We girls instigated . . . to present a resolution at a regular meeting providing that girls as well as boys should be appointed for declamations and debates. Upon this the teachers all arose en masse, and declared that they would leave the society if we persisted in our resolution. . . . We were thus suppressed, and my first effort for the equality of the sexes was unsuccessful. (Willis 7)

Brown's memory reveals the complex intersections of gender and delivery on the academic platform. First, it indicates that by the mid-nineteenth century, schoolgirls reading onstage had become a commonplace and widely accepted pedagogical practice. It also shows that reading was one of a narrow set of discursive genres considered acceptable for young women on school stages; the vast majority—including debate, declamation, extemporaneous address, and oratory—were coded as masculine and, therefore, discouraged. Finally, Brown's story suggests that when young women challenged gendered discourse conventions on academic platforms, they provoked strong reactions from educators and educational institutions alike.

This chapter examines gender and the academic platform, a term encompassing all of the curricular and extracurricular sites and activities that permitted pupils to practice the arts of oral expression, including formal classroom exercises, school exhibitions, college commencements, and literary club events. The academic platform is significant because it provided middle- and upper-class schoolgirls experience in addressing real audiences. My analysis begins with late-eighteenth-century district schools, venture schools, and ladies' academies, which adopted the tradition of school exhibitions from boys' schools and men's colleges (see fig. 2.1). School exhibitions required students to display their learning orally and publicly, and these events proved extremely popular, attracting large, influential, mixed-sex audiences from surrounding communities. From the first, schoolgirls were permitted to compose exhibition-day essays, and they frequently used these opportunities to explore such topics as women's roles and education. However, in many regions and school settings, controversy raged over the propriety of young women reading original compositions to exhibition audiences. Fearing such display might damage the delicate, modest, and retiring feminine character, some schools required male surrogates to deliver young women's essays for them on public days. In general, though, by the mid-nineteenth century, primary- and secondary-level girls had secured the right to write for and read from school stages. Once women entered American colleges, however, the academic platform once again became a contested site, rife with tensions over gender, education, power, and discourse.

To date, the most provocative analysis of gender and the antebellum college platform appears in Robert Connors's *Composition-Rhetoric: Backgrounds, Theory, and Pedagogy* (1997).[1] He argues that women's entry into higher education transformed the entire college curriculum over the course of the nineteenth century. Traditionally, American colleges had focused on preparing men for public life through the study of rhetorical theory and oratory, an education demanding oral, public, and agonistic modes of learning and practice. These pedagogical ends and means came into question once women began to enter college classrooms in the 1830s. Because it was considered inappropriate for men and women to compete for verbal supremacy in academic settings, the college curriculum gradually deemphasized "masculine" modes of oral display associated "with combat and contest" and "the ethos-based worlds of public affairs and government" and instead promoted "feminine" modes of reading and writing associated with silence, harmony, and solitude (44–68). Thus, oratory and debate were pushed to the margins while composition and literary analysis moved center stage as subjects of study.

Connors's feminization of rhetoric theory has elicited strong reactions from feminist scholars, including Suzanne Bordelon, Sharon Crowley, Lisa

Fig. 2.1. Young ladies on the academic platform, 1816. Jacob Marling's *The May Queen*. Courtesy of the Chrysler Museum of Art, Norfolk, Virginia.

Mastrangelo, Roxanne Mountford ("Feminization"), and Lisa Ricker. At root, they take issue with Connors on two counts. First, they charge that he over-simplifies causes of the curriculum's shift from an oral to a written focus by overlooking such factors as the influence of Romanticism and influx of students of different classes into American colleges. Second, they note that he slights evidence of nineteenth-century women's rhetorical efforts and accomplishments in genres and domains coded as masculine. I would add a third criticism concerning Connors's gendered categories of discourse and the distinctions he draws between "masculine" and "feminine" genres. Connors (drawing upon Walter Ong's scholarship) identifies writing as a feminized rhetorical practice that became acceptable for women sometime during the medieval period. This broad generalization, however, is not supported by E. Jennifer Monaghan's careful research into literacy practices in colonial America, which indicate that writing was considered a masculine job skill and was, therefore, largely withheld from women until well into the eighteenth century (see "Literacy Instruction"). Furthermore, Connors describes reading as a silent, solitary, and feminine genre. However, as I argue in chapter 1, reading was actually viewed as an oral and communal skill until late in the nineteenth century, and far from promoting silent abilities, school readers actually provided American schoolgirls with their first consistent exposure to elocutionary principles. In other words, neither reading nor writing was necessarily the irenic, personal, feminine domain that Connors claims they were.

In response to criticisms like these, Connors refined and clarified his position, observing that

1. Between 1820 and 1910, women entered American post-secondary education in both all-women's colleges and in coeducational settings.

2. Between 1820 and 1910, rhetorical education in American colleges shifted powerfully from its 2,500-year-old traditional concern with oral, argumentative, non-personal discourse to a new concern with written, multi-modal, and more personalized discourse. "Rhetoric" became composition, and the remnants of the oral rhetorical tradition were marginalized as elocution and dramatic recitation. ("*Adversus*")

He concludes by claiming "*some* causal correlation" between women's entry into college classrooms and changes in the traditional focus of rhetorical education (emphasis added).

Although initially dubious about Connors's feminization of rhetoric theory, I now accept his modified claim that the nineteenth-century curriculum changed shape, at least in part, in response to women's admission into American colleges. However, I also believe that he misjudges the reasons motivating that change. Connors interprets rhetoric's shift from an oral to written focus as an effort to accommodate women's presence in higher education, but it can also be read as an effort to withhold from women knowledge of and practice in the arts of public expression. Carrying forward the notion of educational backlash introduced in chapter 1, I argue that antebellum educators became increasingly vigilant of young women's access to and delivery on academic platforms as elocutionary instruction bore unanticipated fruits. Once American women began to adapt the discursive abilities acquired in sanctioned school settings to previously prohibited public venues, educational authorities reacted with alarm and attempted to restrict female students' rhetorical practice in classrooms and on academic platforms. While some young women accepted limited rhetorical opportunities, others combated institutions and, when necessary, created extracurricular alternatives in order to acquire the full elocutionary training and practice they desired.

Throughout this chapter, I question Connors's view of the academic platform as a quintessentially masculine site of contentious verbal display, a view that has two very unfortunate consequences: First, it minimizes the fifty-year history of young women's performances on school stages predating their college admission in the 1830s, and, second, it oversimplifies the rich and complex convergence of gender, power, and delivery on college platforms afterwards. To explore these matters, I begin by examining how and why the academic platform became a prominent feature of female education in the late eighteenth century and then turn to antebellum women's experiences on college platforms.

Schoolgirls on the Academic Platform

Growing interest in women's education over the course of the eighteenth century led to expanded schooling options, prompting girls' admittance into district schools and venture schools, stimulating the development of ladies' academies, and providing middle- and upper-class girls greater access to formal learning. Lacking precedents for educating young women, coeducational and female academies initially imitated the pedagogical methods employed in boys' schools, adopting the English (rather than the classical) curriculum and offering classes in rhetoric, reading, pronunciation, and elocution (Nash 244–45). Typically, students' elocutionary training and practice began in the classroom. Teachers would, first, demonstrate how to deliver selections of prose, poetry, or oratory, and students would then select a passage, memorize it, and, when ready, recite it to the class. Alex Graydon's account of his early education provides a sketch of standard classroom procedure: "Each scholar . . . ascended the stage, and said his speech. . . . The speech was carefully taught him by his master, both with respect to its pronunciation, and the action deemed suitable to its several parts" (qtd. in Michael 287). Following classroom recitations, teachers would critique students' delivery. These regular classroom exercises led up to quarterly or annual school exhibitions at which students displayed their knowledge and abilities by, among other things, reciting memorized passages or reading compositions to assembled families, friends, neighbors, and officials.

In addition to adopting the English curriculum, classroom recitation exercises, and exhibition days from boys' academies, coeducational and female academies also embraced emulation, a pedagogy that encouraged student competition in the classroom and at school events. During classroom recitation exercises, for example, students who performed well advanced to the "head" of the class while those who did poorly inched toward the "foot." Emulation was a feature of school exhibitions as well, with awards and honors crowning the finest scholarly and rhetorical achievements. To illustrate, the Albany Female Academy held a public examination each July and awarded premiums for "proficiency in the various subjects of study" to students in the lower grades and "testimonials" signed by board members to those in the upper grades. Additionally, a gold medal went to the writer of the best original composition and to the top student in mathematics (Sizer 173). Late-eighteenth-century educators held that such incentives motivated students to learn and perform to the best of their abilities, so they encouraged both girls and boys to strive for public recognition and awards, a curious practice given prevailing gender constructs promoting feminine modesty and retirement. Apparently, educators initially had few qualms that "school competition and public rewards might be inappropriate for creatures . . . destined to live quiet, domestic lives" (Green 132). Not only were girls permitted to compete for prizes but they were also required to display their intellectual, written, and elocutionary talents at school exhibitions, a pedagogical practice that provided many young women with their real introduction to public reading and speaking.

One of the earliest accounts of schoolgirls onstage comes from William Woodbridge, an educator who ran a venture school for young ladies in New Haven, Connecticut, between 1779 and 1780 (Brickley 43). Twenty young women attended the school five nights a week for twelve weeks, studying grammar, geography, and composition. Woodbridge describes the school's closing ceremonies:

> At the end of the term, in the presence of the faculty of —— —— College, the parents, and others, [my pupils] passed an examination that did them honor, and delivered addresses of their own composition. Each brought her essay or letter, neatly copied, for the perusal of the spectators. (qtd. in Woody 1: 137)

Typically at these examinations, an authority (a school principal, visiting trustee, or college professor) posed questions about a school subject to a pupil, who then attempted to answer or solve the question and thus demonstrate her knowledge. Even more intriguing was the practice of allowing young women to read or, occasionally, orate original compositions on the academic platform. Records from the Young Ladies' Academy of Philadelphia suggest that schoolgirls used such opportunities to examine civic and social issues pertaining to women.

Unlike Woodbridge's short-lived venture school, the impressive history and accomplishments of the Young Ladies' Academy of Philadelphia reflect mounting interest in women's education during the early national period. Directed by John Poor, the academy opened in 1787 with the blessings and financial support of the city's most prestigious citizens and, after obtaining a charter in 1792, became the first incorporated school for women in the United

States (Savin and Abrahams 59). Although the Young Ladies' Academy offered standard ornamental studies in foreign language, music, dancing, and drawing, it also instructed girls in more substantial subjects, including arithmetic, science, reading, composition, spelling, English grammar, rhetoric, geography, and history (Savin and Abrahams 60).

The academy held public examinations twice yearly, at which the principal and assorted "trustees read papers submitted anonymously by the girls and heard them spell, read, and otherwise demonstrate what they had learned" (Gordon, "Young" 80). The best performer in each category earned a premium of merit while girls displaying broad knowledge of the subjects taught at the academy received diplomas (Savin and Abrahams 61–62). Students vied for these awards with great earnestness, and trustees encouraged the girls' competitive spirit, for example, by praising "combatants" for having "nobly contended for the prize with very formidable and determined opponents, who disputed the ground with you, inch by inch, with praise-worthy perseverance and undaunted fortitude" (qtd. in Nash 249). The highest honor bestowed by the academy violated feminine norms even more spectacularly: At each year's commencement exercise, two girls were selected to deliver original orations to the audience.

Ann Gordon describes these speeches as formulaic, constructed according to rhetorical prescription, and self-conscious of the "unique public character of their performance" ("Young" 81–82). Furthermore, she argues that the "fate of oratory as a school subject" at the Young Ladies' Academy of Philadelphia reveals hard facts about women's limited options after graduation:

> Oratory and rhetoric capped boys' education; it forced a student to apply everything he had learned at school in order to prepare interesting and effective speeches, but more important, it set him up for assuming leadership after school by the devices he had learned about persuasion. . . . [T]his purpose disappeared entirely at the [Young Ladies'] academy, and oratory became a means to a pedagogical end, like learning the rules of grammar. ("Young" 77)

The benefits of young women's knowledge of rhetoric and oratory, in other words, consisted entirely of increased mental discipline because they lacked opportunities to use their skills outside the academy. Gordon's insights into gender inequities are, of course, accurate. However, I would argue that schoolgirls' delivery of original addresses, far from being an empty pedagogical exercise, represents a significant moment in the course of American women's entry into the public realm. The commencement orations at the Young Ladies' Academy of Philadelphia were important, first, because they provided young women with a public platform and, second, because of the influential audience they attracted. Jacob Hiltzheimer's diary of 1794 indicates that the schoolgirls' orations were so popular that they literally ground state government to a halt: "At noon the [Pennsylvania] House adjourned, and the members with their Speaker attended the Commencement at the Methodist Church on Fourth St., where several young ladies from Mr. Poor's Academy spoke before a large audience" (qtd. in Savin and Abrahams 62).

Young women selected to deliver commencement orations frequently used the occasion to examine the politics of gender. In her 1792 address, for instance, Molly Wallace analyzes prejudice regarding the woman rhetor. Wallace begins meekly, seeking the audience's sympathy rather than provoking its outrage at her own audacity:

> The silent and solemn attention of a respectable audience, has often, at the beginning of discourses intimidated, even veterans, in the art of public elocution. What then must my situation be, when my sex, my youth and inexperience all conspire to make me tremble at the talk which I have undertaken? . . . With some, . . . it has been made a question, whether we ought *ever* to appear in so public a manner. Our natural timidity, the domestic situation to which by nature and custom we seem destined, are, urged as arguments against what I have now undertaken:—Many sarcastical observations have been handed out against female oratory: But to what do they amount? Do they not plainly inform us, that, because we are females, we ought therefore to be deprived of what is perhaps the most effectual means of acquiring a just, natural and graceful delivery? No one will pretend to deny, that we should be taught to read in the best manner. And if to read, why not to speak? (Gordon, "Young" 87)

Wallace questions the logic of teaching girls to read well and then denying them the opportunity to speak publicly, refuting the charge that oratory "unsexes" women and drives them to "harangue at the head of an Army, in the Senate, or before a popular Assembly." She also reassures her audience that elocutionary training will not inspire women to reach for oratorical heights reserved exclusively for men: "[W]e look not for a female Pitt, Cicero, or Demosthenes." Nevertheless, young women's public speech teaches them important lessons that cannot be learned by precept or observation. Wallace defends her own oratorical performance here, but in the end, her argument is cautious and muted. Although ultimately restricting women's eloquence to private domains, she still manages to make a convincing case for the value of extending oratorical learning and practice to schoolgirls.

When Priscilla Mason delivered her oration in 1793, she examined the issue of women's oratory with greater critical acumen. She starts by establishing that women's "right to instruct and persuade cannot be disputed, if it shall appear, that [they] possess the talents of the orator—and have opportunities for the exercise of those talents" (Gordon, "Young" 90). Mason proceeds to prove that women do indeed possess the requisite oratorical talents—"power of speech and volubility of expression," personal attractiveness, and "popular and practical" knowledge. She then protests that they have no theater in which to employ their skills: "The Church, the Bar, and the Senate are shut against us. Who shut them? *Man*; despotic man, first made us incapable of the duty, and then forbid us the exercise. Let us by suitable education, qualify ourselves for those high departments—they will open before us." Mason charges men with engineering women's marginalization and oppression and then promises that education will prompt shut doors to "fly open before us," a hope that is both poignant and premature. As Gordon notes, upon graduation, women had virtually no public avenues for employing the elocutionary talents developed in the course of their schooling. Nevertheless, Mason's delivery embodied her belief that new possibilities would present themselves to educated women and served as a harbinger of their future accomplishments.

In *Imagining Rhetoric: Composing Women of the Early United States* (2002), Janet Carey Eldred and Peter Mortensen observe that schoolgirls' opportunities to stand and speak publicly on academic platforms reflected progressive tendencies in women's education, encouraged by such influential writers as Benjamin Rush and Judith Sargent Murray. However, severe limitations imposed on women's delivery effectively nullified any threat it might pose to the status quo:

> The carnival specter of the female orator . . . was limited to classroom lessons and commencement exercises. True, these exercises, open to the public, challenged received notions of gender, but only for one day, after which . . . orators resumed their roles as daughters and sisters, preparatory to their roles as wives and mothers. And even on that day they had to share the stage with classmates who delivered more appropriately "female" performances: musical pieces and recitations of sentimental and religious poetry. (8)

Despite the restrictions surrounding women's public speech—their oratory tolerable only so long as it was presented as fleeting, carnivalesque amusement—gradual changes in taste and decorum took place as generation after generation of American schoolgirls practiced delivery on academic platforms.

By the early decades of the nineteenth century, exhibitions at coeducational schools, ladies' seminaries, and women's colleges had become commonplace and popular "high-stakes performances: "In an era when few forms of public entertainment were available, the examinations in some cases assumed the form of a spectacle" (Tolley, "Science" 145). Accounts of these events sprinkle the letters, journals, newspapers, and memoirs of the day. In 1848, for example, Antoinette Brown, on a break from her theological studies at Oberlin College, attended school examinations in her hometown of Henrietta, New York, and deemed the events significant enough to merit mention in letters to former classmate Lucy Stone: "We have had a fine Common School Celebration. Half the town were assembled together. The Academy examination came off last Thursday & Friday. The ladies read price essays. My Sister Gus took the prize" (Lasser and Merrill, *Soul* 38).[2]

Nineteenth-century school exhibitions were elaborate affairs, often lasting two to three days and, in addition to the examinations themselves, included orations, concerts, art shows, processions, and parties. The events attracted spectators from near and far and were a social highlight of the year. Elizabeth Cady Stanton, later an accomplished speaker and writer for woman's rights, attended Emma Willard's Troy Female Seminary in the early 1830s. Forty years after her enrollment, Cady Stanton could still recall the drama surrounding seminary examinations:

> This was the great event of the season to many families throughout this State. Parents came from all quarters; the *elite* of Troy and Albany assembled here. Principals from other schools, distinguished legislators, and clergymen all came to hear girls scan Latin verse, solve problems in Euclid, and read their own compositions in a promiscuous [i.e., mixed-sex] assembly. A long line of teachers anxiously waited the calling of their classes, and over all, our queenly Madame Willard presided with royal grace and dignity. Two hundred girls in gala attire, white dresses, bright sashes, and coral ornaments, with their curly hair, rosy cheeks, and sparkling eyes, flitted to and fro, some rejoicing that they had passed through their ordeal, some still on the tiptoe of expectation, some laughing, some in tears—altogether a most beautiful and interesting picture. (*Eighty* 441)

The account captures the combined festivity and desperation of the academic platform on public days.

Opinions differed concerning the kinds of discursive activities considered [in]appropriate for female students onstage, opinions that varied greatly according to region. Southerners, for instance, may have been more accepting of schoolgirls' elocutionary display than northerners, in part, because southern women had fewer opportunities for later adapting their abilities to the professional or public sphere. Therefore, female students in the South

> were never prevented from reading their compositions at public exercises.... Whereas Northern society valued sober, cautious, and dignified behavior growing out of middle-class lifestyles, the Southern ideal was more expressive. Parents, young men, and family friends wanted to enjoy the refined gestures and stylized movements that denoted the Southern belle, with her allusions to the wisdom of the ancients, references to classical antiquity, homage to home, and allegiance to the South. To receive one of the honors of the school meant bestowing honor on family as well. (Farnham 91)

Southern women's display of learning and eloquence onstage was interpreted as a sign of class and distinction rather than as a threat to the established gender hierarchy.

Northern schoolgirls, on the other hand, encountered radically different institutional and social constraints. To illustrate, at the Litchfield Female Academy in Connecticut, select students were asked to write compositions for the yearly exhibition. Essays were evaluated by judges, and winning selections were read aloud to exhibition-day audiences, not by the writers themselves but by male judges or instructors (Brickley 211–12). However, although Litchfield girls were not permitted to read their own compositions to spectators, they were encouraged to act in dramatic skits written by the school's preceptress, Sarah Pierce, a puzzling distinction regarding feminine propriety onstage. A similar attitude prevailed at the Boston girls' school run by Susanna Rowson, the actress, playwright, and novelist turned educator. Her theatrical background resulted, naturally enough, in an emphasis on the arts of oral expression and in spectacular yearly exhibitions. In 1802, she hired Boston's Franklin Hall to stage her academy's first gala, and the event attracted "a large and fashionable audience" who watched young ladies perform sketches written by Rowson herself (Nason 109). By 1804, the academy's exhibition was engaging "the attention of the public quite as much as the commencement at the college in the neighboring town of Cambridge," and by 1807, Rowson was charging fifty cents' admission to the event (Nason 122, 155). Apparently, the discursive genres deemed acceptable for schoolgirls onstage—whether oratory, reading, declamation, or acting—changed markedly with time period and location.[3]

Educators understood the value of inviting the public to observe student performances, for if students did well, a school's reputation grew and attracted new pupils. Emma Willard, who founded the Troy Female Seminary in 1821, believed that students' stellar performances at public exhibitions demonstrated women's intellectual capacity as well as the soundness of her educational methods: "I depend upon my examinations not only for the reputation of my school, but for ultimately effecting change in the system of female education, which I believe to be of great importance, not only to my own sex, but to society in general" (qtd. in Lord 46). The Troy Female Seminary held exhibitions twice yearly, in February and July, and the events typically spanned eight days (Lutz, *Emma Willard: Pioneer* 92). Examinations were conducted at the center of a large room flanked with benches and decorated with students' artwork (see fig. 2.2). Examiners sat at the center of the room behind a long table and were approached by pairs of girls, who might be asked to solve mathematical problems, analyze passages, recall historical facts, or draw maps. The exhibition attracted a large and influential audience, including "members of the legislature, governors, and Supreme Court Justices" (A. Scott 688). It also drew visiting educators, who had the power to adopt Willard's pedagogical principles and methods at their own institutions and thus disseminate her views on women's education throughout the country.

Hoping to impress this prestigious assembly, Willard staged seminary examinations carefully to emphasize her students' femininity, an important consider-

Fig. 2.2. The exhibition room at the Troy Female Seminary. From Fairbanks's *Emma Willard and Her Pupils* (1898). Courtesy of Nancy Iannucci, Archivist/Librarian, Emma Willard School, Troy, New York.

ation given prevailing views that learning masculinized women. Willard addresses this misperception in her treatise "A Plan for Improving Female Education" (1819), in which she stresses the importance of providing young women with opportunities for rigorous study while also ensuring that their curriculum is "as different from [that] appropriated to the other sex, as the female character and duties are from the male" (46). She acknowledges concerns regarding the propriety of young ladies' oratory and concedes that "public speaking forms no part of female education. The want of this mode, might, however, be supplied by examinations judiciously conducted [. . . before] Persons of both sexes" (68). Willard is careful to distinguish between oratory and school examinations; in fact, she suggests that examinations somehow substitute for (rather than encourage) public speaking and thus actually diminish education's potential threat to the feminine character.

Willard's preoccupation with preserving students' feminine ethos reflected mounting unease among nineteenth-century educators, who began to question the wisdom of teaching schoolgirls with pedagogical methods imported directly from boys' academies. As Nancy Green details in "Female Education and School Competition: 1820–1850," debate raged in educational journals of the 1820s concerning the adverse effects of emulation (or competition) on young women's moral integrity, a symptom of the changing social and ideological climate:

> Reformers had advocated the extension of schooling to females in order that their moral role in society might be enhanced; yet schools, reflecting the competitive aspects of male society, might inadvertently destroy those very qualities men most valued in women. Women were, at least according to the men who wrote about them, "naturally" submissive, forbearing, quiet and self-sacrificing; but this inborn character was surprisingly susceptible to corruption by the wrong influences. (135)

Antebellum educators worried that competition would encourage schoolgirls to develop "unnatural" qualities like "selfishness, envy and aggressiveness" and thereby damage the delicate female character. Like the practice of emulation, school examinations also underwent critical scrutiny at this time for their potentially harmful effects upon young women. Public performance had the potential to stimulate self-confidence rather than self-abnegation, assertiveness rather than compliance, expressiveness rather than receptiveness in schoolgirls, so it, too, became suspect.

Where did Willard stand on the issue of femininity and rhetorical display? Frankly, it is difficult to tell. Researchers Alma Lutz and Lillian O'Connor contend that Willard staged public examinations so as to eliminate either the possibility or impression of schoolgirls orating to an audience. She did, however, permit emulation to a degree. Although awards were not issued, the finest student essays were read aloud at seminary examinations, however, not by the authors themselves "as this would have been too great a strain on the modesty of young ladies. Everything was done to keep girls from becoming too bold or forward" (Lutz, *Emma Willard: Pioneer* 93). Contrary to O'Connor's and Lutz's accounts is that of former pupil Elizabeth Cady Stanton, who recalled girls "read[ing] their own compositions in a promiscuous assembly" at public examinations as well as regular opportunities to deliver essays to classmates at school gatherings (441, 38). Furthermore, not only was elocution a required course at the Troy Female Seminary but advanced students also studied rhetoric, reading Hugh Blair's *Lectures on Rhetoric and Belles Lettres* and Samuel Newman's *A Practical System of Rhetoric* (O'Connor 29; Fairbanks 16).[4] Such conflicting accounts of Willard's educational purposes and practices point, yet again, to the disruptive potential of the academic platform, which, because of its implications regarding women's roles and rights, had to be renegotiated in each context.

Far from simply being a masculine venue for masculine forms of public display, the academic platform allowed schoolgirls to exercise their elocutionary abilities and practice addressing audiences. Although the types of rhetorical performance deemed appropriate for young women varied according to institution, region, and time period, by the 1820s, American schoolgirls had been delivering discourse on academic platforms for nearly four decades, all the while being admonished to restrict their eloquence to home and hearth. As antebellum women began to use their academically acquired speaking skills to address civic, religious, and political issues in public spaces, educators became alarmed at the revolutionary potential of the academic platform. Classes instructing schoolgirls in the arts of oral expression, exhibitions affording them practice in public reading and speaking, and educated mothers who modeled eloquence for their daughters had all contributed to women's entry onto public platforms. In response, educational institutions began to police young women's access to and performance on academic platforms more rigorously, a policy that erupted in controversy when women entered American colleges in the 1830s.

College Women on the Academic Platform

Recognizing that late-eighteenth- and early-nineteenth-century young women had opportunities to practice elocution in classrooms and on academic platforms is not to suggest that they received a rhetorical education equal to that provided young men in Latin schools and colleges. Compare, for example, the rhetorical education that woman's rights rhetor Cady Stanton received at the Troy Female Seminary with the "thorough training in rhetoric, oratory, and declamation" that abolitionist orator Wendell Phillips received at Harvard:

> Not only did he study outstanding books on the theory of public address and of writing . . . and listen to lectures on Rhetoric by Professor Channing, but throughout the four-year course he was required to engage in very frequent practice. We must remember, also, that a considerable part of the study of Latin and Greek was really a study of oratory and theories of public address. . . . During his three years in the law school, he continued to practice the art of speechmaking in the Moot Court. In all this experience, he had excellent training, which was the foundation of his later success as a public speaker. (Brigance and Hochmuth 1: 333)

The contrast between Cady Stanton's and Phillips's formal preparation makes all the more remarkable nineteenth-century women's courage in taking to the public platform. With their entry into American colleges in the 1830s, however, antebellum women could hope for an advanced rhetorical education for the first time.

Extensive training in rhetoric, recitation, debate, argument, and oratory characterized the college experience at the outset of the nineteenth century. But once women joined men in college classrooms and on school stages, students' struggle for verbal dominance was no longer comfortable or desirable. Robert Connors argues that the college curriculum changed shape in response to women's entry into the academy and that nonconfrontational activities like composition and literary study gradually replaced oral exercises like declamation and debate (*Composition* 44–68).

Connors's feminization of rhetoric theory is at once probable and problematic. On the one hand, antebellum women's rhetorical delivery became ever more suspect as the cult of true womanhood grew dominant. The feminine virtues of purity, piety, submissiveness, and domesticity were fundamentally incompatible with the masculine demands of public speaking, which required extroversion, assertiveness, intelligence, and passion (Welter 152). Therefore, as domestic ideology took firm root in the culture, women's delivery increasingly looked like outright gender subversion. Furthermore, as Susan Zaeske details in "The 'Promiscuous Audience' Controversy and the Emergence of the Early Woman's Rights Movement," while antebellum women's delivery to other women was considered acceptable, their delivery to mixed-sex (or promiscuous) audiences elicited alarm, a consequence of "deeply-rooted myths about women and their proper role in politics" (197). Although the word *promiscu-ous* originally denoted something "of a mixed nature," it acquired negative con-notations with antebellum women's ascendancy to public platforms. Thereaf-ter, women (but not men) who addressed mixed-sex audiences risked being viewed as heretics defying biblical mandates dictating their public silence, as loose or promiscuous women seeking men's attention, or as unnatural "mas-culine" women: "[O]pponents used the injunction against addressing 'promis-cuous audiences' to contend that no woman could be virtuous if she stepped outside the domestic sphere by engaging in activities such as pubic speaking" (198, 203). Therefore, college educators' decision to deemphasize the oral elements of the rhetoric course and thus spare women the need for rhetorical display can be viewed as efforts to accommodate feminine gender and discur-sive norms, in which case, Connors's feminization thesis makes sense.

However, there are serious shortcomings to this argument as well. First, Connors minimizes women's mixed responses to oratory's erasure from the curriculum. While some college women willingly relinquished elocutionary opportunities on academic platforms, a matter to be discussed shortly, oth-ers insisted on equal access to curricular and extracurricular rhetorical activi-ties. Second, Connors overlooks alternative explanations for oratory's removal from the heart of college education. Although he suggests that the college cur-riculum changed shape in order to accommodate women's presence in higher education, I believe the historical record supports another motive for oratory's elision, namely, withholding from women formal training and practice in pub-lic speaking.

I illustrate these points by examining practices at two coeducational col-leges. Granted, a number of women's colleges opened between 1839 and 1860, but I have concentrated on the coeducational experience chiefly because early women's colleges fell short of providing a separate but equal higher educa-tion. This failing resulted from a cluster of factors, including incoming stu-dents' inadequate preparation for college work, female colleges' consequent lowering of admission standards and simplification of the curriculum, and female institutions' perennial struggle to obtain adequate funding (Woody 2: 140–50). For these reasons, antebellum women generally obtained a better education at coeducational colleges, and my analysis focuses on two of the earliest, Oberlin and Antioch.

Oberlin College

The first coeducational college in the United States opened its doors in the Ohio backwoods on 3 December 1833. Dedicated to the mission of disseminating ministers and missionaries throughout the West and the world, Oberlin College also committed itself to educating women and African Americans, admitting them alongside men. The college's first circular (1834) proclaimed the institution's ambition to elevate "the female character by bringing within the reach of the misjudged and neglected sex all the instructive privileges which hitherto have unreasonably distinguished the leading sex from theirs" (qtd. in Fletcher 1: 373). Lacking a coeducational predecessor, Oberlin had to determine on its own which "instructive privileges" would be extended to or withheld from "the misjudged and neglected sex" in terms of the curriculum, classroom, and school stage, a difficult and often contentious process.

Regarding the curriculum, a two-track system divided along gender lines quickly evolved:

> The classical [or collegiate] course, leading to a bachelor's degree, included Greek, Latin, and Hebrew; mathematics, astronomy, and "natural philosophy"; chemistry, geology and biology; logic and rhetoric; and weekly lectures on the Bible. The literary course omitted the more rigorous subjects—classical languages, rhetoric, and advanced mathematics—and substituted for them English poetry, American history, and art. The literary course was designed for women students, and led only to a diploma, not a degree. (Cazden 25)

Although most women pursued the literary or ladies' course, Oberlin remained true to its commitment by allowing the few who desired more challenging study to pursue the AB or bachelor's degree. In terms of student distribution, the two-track system led to women only in ladies' course classes and primarily men (with an eventual sprinkling of women) in classical or collegiate classes. Despite women's access to both the classical and literary courses, their rhetorical education was not equivalent to that offered male students either in the classroom or on the academic platform.

Oberlin's policy on delivery was informed by St. Paul's injunction that women should "learn in silence with all submissiveness" and by the assumption that women's rhetorical training was unnecessary as they were barred from activities and professions requiring public speech. The ladies' course, therefore, "prepared women to be good wives for professional men—and to teach before marriage. It did not, however, prepare them to engage in the world of public discourse as ministers, lawyers, scientists, or other professionals, as the men's curriculum was preparing the male students" (Royster 189). Oberlin's curriculum supported emerging domestic ideology by situating women's primary purpose within the home, and it educated women not for equality's sake but for "intelligent motherhood and a properly subservient wifehood" (Fletcher 1: 291). Following from this, elocutionary and rhetorical training in the ladies' course emphasized reading and composition while that in the classical course stressed writing, discussion, oration, debate, and declamation. The 1838 "Young Ladies' Course of Study," a publication detailing required coursework and activities, indicates that female students attended "the regular recitations of the college Department" and observed the performances of their male counterparts rather than performing themselves (Hosford 41). Although the ladies' course did not provide extensive rhetorical training, it did assign such prominent rhetorics of the day as Whately's *Logic* and *Rhetoric*, Paley's *Evidences*, and Butler's *Analogy* (Royster 190). Initially, then, Oberlin women learned about rhetoric and elocution indirectly through their readings and observations of men's recitations.

Uncertainty regarding men and women's comportment in coeducational classrooms created great discomfort at times. In 1839, professor Asa Mahan invited ladies' course students to attend one of his (predominately male) college classes in the belief that the women's presence would exert a beneficial influence upon the men. Mahan also suggested that the visiting women might gain valuable elocutionary experience by reading their compositions aloud in class. The women students disagreed, and twenty-three petitioned Oberlin's faculty, protesting Mahan's proposal and arguing that modesty prevented their reading to men in the classroom (Ginzberg, "Joint" 73). Ladies' course students essentially policed themselves in order to conform to the dictates of true womanhood. Although some professors labeled such resistance "false modesty," the young women's objections were respected, and their oral participation in coeducational classes became optional. Soon the assumption that women would choose to remain silent in mixed-sex classes prevailed across campus.

Many Oberlin women upheld feminine discursive norms, but others desired an equal education in all areas, including debate, oratory, and declamation. Oberlin women's right to pursue the AB degree became official in 1837 when the college acknowledged women students in its "College Course of Study," a publication detailing the track's required coursework and activities. Students in the classical course read Whately's *Logic* and *Rhetoric* and participated in exercises designed to promote oral and written competence: "Compositions and either extempore discussions or declamation weekly throughout the course. For the last two years, the Students will declaim their own Compositions" (qtd. in Hosford 74). On paper, then, women pursuing the AB degree received rhetorical instruction and training throughout the four-year course; in practice, however, the college as a whole did not support their discursive efforts, as Elizabeth Prall's experiences in the rhetoric classroom indicate.

Prall was one of the first women to enroll in Oberlin's classical course and earn a bachelor's degree. The difficulties confronting a solitary woman in a classroom of men is rendered vividly in tutor James Fairchild's account of one of her recitations:

> Miss Prall presented the character of Elizabeth of England, quite a pretty composition, but near the close she took occasion to make a remark or two on "Woman's Rights." Speaking of Elizabeth's visit to Oxford she says, "Strange that woman in monarchical England should be permitted to address vice-chancellors and doctors at Oxford University, and in Latin, too, while in liberty-loving America she is not permitted to speak in her own tongue, among the populace, to defend her own rights." The matter passed off with a laugh, but a discussion soon followed which involved the woman's rights question. Messrs. Bancroft, Fisher, Dougherty, and Kedzie, one and all came out so ungallantly against Miss Prall's sentiments that the poor girl cried sadly. I understood it all as a joke until I saw by Miss Prall's tears that she felt a little serious about it. (qtd. in Hosford 66)

Fairchild's patronizing attitude toward women's rights and oratory unfortunately persisted throughout his career at Oberlin, first as a tutor, then as a professor, and, finally, as college president.

Matters had not improved much by the time of Lucy Stone's and Antoinette Brown's arrival in the 1840s. Twenty-six-year-old Stone entered Oberlin hoping to obtain the education and training necessary to become a speaker for abolition and woman's rights, and she had overcome considerable obstacles to get there. Stone's father, for example, had generally disapproved of her educational ambitions, so as a child, she had gathered and sold nuts and berries in order to purchase schoolbooks and supplies. At sixteen, after completing district school, she started teaching, beginning a cycle of work and study that would last nearly a decade. Stone would teach until she accumulated enough money to quit her job and attend a nearby academy for a quarter or two. In this manner, she studied at the Quaboag Seminary, the Wilbraham Academy, and Mount Holyoke Seminary. After nine years, Stone had learned enough Latin, Greek, math, and rhetoric to pass Oberlin's qualifying exams and, in 1843, gain admittance as a first-year student in the classical course (Blackwell 20–40; Kerr 21–28).

One of Stone's classmates at Oberlin, Antoinette Brown, also felt called to public speaking. From youth, she had been an active and vocal church participant, "speaking often in informal prayer meetings . . . and taking for granted that God's call was not limited by gender" (Cazden 15). Although Brown's neighbors assumed she would channel her religious enthusiasm by becoming a minister's wife, she aspired to become a minister herself. Brown entered Oberlin in 1845, determined to gain admission into its theology department after completing the ladies' course.[5]

Stone and Brown joined forces in order to obtain rhetorical training and practice. After Asa Mahan's earlier efforts to integrate women into the classroom ended in failure, Oberlin faculty voted to release (or exclude) women from oral participation in mixed-sex exercises, discussions, and debates. Stone and Brown persuaded professor James Thome to allow them to debate each other rather than simply listening to the debates of their male colleagues, and by all accounts, their performances were "exceptionally brilliant" (Kerr 37). Reaction, however, was swift. According to Alice Stone Blackwell, the Ladies' Board, which supervised Oberlin's women students, "immediately got busy, St. Paul was invoked, and the college authorities forbade any repetition of the experiment" (61). Stone lamented in a letter home, "I was never in a place where women are so rigidly taught that they must not speak in public" (qtd. in Blackwell 71).

In an effort to supplement their limited opportunities for public speaking, Stone and Brown founded a secret debating society for women in May 1846, which met surreptitiously either in the woods or in a home off campus. Stone opened the first meeting with a statement of purpose: "We shall leave this college with the reputation of a thorough collegiate course, yet not one of us has received any rhetorical or elocutionary training. Not one of us could state a question or argue it in successful debate. For this reason I have proposed the formation of this association" (qtd. in Blackwell 61). Debate topics ranged from "Egotism" and "The Qualifications of a Minister's Wife" to woman's rights, and within a few months, Stone developed enough confidence to deliver her first public address. On 1 August 1846, she stood on a public platform, read an address to a local antislavery group, and embarked upon her rhetorical career (Cazden 28).

Like the debating society founded by Stone and Brown, extracurricular literary societies also provided Oberlin women opportunities to develop oral competence and gain recognition for their scholastic achievements. The Ladies' Literary Society (LLS), for instance, played a crucial role in initiating women's participation in Oberlin's graduation ceremonies. Throughout the 1830s, Oberlin women began and ended their studies invisibly, their completion of the ladies' course receiving no official recognition whatsoever. In 1840, the LLS sponsored the first commencement ceremony for graduates of the ladies' course. The gala began with a procession of female students attired in white dresses with blue sashes. The ceremony included prayers and musical interludes and reached its culmination when women graduates mounted the academic platform and read original compositions to a mixed-sex audience estimated at three thousand. Following the readings, Oberlin's president awarded graduates a testimonial and certificate acknowledging their completion of the ladies' course. In 1843, Oberlin integrated the LLS exercises into its regular commencement ceremonies, and thereafter, the ladies' course graduation took place the day before that of the classical course (Hosford 49–53; Fletcher 2: 831–33).

The college confronted especially thorny issues regarding gender and the academic platform once women began to graduate from the classical course. In 1841, Mary Hosford, Elizabeth Prall, and Caroline Rudd became the first women to earn the AB degree in the United States (Cazden 25). However, although ladies' course graduates might stand upon a stage and read compositions to friends, families, trustees, and college supporters, it was considered inadvisable for AB women graduates to do the same. Oddly enough, the mixed composition of the audience did not concern Oberlin officials as much as the composition of the academic platform itself:

> [W]hen the graduates of the Ladies' Literary Course took their diplomas, the persons on the platform were all women, except the president; and when the students of the regular classical course received their degrees, the persons on the platform were almost all men. Hence on the one occasion it was thought permissible for a woman's voice to be heard, while on the other it would have been considered a direct defiance of a divine command. (Blackwell 73)

Oberlin first suggested that AB women read their essays with ladies' course graduates on the evening prior to the classical course ceremony and then receive their degrees the next day with their male cohorts. The ABs rejected this proposal, so a compromise was reached:

> To avoid the impropriety of having the young ladies read from a platform arranged for the speaking of young men, and filled with trustees and professors and distinguished gentlemen visitors, the essays of the lady college graduates were read by the professor of rhetoric, the young women coming upon the platform with their class at the close to receive their diplomas. (James Fairchild qtd. in Hosford 67–68)

Despite the restrictions placed on their delivery, AB women, nevertheless, used the occasion to discuss issues of importance to them. Mary Hosford, for example, penned "A Young Lady's Apology for Pursuing the Classical Course of Study," a defense of her decision to obtain a college degree. Professor John Morgan then read the address to the commencement audience, apparently with less than stellar results (Hosford 68). The *Ohio Atlas* remarked that the women's essays would have been better if "spoken with all the spirit and life which the feeling of maternity could not have failed to produce, instead of being condemned to an indifferent reading by a Professor who had nothing to do with the composition" (qtd. in Fletcher 2: 835).

Lucy Stone viewed her 1847 graduation from the classical course as an opportunity to challenge Oberlin's stance on women's delivery, as she explained in a letter home: "We are trying to get the faculty to let the ladies of our class read their own pieces when they graduate. They have never been allowed to do it, but we expect to read for ourselves, or not to write" (qtd. in Blackwell 67). Stone's entire class asked the faculty and Ladies' Board to reconsider their position on AB women's participation in commencement-day exercises, but the petition was rejected. In response, Stone and many of her classmates, both male and female, refused to write or deliver graduation pieces in order to protest the unfairness (Blackwell 73). Women ABs continued to have their graduation essays read by proxy until 1858 when officials ruled that women might read (but *not* orate) their own compositions. This revised tradition remained intact until Harriet Louise Keeler's graduation in 1874:

> Demurely [Keeler] tripped upon the stage, holding the conventional pages like the other sweet girl graduates. Demurely she read the first sentence, eyes modestly fixed upon her manuscript—and then the paper was discarded, the brave eyes swept the rows of startled faces, and the sweet girl graduate addressed the audience! (Hosford 102)

After Keeler "cast aside her written part and orate[d] like an Oberlin man," the ban on women's speech was lifted although school officials continued to view women's oratory as an act of questionable taste (Solomon, "Oberlin" 83).

Following her 1847 graduation, Stone realized her lecturing ambitions by becoming an agent for the American Anti-Slavery Society. Antoinette Brown completed the ladies' course that same year but remained at Oberlin to pursue her own dream of studying theology. The college permitted interested women to attend theology classes, assuming that their learning would be for domestic use only. Brown's classmate Lettice Smith, for instance, was studying theology in order to prepare herself for life as a minister's wife (she married Thomas Holmes, a divinity student at Oberlin). Brown's determination to become a minister herself, however, was an entirely different matter. The college had no intention of training women professionally for the ministry, so

Brown's presence in the theology department presented Oberlin with an ethical dilemma. Although committed to providing women access to higher education, Oberlin considered certain occupations and roles unsuitable for them. In consequence, throughout her three years of theological study, Brown confronted two interrelated obstacles: Oberlin's resistance to women's full participation in public speaking exercises both in and out of the classroom and its refusal to recognize her officially as a theology student.

The first in a long series of negotiations began when Brown applied for admission to the theology department in the fall of 1847. As figure 2.3 indicates, Oberlin preferred to list Brown as a resident graduate in the ladies' department rather than as a student in the theology department, thereby granting her semi-official status as a visitor but circumventing the issue of her professional goals.

Brown's ambiguous position in the theology department had ramifications in the classroom as well. In-class exercises like extemporaneous speaking, declamation, and debate prepared theology students for the pulpit; however, because women were exempted from oral display before male classmates, Brown had difficulty acquiring the necessary practice. During her first semester of study, for example, she took a class with theology professor Charles Finney, who asked students to share their motivations for becoming ministers. One by one, male students gave their accounts until, near the end of the class period, Finney called for anyone who had not yet spoken to take a turn. When someone mentioned that only Lettice Smith and Brown remained, Finney grew flustered, as Brown recounted in a letter to Stone:

> [Finney] looked as though he did not know what to say & the next time said, "O we dont call upon the ladies." They had all told me we should have to speak & I felt so badly at what he said that I just began to cry & was obliged to leave the room. It was the first & last time that I have cried about anything connected with this matter. . . . After I went out they talked over the matter & it seems Prof. Finney did not know we were members of the department in any other sense than the other ladies are who go in to hear the lectures. . . . He said he was willing any lady should speak if she wished to & If we were members of the department he should like to know it. (Lasser and Merrill, *Soul* 41)

Finney's support would prove crucial to Brown because of his great influence at Oberlin, his evangelical vision having in large measure inspired the college's original mission. Furthermore, the unorthodox roles assumed by Finney's first and second wives suggest that he was generally well disposed toward socially engaged women. Finney's first wife, Lydia Andrews, not only edited *The*

YOUNG LADIES' · COURSE.

RESIDENT GRADUATES.

Names.	Residences.
Antoinette L. Brown,*	*Henrietta, N. Y.*
Lettice S. Holmes,*	*Ann Arbor, Mich.*

*Pursuing Theological Course.

FOURTH YEAR.

Names.	Residences.
Rebecca Bebout,	*Savannah.*
Mary E. Cone,	*Bristol, Ill.*
Helen M. Cowles,	*Oberlin.*
Minerva P. Dayton,	*Piqua.*
Harriet A. Green,	*Newberry.*
Sally Holly,	*Rochester, N. Y.*
Amanda Parmelee,	*Oberlin.*
Clarinda Parmelee,	*Oberlin.*
A. R. Skinner,	*Chelsea, Vt.*
Lucy A. Stanton,	*Cleveland.*
Eunice Thompson,	*Medina.*

Fourth Year Ladies, 11.

Fig. 2.3. Oberlin's Young Ladies' Course Catalogue, 1849–1850.
Courtesy of the Oberlin College Archives, Oberlin, Ohio.

Moral Advocate but also established women's prayer groups and instructed the young. His second wife, Elizabeth Atkinson, fully supported Finney's evangelical work and frequently participated in religious meetings as her husband's partner and equal. During the couple's 1849–51 tour of England, for instance, she and Finney jointly led prayer meetings so often that "it was hard . . . to distinguish who was the minister" (Solomon, *In the Company* 38). Furthermore, Finney's acceptance of women's activism influenced the college's policies, especially during his various terms as college president between 1851 and 1865 (Lasser and Merrill, *Soul* 89–90). Therefore, after a somewhat awkward beginning, Brown was free to participate in all classroom exercises, and Finney challenged her to grow as an orator, frequently calling on her to speak at public prayer meetings.

Although Finney encouraged her, other faculty members did not, a fact that became apparent when Brown sought admission into the Theological Literary Society, an extracurricular club that sponsored discussion, oration, and declamation. The society's advisor—John Morgan, professor of New Testament literature—openly opposed Brown's delivery in and out of the classroom, as she related in a letter to Stone:

> Prof Morgan said if he was the teacher he would not let me sustain any other relation to the department than the ladies to the college classes i.e. he would have no discussion or declamation from the ladies but as it was a society the members had a right to say what I might do & they were too evenly divided to prevent me from speakin[g]. He said he respected me none the less for my views—that he would not criticize me any more severely than he would if I were a gentleman. . . . Lettice & I may have every privilege now promised us except delivering our own sermons. We have nothing to do with that this year & though Prof Morgan says no we shall not do it he may change his mind or rather his *conscience* before then. (Lasser and Merrill, *Soul* 42–43)

Because only its advisor and half its membership opposed her participation, Brown was permitted to join the extracurricular group, making her the only Oberlin woman ever admitted to a male literary society (Fletcher 1: 293).[6]

Although Brown's enthusiasm and determination helped her to obtain, in some measure, the education she desired, two years of solitary struggle with institutional prejudice and resistance finally took its toll, leaving her tired and discouraged. When Augusta Brown, Antoinette's sister and a fellow Oberlin student, developed symptoms of severe tuberculosis in 1849, Antoinette left college to accompany the patient home. She spent the winter nursing Augusta and pondering whether to return to Oberlin or finish her theological studies elsewhere. In the end, Brown opted to return in the spring of 1850 and complete her last semester, a decision that even a staunch supporter like Stone adamantly opposed. She interpreted the college's refusal to recognize Brown officially as an unforgivable affront:

> Nette I am so sorry you are at Oberlin, on terms which to me seem *dishonorable*. They trampled your womanhood, and you did not spurn it. I do believe that even *they* would have thought better of you if you had staid away. O Nette, I am sorry you returned, but for all this you KNOW I *love you dearly*, and will say no more about it. . . . I shant ever take a second degree and regret, deeply regret, that I ever took any. (Lasser and Merrill, *Soul* 69)

Unfortunately, little improved upon Brown's return.

Oberlin continued to hedge regarding Brown's status in the program. During the final term of study, it was standard practice for the Lorain County Congregational Association, staffed largely by Oberlin faculty, to issue preaching licenses to theology students and thereby authorize them to deliver sermons in local churches. Although Brown applied for a license, the association sidestepped the controversial issue of women's ministry by advising her to preach if she must but to do so without its endorsement (Cazden 50). Despite her lack of a license, she managed to gain some experience that spring by lecturing on temperance and preaching in small churches nearby.

Brown completed the theology course in 1850, but Oberlin refused to award her a diploma, ordain her as a minister, or grant her a role in its commencement exercises. She left college with nothing but the knowledge and training she had managed to acquire. Biographer Elizabeth Cazden observes that Brown confronted a classic double bind, one common to those who defy gender barriers. On the one hand, by studying without official recognition, Brown appeared to accept Oberlin's unjust treatment; on the other hand, had she quit in protest, as Stone urged her to do, Brown would not have obtained the education and experience needed to enter the ministry, her long-standing ambition (49). Although she lacked a degree, a small church in South Butler, New York, nevertheless, ordained Brown in 1853 and made her the first Congregational woman minister in the United States. Furthermore, she eventually received recognition from Oberlin as well. In 1878, the college awarded her an honorary master's degree, adding her name to the list of theology school graduates of 1850, and in 1908, nearly sixty years after she had completed her studies, it awarded the eighty-three-year-old an honorary doctorate of divinity, both belated tributes to her groundbreaking accomplishments (Cazden 192, 251).[7]

In review, Oberlin women negotiated gender issues surrounding the academic platform in their exchanges with students, faculty, and administrators. As this section has suggested, college women had varied responses to the prospect of equal participation in mixed-sex classrooms and on school stages. Some chose silence, others speech; some preferred separate and distinct forms of rhetorical education, others joint and identical; some insisted on their right to deliver rhetoric with men, others on their right to deliver without them. In any case, the rhetorical impediments confronting college women were far more complicated than simply obtaining the right to address mixed-sex audiences. Furthermore, regardless of institutional intent or arrangement, one fact remained constant: Whenever women approached the academic platform, issues of power, gender, and discourse inevitably erupted. Their experiences at another coeducational college in Ohio—Antioch—illustrate precisely this point.

Antioch College

Antioch College opened in Yellow Springs, Ohio, in 1853, twenty years after Oberlin, and benefited from its predecessor's experiences with coeducation and the academic platform. Antioch was committed to providing men and women with the same high-quality education. Unlike Oberlin, which offered women a separate track of study, all Antioch students followed a curriculum leading to the bachelor's degree. Antioch women participated fully alongside men in classrooms, examinations, and commencement exercises, where graduates read original essays regardless of gender (Stein 54). Furthermore, both men and women were active in extracurricular literary societies. However, despite Antioch's dedication to the equal education of the sexes, the college occasionally fell short of its ideals in practice, some of its inconsistency and ambivalence traceable to the views of its first president, Horace Mann.

Mann was "the best-known educator of his age," a man whose stellar reputation derived from pioneering a system of common and normal schools in Massachusetts, editing the influential *Common School Journal* for nearly a decade, and serving as a legislative representative for Massachusetts at both the state and national levels (Rury and Harper 482; Lach 426). Mann explained his stance on women's education in a series of lectures later published as *A Few Thoughts on the Powers and Duties of Women* (1853): "The female has every natural right to a full and complete mental development [as that] which belongs to the other sex" (57). He protested woman's exclusion from higher education, noting that in most colleges we lose sight of the female portion of the race altogether. From an examination of their catalogues, or a visit to their halls, we should infer that woman had been expatriated from creation, or had never belonged to it. Neither as student nor as teacher does she appear on academic rolls, or in academic chairs. (*Few* 59)

Mann was, in part, drawn to the presidency of Antioch as a means of redressing these wrongs. Antioch offered qualified women and men access to the same demanding curriculum, including the study of Latin, Greek, English, history, philosophy, mathematics, and natural science (Messerli 543). The English course emphasized oral and written communication rather than literature and demanded weekly rhetorical exercises throughout the four years of study (Vallance 314). Mann's hiring practices reflected his beliefs as well. Although Oberlin had hired women to instruct students in the ladies' course, Mann hired the first female professors expected to teach mixed-sex classes. Rebecca Pennell, one of Antioch's original faculty, taught moral philosophy, didactics, and civics; Lucretia Crocker taught mathematics and philosophy between 1857 and 1858; and Rebecca Rice, an Antioch graduate of 1860, taught mathematics and physics beginning in 1866 (Rury and Harper 484–85). (In figure 2.4, Rice is seated on the far left in the bottom row.)

Mann's conviction that there were essential differences between the sexes, however, tempered his commitment to equal education. God, according to Mann, "created the race, Male and Female, ON THE PRINCIPLE OF A DIVISION OF LABOR" (*Few* 17). They were to fill distinct but complementary roles in their respective spheres, women destined for "the fireside, the cradle and the nursery, which involve the least of glare and notoriety, and the most of retirement and reserve," men ordained for "those spheres which demand most of an iron sternness and persistence of will, and a hard intellectual fibre, as tough and as tearless as whip-cord" (*Few* 106–7). Mann's stance on women's public involvement followed from these beliefs. Although he expressed outrage at women's exclusion from the most "honorable and lucrative" occupations, he did not advocate their equal access to the professions (*Few* 63). Women were well adapted to bookkeeping (so long as the work was not "performed in a crowded shop or public counting-room"), clerking "in shops where female customers mostly resort," teaching, pharmaceutics, interior design, the ministry, and even medicine (*Few* 76–95). However, they were constitutionally ill equipped for such professions as the military, law, and, most especially, politics: "Politics! Politics!! That any mortal who has ever lived within the roar and stench of that black and sulphurous lake should desire to see woman embarked upon its tumultuous and howling waters, is a mystery past finding out" (*Few* 97). Mann believed that women's political involvement would ulti-mately produce sexual degeneracy, disordered families, and social chaos, so rather than permitting internal division and gender confusion to destroy the nation, he urged men to resign from politics should women successfully "make a sortie upon the political rostrum, and invade legislative halls" (*Few* 104). He felt strongly that "woman's rights" women, proponents of equal occupational and political rights, were dangerously misguided; therefore, it is ironic that Mann's relatively liberal stance on education attracted precisely this sort of woman to Antioch. Not too surprisingly, the inevitable conflicts arising be-tween Mann and women at Antioch became most readily apparent in matters related to the academic platform.

An early squabble arose over the college's lecture series, which invited prominent speakers like Henry Bellows, George Curtis, and Amory Mayo to visit and address students and faculty (Stein 65–69). When student Olympia Brown protested the absence of women lecturers, she was informed that "there were no women comparable to the men they had secured" (Willis 15). Brown believed otherwise, so she gathered together other women students and ex-plained her objections to them: "I said there were Susan B. Anthony, Eliza-beth Cady Stanton, Lucy Stone, Antoinette Brown, anyone of whom would compare very well with the men of the course, and that what we had to do now was to raise the money, and select the speaker. They all agreed." The group invited Antoinette Brown to Antioch, raising funds and making arrangements for her to deliver a lecture and sermon. When Antioch refused to grant her use of the college chapel, the group arranged for her to preach in a nearby Yellow Springs's church instead. Seeing a woman deliver a sermon altered the course of Olympia Brown's life: "It was the first time I had heard a woman preach, and the sense of victory lifted me up. I felt as though the Kingdom of Heaven were at hand" (Willis 15). After graduating from Antioch with a bachelor's degree in 1860, Brown studied theology at St. Lawrence Univer-sity and, in 1863, became the first woman to be ordained as a Universalist min-ister (see fig. 2.4). She pursued a twenty-five-year career in the ministry until 1887, when she resigned in order to dedicate herself fully to promoting woman suffrage. Antoinette Brown's visit clearly affected women students deeply; furthermore, it indicates that they were capable of swift and decisive collec-tive action, a skill apparent in their literary society efforts as well.

Extracurricular literary societies abounded at Antioch. The 1850s alone witnessed the founding of the Alethezetean, Amphychtion, Star, Crescent, Adelphian Union, and Franklin literary societies (Vallance 383–85). Most of these organizations consisted of separate but cooperating men's and women's

Fig. 2.4. Olympia Brown and Antioch's class of 1860. Wrapped in a paisley shawl,
Brown is the third person in from the left in the second row from the bottom.
Image Courtesy of Antiochiana, Antioch College.

branches that shared meeting rooms, maintained libraries, funded speakers'
visits, and cosponsored public exhibitions. Literary societies gave students a
weekly platform on which to practice rhetorical precepts learned in the classroom. Students debated, orated, lectured, and read compositions on subjects
of their own choosing, often social, philosophical, or political issues of the day.

To illustrate, weekly meeting records for the Crescent Society, the women's
affiliate of the men's Star Society, show that woman's rights and gender relations were central topics of discussion. Between 1855 and 1857, the Crescent
Society's secretary book indicates that female members debated the following topics: "no true woman will be dependent on man for her support";
"women should universally adopt the Short [Bloomer] dress"; "it is the duty
of every woman to devote her time, talents & energies, entirely to advancing
the woman's rights cause"; "woman was made to please man, and therefore
man is the proper umpire for determining her sphere"; and "the study &
practice of law does not [fall] within the province of woman" (Stein 6–7). The
Crescents also sponsored women speakers, for example, inviting Antioch
alumna Mahala Jay to lecture on 13 June 1860 and subsequently publishing
her address. Such issues and efforts suggest that female students embraced a
radically different conception of women's roles than that forwarded by college president Horace Mann.

Students' weekly literary society meetings prepared them for quarterly and annual public exhibitions, events that attracted large audiences from Yellow Springs and beyond. Local, regional, and even national newspapers covered the exhibitions, with reviews appearing in Springfield's *Evening News and Journal*, the *Cincinnati Gazette*, and the *Saturday Evening Post* (Stein 18; Rury and Harper 497; Stein 20). Antioch managed issues concerning gender and delivery quite differently than Oberlin. Typically, the men's and women's branches of an Antioch literary society—say, the Stars and the Crescents—cosponsored exhibitions and anniversaries, and members performed together before promiscuous (mixed-sex) audiences.

Given Antioch's tolerance of a mixed-sex academic platform, it is somewhat puzzling to learn that the college discouraged cooperating literary society branches from holding joint weekly meetings, a policy that created tension between faculty and students in the 1850s. Recurrent conflicts involved the Alethezetean Society, Antioch's first literary club founded in 1853. It consisted of segregated male and female branches that initially met separately each week; however, by the fall of 1854, it was apparent that there were not enough members to sustain the women's branch. The two branches voted to unite, and in February 1855, they submitted a petition to faculty detailing the merger and requesting permission to meet weekly as a coeducational society. Faculty promptly rejected the petition, citing the impropriety of men and women meeting without adequate supervision, a decision that created uproar among the Alethezeteans and prompted nearly a quarter of its members to resign from the society in protest (Stein 44–46; Rury and Harper 494–95). Mann's commitment to ensuring "relations of delicacy and purity between the sexes"—in other words, his fear that the sexual impulse would run rampant among unsupervised men and women—likely accounts for Antioch's decision to prohibit coeducational meetings but condone mixed-sex exhibitions (Mann, *Dedication* 118).[8]

After the rejection of its 1855 petition to merge branches, the Alethezetean women's group languished for a time, but within a year, efforts were underway to revive it. A renewed women's branch asked faculty for permission to hold a public exhibition in June 1857, but the request was denied. The group promptly submitted another petition specifying a September date instead. As faculty delayed responding to the second request, the women's branch grew irate. Member Nancy Leavell sent a letter to faculty arguing women students' right to access the academic platform:

> We feel that in accordance with the principles upon which Antioch College was founded, that you have no right to deprive the ladies of the Institution any

opportunities for educational or literary improvement which you freely bestow upon the gentlemen.... Sirs, the only request we have to make is, that you will make known to us at an early date whether or not the ladies connected with this Institution shall hereafter have the same privileges as the gentlemen. (qtd. in Stein 52–53)

The faculty's eventual answer was, again, no. (Leavell, by the way, also appears in figure 2.4. She is the third person in from the right in the third row from the bottom.)

If the Alethezeteans interpreted the faculty's decision as discriminatory and inconsistent with Antioch's commitment to equal education, others viewed the issues at stake quite differently. Both Moses Cummings, editor of the *Christian Palladium*, and Stephen Weston, author of "History of Antioch," saw the petitions' rejection as an attempt to quell woman's rights sentiments on campus, arguing that "ultras" (or extremists) dominated the Alethezetean women's branch (Stein 55). Complicating this explanation, however, is the fact that another women's branch, the Crescents, obtained permission to hold a joint exhibition with its male counterpart, the Stars, just after faculty denied the women Alethezeteans' first request for a June exhibition (Stein 52). As the club records detailed earlier indicate, the Crescents regularly examined woman's rights issues at its weekly meetings and sponsored events. Given faculty support for the Crescents' petition and rejection of the Alethezeteans', it seems unlikely that Antioch was attempting to suppress woman's rights advocates. The Alethezeteans' interpretation of events may finally prove more sound, namely, that the real issue at stake concerned women's efforts to access the academic platform independently, without the cosponsorship of an affiliated men's branch.

In response to the faculty's rejection of its second petition, the women's Alethezetean Society dissolved itself. It also expressed its displeasure at the college's first commencement exercise, an important social and symbolic occasion. Draped in black, the color of mourning, the disbanded Alethezeteans displayed themselves prominently in the front row of the chapel, their somber dress a form of visual protest that received mention in a number of newspapers, including the *Cincinnati Gazette* (Rury and Harper 497). Although he officially minimized the significance of the event, Mann resented the negative publicity. His wife, Mary Mann, affords readers a glimpse into her husband's response to the Alethezetean affair (however, she conflates two incidents—the 1855 petition for coeducational meetings and the 1857 petition for a women-only exhibition):

Outside, "women's-rights" women of the ultra stamp increased the difficulties for him [Mann] by coming upon the premises, and promulgating their heresies against good manners. On one occasion, when the faculty had decided that it was best the young ladies and gentlemen of the literary societies would no longer hold their ordinary meetings together, but should meet separately, except on their public days, some women of this class felt that their rights were denied them,—"rights" being sometimes interpreted to mean, *just what I choose to do*. To avenge their wrongs, they induced the whole society to appear dressed in deep mourning on a very public occasion, when their united literary societies were addressed by a stranger. The faculty took no notice of it except by a good-natured smile, thinking the most salutary punishment would be to leave them to the public ridicule, without giving them the solace of being martyrs. The most prominent offender soon concluded to leave an institution where she was subject to such *oppression*. (526-27)

Mary Mann dismisses the Alethezeteans as "ultras" who ascribe to annoying "heresies against good manners" and seek selfish ends of doing "*just what [they] choose*." Their decision to wear mourning to a prominent public event is treated as the act of willful children, one that wise, parental faculty ignore with "good-natured" smiles. At no point does she suggest that either her husband or the faculty seriously consider the perspective of the Alethezeteans. Nonetheless, although denied access to the academic platform, women students used audience space and the rhetoric of dress to express a complaint that the press, if not officials at Antioch, perceived clearly.

Although Antioch pledged itself to educational parity in the classroom and on the college platform, it did not sustain that commitment fully, and literary societies became the lightning rod for ideological inconsistencies. In the Alethezetean affair, Antioch denied women the opportunity to speak from an academic platform filled with members of their own sex, a prospect that would not have been the least bit disconcerting at Oberlin. Antioch's decision to support mixed-sex exhibitions but prohibit women-only events makes sense only if we recognize that the convergence of gender and delivery on academic platforms inevitably produced power struggles, even among those with good intentions.

American rhetors have traditionally had recourse to five occasions or settings for public speech: the legal, the legislative, the popular, the religious, and the academic (Bohman 22). Although women were largely excluded from legal, legislative, and popular forums until the second quarter of the nineteenth century, they gained access to religious and academic platforms much earlier, and these sites became important training grounds. The academic platform, in particular, allowed generations of women to hone their skills of oral expression and practice addressing large, mixed-sex, influential audiences. However, when schoolgirls' elocutionary exercises eventually translated into women's public discourse, ideological conflicts among educators, pupils, and the public led to curricular and pedagogical reform, especially at the college level.

Over the course of the nineteenth century, rhetorical instruction in American colleges altered dramatically, a change that has been thoroughly documented by Albert Kitzhaber, Nan Johnson, James Berlin, and Robert Connors. Connors argues that between 1820 and 1910, rhetoric shifted from an oral to a written focus in response to women's entry into American colleges, and he interprets oratory's purgation from the curriculum as an attempt to reduce the climate of competition, disputation, and vainglorious display that had traditionally characterized higher education:

> Contestive, combative educational methods that had worked satisfactorily for all-male schooling now came to seem violent, vulgar, silly. A man could attack another man verbally, and was expected to do so, but to attack a woman, either physically or intellectually, was thought ignoble. As more women entered colleges, their influence—both tacit and explicit—caused the abandonment of the agonistic tradition and the evolution of less overtly contestive educational methods. (*Composition* 26–27)

In order to accommodate both men and women, rhetoric shed its contentious oral components and adopted a new theoretical base, set of pedagogical strategies, and disciplinary status within the academy (*Composition* 24). If Connors is correct in positing that women's entry into the academy prompted curricular change, then I would complicate his thesis by adding that rhetoric's transformation served a dual purpose, not only accommodating women's presence in American colleges but also limiting their knowledge and practice of privileged genres like oratory, debate, and argument.

Oratory's removal from the heart of the college experience may also have resulted, in part, from an educational backlash that developed in response to antebellum women's heightened public profile. Once women began to cross gendered boundaries in order to speak in public venues, educators became nervous and attempted to restrict young women's activities on the academic platform. Backlash is evident in educators' debates about the adverse effects of emulation and public performance on feminine character, an educational concern that emerged contemporaneously with women's burgeoning activities in legislative, popular, and religious forums. Backlash is apparent, too, in the policing of female students' access to and performance on academic platforms in coeducational colleges like Oberlin and Antioch. Backlash is also indicated by the frequency of student/faculty disagreements over the types of discursive activities deemed [in]appropriate for women onstage, whether reading, oratory, debate, declamation, drama, or silence. Finally, backlash is suggested by young women's founding of extracurricular literary societies and debate clubs in an effort to circumvent institutional restraints.[9]

My argument regarding academic backlash receives further support from Catherine Brekus's observations of the religious platform during the antebellum period. In *Female Preaching in America, Strangers and Pilgrims, 1740–1845* (1998), she identifies a similar reaction underway among Protestant sects once supportive of women's preaching:

> [The backlash] began among socially conservative ministers and lay people . . . who were alarmed by the growing popularity of female evangelists, and it accelerated under the leadership of Methodists, African Methodists, Freewill Baptists, and Christians who wanted to build their small, countercultural churches into successful denominations. [To accomplish this end, . . .] they traded their tradition of female evangelism for greater power and respectability. (271)

Women's preaching became verboten. Furthermore, because male clergy crafted church histories that supported this stance, the tradition of Protestant women's witnessing was soon "erased from public memory," producing "historical amnesia" regarding their practices and accomplishments (Mountford, *Gendered* 11).[10] Ministers not only discouraged women's preaching but their public speaking as well. In the late 1830s, as women became active as antislavery lecturers, their efforts drew fire from Congregational ministers, who issued a pastoral letter warning that "when [woman] assumes the place and tone of man as a public reformer . . . her character becomes unnatural" and destroys "that modesty and delicacy which is the charm of domestic life, and which constitutes the true influence of woman in society" (Ceplair 211). Because Protestant groups founded and funded many of the early coeducational colleges (Congregationalists supported Oberlin, and the Christian Connexion and Unitarians supported Antioch), the churches' growing conservatism likely contributed to educators' discomfort with women's delivery on academic platforms.

Therefore, I posit that antebellum women's movement into new rhetorical arenas—from college classrooms to public stages—had a significant impact on education and that both the college curriculum and academic platform changed in ways that made it more difficult for young women to access elocutionary instruction and practice. However, despite social and educational resistance, many American women fought for knowledge, training, and experience in the arts of oral expression whether they aspired to the home, the professions, or the public platform. Indeed, the efforts of antebellum women like Lucy Stone, Antoinette Brown, Olympia Brown, and the Alethezeteans, far from representing the efforts of an extremist element, helped subsequent generations of college women obtain more equitable rhetorical opportunities both in and out of the classroom.

3

Performing Gender and Rhetoric
"Feminine" and "Masculine" Delivery Styles

A crimony over antebellum women's public involvement became apparent
during the 1830s and created tension within the ranks of activist women
themselves. Antislavery women, for instance, complained that they were com-
pared unfavorably to "benevolent" women, members of moral and philanthropic organizations dedicated to such concerns as "caring for widows and
orphans, assisting the aged, [and] providing health care to pregnant women"
(Boylan, "Women" 364). More than a hint of this discord is audible in Maria
Weston Chapman's 1836 report to the Boston Female Anti-Slavery Society, in
which she protests the preferential treatment accorded benevolents: "[N]o
clergyman has been censured for reading the notification of the annual meeting of the Fatherless and Widows' Society [a benevolent organization], with
the name of their lecturer. . . . *Those* ladies are designated as 'women, stepping gracefully to the relief of infancy and suffering age,' and their treasury
overflows with the donations of an approving public" (qtd. in Ginzberg,
Women 33). The money and approbation showered upon benevolent women
resulted, in part, from their upper-class affiliations and consequent access to
and influence upon decision makers. Additionally, however, their efforts were
advanced by a distinct manner of delivery that permitted them to present their
public efforts as extensions of (rather than departures from) women's domestic
sphere. Collectively, their social connections, feminine ethos, and muted delivery style contributed to their rhetorical successes, evidenced by the award-
ing of legislative charters, acquisition of public funds, and passage of laws
benefiting their organizations and societies.

Antislavery women, on the other hand, were commonly "thought to act
with undue publicity" (Chapman, qtd. in Ginzberg, *Women* 33). Scholars have
argued that negative perceptions of abolitionist women stemmed from their

more humble, middle-class backgrounds, which meant that they lacked connections to the political and social elite enjoyed by benevolents and so had to use more public methods of persuasion (see Boylan's "Timid Girls" and Ginzberg's *Women and the Work of Benevolence*). Abolitionist women compensated by taking to the streets, to fairs, to conventions, to public platforms, and to print in order to broadcast their opposition to slavery, thereby employing more direct (and conventionally masculine) means of rhetorical engagement. Indeed, during the 1830s, two distinct manners of delivery became available to women, ones that I term the *feminine* and *masculine* delivery styles.

These stylistic options grew out of the surrounding social context, which determined the genres of rhetorical performance deemed acceptable for men and women. Of course, the available genres were influenced by gender ideology, and during the antebellum period, public speaking was perceived as a "masculine domain":

> Speakers are expert and authoritative; women are submissive. Speakers operate in the public sphere; women's concerns are domestic. Speakers call attention to themselves, aggressively take stands, affirm their expertise; "true women" are retiring, their influence is indirect, they have no expertise on matters outside the home. The public realm is driven by ambition; similarly, speaking is competitive, energized by the desire to persuade others. These are traditionally masculine traits related to man's allegedly lustful, competitive nature. (Campbell and Jerry 125)

When antebellum women spoke for persuasive purposes in spaces gendered as masculine, they defied dominant gender ideals mandating their public silence, a rhetorical constraint that posed serious obstacles to their effectiveness. Therefore, first and foremost, women rhetors had to discover means to justify their speech and participation in extradomestic affairs, a task that required considerable ingenuity:

> The discovery of the available means was for Aristotle an act of invention that always assumed the right to speak in the first place and, even prior to that, assumed the right to personhood and self-representation, rights that have not long been available to women. . . . The act of invention for women, then, begins in a different place . . . women must first invent a way to speak in the context of being silenced and rendered invisible. (Ritchie and Ronald xvii)

A number of antebellum women selected the available (and gender-appropriate) means of indirect influence rather than direct persuasion and devised a manner of rhetorical presentation to match, one that simultaneously subverted social norms dictating women's silence and invisibility and cloaked the public and persuasive nature of their discourse.

Rhetorical efforts of the American Female Reform Society (AFRS) exemplify this distinctive feminine style. The New York AFRS branch regularly sent female representatives to the state capitol in Albany to monitor and promote relevant legislation. In 1848, they ensured passage of antiseduction laws and, in the 1850s, petitioned the state for financial support. AFRS representatives Mary Hawkins and Elizabeth Seldon Eaton frequently updated the home office on their methods and progress, noting, for example, that their legislative lobbying

> had been pursued "discreetly" and that [they] had been introduced to the politicians by their husbands. Apparently the ends justified the means, for the society proudly announced that the women had convinced two-thirds of the senate and three-fourths of the house to sign their petition for assistance. Of course, they added, they had achieved this result "with scrupulous regard to woman's sphere." The women modestly commended themselves on a good result quietly obtained. (Ginzberg, *Women* 78–79)

Obtaining results "quietly" and with "scrupulous regard to woman's sphere" perhaps best encapsulates the goals of the feminine delivery style. Hawkins and Eaton's legislative efforts display many of the style's characteristic features, such as asking male family members to support and promote women's public efforts, employing conversation rather than oratory, and avowing a commitment to conventional gender roles while behaving contrary to them.[1]

However, not all antebellum women rhetors embraced the feminine delivery style. Typically, it was employed by more conservative women who, as Anne Boylan observes, "accepted the convention that women's sphere was the home and the church, and . . . used that convention to undertake public actions as wives, mothers, and daughters." In contrast, more liberal women, many of whom were involved in the antislavery movement, privileged the individual over her gender-assigned role and repudiated the notion of separate spheres altogether, instead asserting "that women as moral beings had as much right as men to speak and act on questions of great public import" ("Timid Girls" 789). This egalitarian stance on gender translated into a different style of delivery, one I describe as masculine because it appropriated postures and prerogatives that had hitherto been reserved almost exclusively for men. Women employing the masculine delivery style, for example, directly delivered their own speeches, addressed same- and mixed-sex audiences in public spaces, and used genres like lecture, debate, and oratory.

This chapter outlines and contrasts the feminine and masculine delivery styles and examines the rhetorical practices of five antebellum women rhetors, Emma Willard, Dorothea Dix, Catharine Beecher, Sarah Grimké, and Angelina Grimké. Willard, Dix, and Beecher used feminine methods of delivery that permitted them to express their ideas in a nonthreatening, indirect manner whereas the Grimké sisters adopted masculine methods that initially created considerable resistance and controversy. At bottom, the feminine style disguised the fact that women were engaged in public discourse, and the masculine style enacted their right to do so. I conclude by calling for scholarly recognition of the feminine delivery style despite its dramatic departures from the traditional fifth canon, which assumes the speaker's direct address of an audience in a public venue. Because the genre and setting were inaccessible or unappealing to many nineteenth-century women, they instead selected alternative means and forged a remarkably creative, highly effective, and widely adopted presentational style. Feminine delivery enabled women rhetors not only to defy dominant gender norms dictating their public silence but also to maintain the appearance of femininity even as they moved and spoke in domains coded as masculine. Unfortunately, to date, the discipline of rhetoric has tended either to overlook this delivery style or else to dismiss it as an odd and quaintly circuitous method of presentation. Recognizing the feminine delivery style and its many practitioners represents an important step toward regendering the fifth canon, requiring scholars to acknowledge the innovative strategies of disenfranchised speakers and to redefine what counts as delivery.

The Feminine Delivery Style

Antebellum women contended with gender conventions that discouraged their participation in the public realm. Many, nevertheless, pursued civic goals, seeking legislative backing for their projects, presenting petitions and memorials to politicians, and soliciting funds for widows and orphans, missionaries and slaves, prostitutes and drunkards. In order to construct convincing feminine ethos while advancing their objectives, some women rhetors eschewed public speaking and instead selected alternate methods of rhetorical presentation looking more like gentle influence than outright persuasion. In this section, I analyze the feminine delivery style of Emma Willard and Dorothea Dix, two rhetors who ostensibly respected antebellum gender norms while advancing educational and social reform.

Emma Willard

Throughout her lengthy career, Emma Willard labored to expand women's educational and professional opportunities. One reason for her success was her manner of delivery, which cloaked the challenge that her views actually posed to the status quo (see fig. 3.1). Willard's rhetorical performances displayed key strategies of the feminine delivery style. She curried the support of influential men, cast her appeals into genres associated with women, asked male family members to promote her projects, emphasized traditional feminine roles even as she practiced nontraditional rhetorical behaviors, domesticated persuasive discourse by delivering it in feminized spaces, enacted the women rhetor as a reader and conversant rather than an orator, and asked men to deliver addresses for her to mixed-sex audiences. The educator, in other words, employed indirect methods of delivery in order to mask her unconventional gender and discursive performances. Before detailing Willard's delivery style, however, I first examine her commitment to and plans for improving women's education, the issue that propelled her into the public, political realm.

Fig. 3.1. Emma Willard. Frontispiece from Fairbanks's *Emma Willard and Her Pupils* (1898). Courtesy of Nancy Iannucci, Archivist/Librarian, Emma Willard School, Troy, New York.

By the early decades of the nineteenth century, the uneven quality of schooling provided in ladies' academies—many stressing ornamental studies like "music, drawing and painting, a bit of French or German, social dancing, and ... needlework" (Dei 243)—had produced reform efforts to improve women's education. Incensed at the contrast between young women's finishing schools and young men's colleges, schoolmistress Willard complained "bitterly [of...] the disparity in educational facilities between the two sexes" (qtd. in Lord 34–35). Discontent prompted her to imagine an alternative, a state-supported women's seminary that would instruct students in geometry, geography, history, and moral philosophy. She detailed her ideas in a document eventually published as *Address to the Public; Particularly to the Members of the Legislature of New York, Proposing a Plan for Improving Female Education* (1819). The *Plan* proceeds along four lines, identifying problems with the current state of women's education, presenting criteria for sound and substantial schooling, outlining plans for a seminary that meets the criteria, and identifying the benefits such an institution would shower upon society.

Aware that women's education had the potential to disrupt established roles and relations, Willard spends a great deal of time reassuring readers that learned women will uphold existing gender hierarchies. She argues that because women's particular mission is to shape "the succeeding generation," it behooves society to educate them for their duties (47). Her seminary's objective is to train schoolgirls for their distinct obligations and sphere; therefore, the school needs to be "as different from those appropriated to the other sex as the female character and duties are from the male" (46). Echoing the sentiments of republican motherhood, Willard links the state of the nation with that of women's education, equates the caliber of its citizens with the learning of their mothers, and, ultimately, creates a convincing case for state-supported women's seminaries (58).

Not only does women's education benefit the country, according to Willard, but it also liberates men from the tedium of teaching, freeing them for more lucrative enterprises:

> If then women were properly fitted by instruction, they would be likely to teach children better than the other sex; they could afford to do it cheaper; and those men who would otherwise be engaged in this employment, might be at liberty to add to the wealth of the nation, by any of those thousand occupations, from which women are necessarily debarred. (72)

Far from usurping male privilege, women's entry into the teaching profession offers freedom and prosperity to men and the nation, a subtle argument that feminizes teaching and makes it an acceptable field for female endeavor. Furthermore, permitting women to teach affords society a necessary safeguard, providing those "master spirits" too ambitious for confinement in the domestic realm with a constructive outlet for their energies:

> To leave such, without any virtuous road to eminence, is unsafe to the community; for not unfrequently, are the secret springs of revolution, set in motion by their intrigues. Such aspiring minds, we will regulate by education, [. . . and] offer them a new object worthy of their ambition; to govern, and improve the seminaries for their sex. (79)

Willard thus dismisses concerns regarding the disruptive influence of erudite women and demonstrates the blessings their education brings to society at large, producing better mothers who in turn raise better citizens, freeing men from the drudgery of teaching, and harnessing the abilities of the nation's brightest women to the instruction of others. Willard's skill in adapting dominant cultural codes and values to her own ends, particularly her negotiation of gender ideology, is apparent not only in the *Plan*'s argumentative acumen but also in her subsequent efforts to win support for the project.

Because the theories, genres, and forums of rhetoric had traditionally pertained exclusively to men, women had to transform masculine elements into feminine forms before they could hope to participate in public discourse. Jane Donawerth has detailed how such eighteenth- and nineteenth-century women as Mary Astell, Hannah Moore, Maria Edgeworth, and Lydia Sigourney "appropriat[ed] rhetorical theory for their own use" and "creat[ed] a tradition of women's rhetoric" ("Conversation" 181–83). These rhetoricians theorized how women might employ the genres of "conversation (domestic discourse), letter writing, and reading aloud" as indirect means of influencing public affairs ("Hannah" 160). These three modes of discourse—correspondence, conversation, and reading—became cornerstones of the feminine delivery style, and Willard used them all to promote her *Plan for Improving Female Education*.[2]

Willard initiated her quest with the letter, a crucial genre for women rhetors. The letter was a communicative form marked as feminine because of its associations with domestic spaces, but it was also a means for expressing women's views to public figures (and, when published, of expressing their views publicly). Willard maintained an active and extensive correspondence with powerful men throughout her career, so it is not surprising to learn that she first advocated the *Plan* in letters to prominent politicians, including Thomas Jefferson, President James Monroe, and assorted governors, congressmen, and judges. New York governor DeWitt Clinton responded enthusiastically to Willard's ideas, encouraging her to move her school from Vermont to New York and urging the New York legislature to improve women's education. Willard strategically reinforced the governor's endorsement by asking friends to write New York legislators and urge them to support women's schooling (A. Scott 686–87). Once her letter-writing campaign was completed, the educator prepared to storm the state capitol in Albany, where her efforts would earn her the distinction of being the first "woman lobbyist" (Lutz, *Emma Willard: Daughter* 65).

When Willard traveled to New York in 1819 to convince the legislature to fund a woman's seminary, her primary goal was to recruit the backing of influential legislators while reassuring them that erudite women posed no threat to the established gender hierarchy. Willard often complained of "the absurd prejudice that, if women's minds were cultivated, they would forget their own sphere, and intrude themselves into that of men," a misconception caused by the indiscretions of a few "masculine" women who had "forcibly broke[n] through every impediment, and rivaled the men even in their own department" (qtd. in Lord 39). Therefore, Willard consistently tried to embody the educated woman as one who both knew and honored her ordained place. Enacting the learned yet subordinate woman while entering political spaces for persuasive ends was no easy task, but Willard staged her rhetorical presentations carefully so as to enunciate her womanliness, always an important objective of the feminine delivery style.

That Willard's husband, Dr. John Willard, accompanied her to Albany contributed greatly to her feminine ethos. His presence allowed Willard to present herself as a "respectable, proper, pious homemaker and wife who was also intelligent and informed because she had been well educated" (Dei 251), thus providing living proof that learning could enhance rather than erode a woman's femininity. John Willard probably contributed to the *Plan's* promotion in other ways as well. A "man of property and considerable attainments," he was an accomplished and prominent physician with a sound understanding of politics acquired from having served as marshal of Vermont and in numerous capacities in the Republican party (Lord 21). Therefore, the educator likely drew upon his political expertise when devising strategies for obtaining legislative funding. Enlisting the aid of male family members to forward women's rhetorical projects is another characteristic of the feminine delivery style.

Throughout her career, Willard used both print and oral media to disseminate her message, "a brilliant tactic" and "canny public relations move" first in evidence at Albany (Dei 248). First, she printed the *Plan for Improving Female Education*, placed a copy on each legislator's desk, and distributed it to bookstores as well, thereby not only ensuring the preservation of her views but also extending their reach to a wider audience (A. Scott 686). Second, she supplemented the textual impact of the *Plan* with her voice. In 1819, a woman directly addressing a legislative body in the state capitol would have been virtually inconceivable because both the genre and space were considered masculine, so Willard instead invited groups of legislators to meet with her privately in homes or parlors to discuss the *Plan*. In this manner, she used domestic surroundings to recast her persuasive discourse into acceptable feminine form—conversation. In addition to holding private, informal talks, Willard also read sections of the *Plan* to legislators, electing to read rather than recite in order to diffuse her persuasive intent. After all, by this time, reading had become a generally acceptable mode of delivery for women. Elocution had been a regular feature of school reading instruction for decades, and the woman reading in the parlor had become a cultural commonplace (see fig. 3.2). Furthermore, Willard's decision to read from a seated rather than a standing position allowed her to avoid the appearance of lecturing or orating to men, for sitting deemphasized her physical presence, masking her body and reducing the need for facial expression and physical gesture. Finally, reading allowed Willard to keep her eyes on the page, making her the object of the legislators' gaze rather than the gazer herself. She thereby enacted a subordinate posture relative to her male audience and reduced the potential controversy of her rhetorical performance. Willard's delivery style allowed her to project a modest yet womanly demeanor while advancing her political objectives, a clever and effective strategy for the times. Such rhetorical uses of domestic settings, conversation, and reading are hallmarks of the feminine delivery style.

Despite the acumen of both the *Plan* and Willard's rhetorical performance, the New York legislature promised but ultimately failed to provide funds for a female seminary, an outcome that forever galled the educator and made her question her original tactics and targeted audience:

> Once I had almost determined to seek permission to go in person before the legislature, and plead at their bar with the living voice, believing that I could throw forth my whole soul in the effort for my sex, and then sink down and die; and thus my death might effect what my life had failed to accomplish. Had the legislature been composed of such men as filled my fancy when I wrote my *Plan*, I could have thus hoped in pleading publicly for women. . . . My present impression is that my cause is better rested with the people than with their

Fig. 3.2. The reading rhetor. Miss Manwaring from Fairbanks's *Emma Willard and Her Pupils* (1898). Courtesy of
Nancy Iannucci, Archivist/Librarian, Emma Willard School, Troy, New York.

rulers. I do not regret bringing it before the legislature, because in no other way
could it have come so fairly before the public. But when the people shall have
become convinced of the justice and expediency of placing the sexes more
nearly on an equality, with respect to privileges of education, then legislators
will find it their interest to make the proper provision. (qtd. in Woody 1: 345)

Willard's eloquence may not have persuaded the legislature, but it did move
the public. Impressed by her reputation and ambitions for women's education, the citizens of Troy, New York, invited her to establish a ladies' seminary
there, built her an impressive edifice to house the institution, and raised more
than four thousand dollars through taxation and subscription drives (Fairbanks 14). The Troy Female Seminary opened in 1821 and quickly became the
nation's premier educational facility for women.

In subsequent years, Willard continued to use her rhetorical abilities to promote women's education as well as the common-school movement. Although these subjects provided her with frequent opportunities for public speaking, she avoided addressing mixed-sex audiences because of the negative moral, sexual, and gender implications the act held for women (Zaeske, "Promiscuous" 203). Pioneering women rhetors found ways to circumvent the promiscuous-audience constraint. Willard, for instance, asked influential men to deliver addresses for her to mixed-sex audiences, a method that I term *surrogate delivery*. Surrogate delivery required a man to serve as a mouthpiece for a woman rhetor, who usually sat silently onstage beside him. The man acted as a medium for the silent woman's message or, to use an analogy from ventriloquism, as the dummy to her master puppeteer. The surrogate's role, however, was far from passive, for he often made important contributions to the rhetorical event itself. Willard acknowledged as much when she incorporated a surrogate speaker's name into the labyrinthine title of one of her published appeals: *Mrs. Willard's Address as Read by the Rev. Mr. Peck at a Meeting Held at St. John's Church, Troy, on the Eve of January 8, 1833, Whose Object as Expressed by Previous Notices Was to Interest the Public in Behalf of Female Education in Greece.* Substituting the Reverend Peck's form and voice for her own allowed Willard to accomplish a number of rhetorical objectives: First, by employing this particular speaker, she gained access to a gendered and normally inaccessible public venue, the church podium; second, she "borrowed" ethical credibility from her surrogate, the Reverend Peck in effect lending his religious authority and the solemnity of sacred space to her appeal; third, she honored dominant notions of feminine propriety by addressing her mixed-sex audience indirectly, thus gaining its good will and support. Willard routinely used surrogate delivery with impressive results. For example, when Elihu Burritt read her address on common schools at an 1840 Connecticut school festival, citizens responded so enthusiastically to Willard's plea for education that they persuaded her to take charge of four district schools and promptly elected her superintendent of the common schools in Kensington, Connecticut (Lutz, *Emma Willard: Pioneer* 104).[3]

As a rhetor, Willard's chief objective was to advance her educational projects in a fashion that promoted the public's perception of her as a knowledgeable yet feminine woman. Although she advocated women's education in public and political spaces, her methods of delivery—which included correspondence, conversation, reading, domestic settings, and surrogate speaking—appeared entirely consonant with prevailing gender norms. Biographer Alma Lutz argues that Willard's accomplishments derived from her ability to "read the signs of the times accurately" and to adapt her rhetorical style and strategy to suit them (*Emma Willard: Daughter* 101). Similarly, Anne Firor Scott observes that Willard was a woman who used "for her own ends social stereotypes about woman's place" and whose true genius may have consisted of finding

> a way to work within the framework of social expectations about women's proper behavior without allowing that framework to hamper seriously her very large plans or limit her ambition. The skill with which she did this is attested by the fact that while she achieved a public career stretching over fifty years, she was seldom criticized for stepping out of her place. (702)

Willard's feminine delivery style played a key role in ensuring her success, allowing the educator to breach gendered constraints quietly in pursuit of her larger goals.

Dorothea Dix

Like Emma Willard, Dorothea Dix also began her professional life as a schoolmistress, but she ultimately devoted herself to improving the treatment accorded the mentally ill in state asylums, prisons, and hospitals. Her introduction to the political process began in 1841 when she witnessed the hopeless condition of the insane incarcerated in Massachusetts jails and poorhouses. Appalled, Dix traveled the state documenting the plight of the mentally ill and their inhumane treatment. She then gathered her evidence into an impassioned memorial, detailing "a sordid panorama of cruelty, filth, and disease" that included such distressing eyewitness accounts of "the miserable, the desolate, and the outcast" as the following: "*Medford.* One idiot subject chained, and one in a close stall for seventeen years" (qtd. in Marshall, "Dorothea" 487). In January 1843, Dix asked a surrogate speaker, Dr. Samuel Howe, to present the memorial to the Massachusetts state legislature, where the speech generated heated debate and resulted in the expansion of the state mental hospital in Worcester. This event marked the beginning of Dix's forty-year commitment to improving mental health care throughout the country.

Dix became one of the most active and influential women rhetors of the nineteenth century. She crisscrossed the nation, visiting asylums and documenting conditions, composing countless memorials demonstrating the need for state-funded mental hospitals, and lobbying politicians at both the state and federal levels to promote legislative change (Marshall, *Dorothea* 99). Between 1848 and 1854, she concentrated her efforts on convincing the federal government to transfer millions of acres of public lands to the states, which would, in turn, sell the land and use profits to establish perpetual endowments for state asylums. Although her memorial passed both the U.S. House and Senate in 1854, it was, unfortunately, vetoed by President Franklin Pierce. Despite its failure, Dix's federal memorial, nevertheless, represents the "most original effort of her lobbying career" and later inspired funding arrangements for land-grant colleges (Brown 148).

Again like Willard, Dix masked her political and rhetorical ambitions with a feminine facade. Contemporaries attested to her gift for merging persuasion with "ladylike propriety." Louisa Hall, for example, described Dix's "beautiful, strong nature, shining through a genuine womanhood," and renowned scientist Benjamin Silliman praised her for possessing "the peculiar tact of a *gifted woman* who preserving perfectly the delicacy and refinement of her sex and combining perseverance and energy and resource with woman's gentleness sways the hearts of *men*" (qtd. in Brown 102, 167). Dix blended womanliness with persuasion by deftly employing the feminine delivery style.

She routinely asked men to act as surrogate speakers and introduce or promote her memorials on the legislative floor. Additionally, she cast appeals into indirect, feminine forms by delivering discourse in private rather than public settings. Biographer Helen Marshall speculates that

> Miss Dix abhorred notoriety and display, and cultivated the virtues of modesty and refinement. She gave no public lectures and . . . rarely spoke in the presence of more than six or a dozen persons. In talking before small groups of legislators that she frequently invited to her hotel, she never made what might be called a formal address. (*Dorothea* 121)

Dix feminized her lobbying efforts by conversing with or reading to select politicians. She describes a typical night's work to correspondent Harriet Hare: "You cannot imagine the labor of conversing and convincing. . . . Some evenings I had at once, twenty gentlemen for three hours, *steady* conversation." Private settings allowed Dix's considerable charisma and eloquence to shine forth and work their magic. She recounts that at the end of one such evening, a politician (who had initially considered her project "all humbug") capitulated entirely and declared, "*I am convinced;* you've conquered me out and out; *I shall vote for the Hospital.* If you'll come to the House and talk there as you've done here, no man that [isn't] a brute can withstand you" (qtd. in Brown 118). Dix's feminine ethos and strategic handling of feminized forms and forums resulted in persuasive presentations that few could resist.

Although highly effective with the feminine delivery style, practical realities were such that Dix could not always accomplish her goals using it. Thomas Brown observes that Dix's political labors were fundamentally "at odds with the dominant rhetoric about womanhood" and that the "contradictions of her culture became the routine stress points of her career, in which she attempted to reconcile femininity and power" (168). When Dix found it impossible to reconcile the two, she usually opted for political expediency. Sometimes, for example, addressing political figures in private settings simply was not effective. During the federal land campaign, she felt isolated from key politicians, so to improve her access, Dix established an office in the Library of Congress, a space she had once described as "too public for ladies" (qtd. in Brown 168). Her stance on addressing promiscuous audiences was likewise contradictory. Although she flatly refused to deliver public lectures or speeches, Dix would address large, mixed-sex assemblies during visits to asylums, reform schools, and prisons, acts she probably justified by defining those sites as private rather than public settings (O'Connor 28; Marshall, *Dorothea* 121). Thus, Dix's practices indicate that women who usually employed a feminine manner of delivery occasionally chose to shift styles and compromise propriety so as to achieve their rhetorical objectives.[4]

Willard and Dix employed the feminine delivery style, a ladylike form of rhetorical subversion. Like them, many other antebellum women also selected feminized genres and settings in order to domesticate and reduce the threat of their discourse. Additionally, they harnessed masculine authority to projects by eliciting letters of support from prominent men; by appearing publicly with brothers, fathers, and husbands; and by asking influential men to deliver addresses for them. Finally, they favored indirect over direct, private over public rhetorical presentation. By cobbling together the available feminine means of persuasion, antebellum women enacted a manner of delivery that ostensibly complemented dominant gender ideology while allowing them to enter previously restricted domains to address public, professional, and political issues—discreetly, of course.

The Style Wars: Masculine Versus Feminine Delivery

By mid-century, the feminine delivery style began to appear antiquated and roundabout in some quarters, a view apparent in an 1853 letter from Benjamin Jones, editor of the *Anti-Slavery Bugle*, to lecturer Lucy Stone. Encouraging her to visit Ohio during an upcoming tour, Jones trumpets changing attitudes toward women's activism and compares old-fashioned to modern styles of rhetorical performance:

> A Women's State Temperance Convention was held in Columbus on the 13th inst., and it was a great one. Lizzie [Jones] and Josephine Griffing addressed

an audience of one thousand in Representatives' Hall. And who does thee suppose presided at that meeting of one thousand men and women? Mrs. Professor Cowles, of Oberlin! Six years ago [educator] Catharine Beecher delivered an address in Columbus, through her brother, she sitting silent in the pulpit by his side. Now the women call meetings, appoint officers, present resolutions, and speak upon them and vote upon them. Church members do these things, and the clergy ask divine blessings upon their proceedings, and there seems to be no thought of their having stepped out of their appropriate sphere. (qtd. in Blackwell 114)

Jones contrasts women who directly address mixed-sex audiences with educator Catharine Beecher's indirect feminine style and associates surrogate delivery with the ancien régime. His comments reflect a divide regarding women's appropriate public conduct, one that had earlier found expression in an 1837 printed debate between the same Catharine Beecher and abolitionist Angelina Grimké.

Numerous scholars have examined the Beecher-Grimké exchanges, including Stephen Browne, Gerda Lerner, Kathryn Kish Sklar, and Jean Yellin. Their works thoroughly detail differences in the two women's views of slavery, feminine character, and women's domestic and political duties. However, a substantial issue still awaits study, namely, how Beecher's and Grimké's ideas about gender informed their divergent delivery styles.

The Masculine Delivery Style

Daughters of a wealthy and aristocratic southern family, Sarah and Angelina Grimké abandoned their South Carolina home and moved to the North to become Quakers, a religious sect opposed to the "peculiar institution" of slavery (see figs. 3.3 and 3.4). The sisters began their speaking careers in late 1836 when they enlisted as the American Anti-Slavery Society's first women agents. Initially, they shared their personal accounts of slavery with other women in parlor talks, which proved so popular that the Grimkés soon moved their meetings to public quarters in order to accommodate the numbers hoping to hear them. From this simple step ensued a series of choices and circumstances that led the sisters to embrace a manner of delivery similar to that employed by men. The Grimkés broke new oratorical ground for women, delivering rhetoric in public settings, directly speaking to mixed-sex audiences, unapologetically addressing political matters, and employing discursive genres conventionally reserved for men, all characteristics of what I term the masculine delivery style.

Fig. 3.3. Sarah Grimké.
Courtesy of the Library of Congress,
Prints and Photographs Division, LC-
USZ61-1608.

Fig. 3.4. Angelina Grimké.
Courtesy of the Library of Congress,
Prints and Photographs Division, LC-
USZ61-1609.

Sarah and Angelina Grimké were certainly not the first women to adopt masculine elements of delivery. Quaker women ministers, evangelical preachers, and lecturers, such as Frances Wright and Maria Stewart, had delivered public addresses to promiscuous audiences well before the Grimkés did so. However, the sisters' rhetorical efforts are particularly significant, not only because their timing, ethos, delivery style, justification, and eloquence provoked such intense public reactions but also because they consciously worked to open doors for subsequent women speakers. Both contemporaries and historians have viewed the Grimkés' rhetorical careers as marking "the *beginning* of the woman's rights agitation in America," adding to their stature as important symbolic figures (Garrison and Garrison 2: 134). Therefore, even though they were by no means its originators, the Grimkés were especially noteworthy practitioners of the masculine delivery style. Additionally, the sisters' stylistic innovations were seen by large numbers of people. Gerda Lerner estimates that during their 1838 New England speaking tour alone, the sisters addressed "eighty-eight meetings in sixty-seven towns. They . . . reached, face to face, a minimum of 40,500 people in meetings. To have reached even half that number would still have been an impressive accomplishment" (227).

To return to the beginning of their public speaking careers, the sisters' first rhetorical efforts were fairly uncontroversial. Privately relating their experiences of slavery to other women drew upon conventions of feminine delivery, relying upon domestic settings and conversational forms and avoiding issues of promiscuous address altogether. When high attendance prompted the sisters to move their talks from private to public venues, some antislavery advisors feared the change would evoke the specter of Frances Wright (a radical woman rhetor of the late 1820s vilified for having abandoned her appropriate sphere) and damage the movement itself (Ceplair 88). Despite these concerns, the Grimkés held their first public meeting in December 1836 and addressed three hundred women for nearly two hours. The talk was considered a triumph by all despite one unsettling incident. Angelina relates that a "warm-hearted Abolitionist had found *his* way into the back pack of the meeting" but adds that he was quickly identified and asked to leave the gathering of women. When fellow antislavery agent Theodore Weld heard of the listener's expulsion, "he exclaimed how extremely ridiculous to think of a man's being shouldered out of a meeting for fear he should hear a woman speak. *We* smiled & said we did not know how it seemed to others, but it lookd *very strange* in our eyes" (Ceplair 89). Such incidents, however, soon became commonplace at the sisters' meetings.

Not only did men continue to appear at the Grimkés' talks but they also arrived in increasing numbers and refused to leave when requested. Angelina describes an early episode in a letter to friend Jane Smith: "We had one male auditor, who refused to go out when [. . . told] it was exclusively for ladys, & so there he sat & somehow I did not feel his presence at all embarrassing & went on just as tho' he was not there" (Ceplair 116). Doing so was no small feat, for women who addressed mixed-sex audiences were considered morally and sexually suspect. Proponents of the feminine delivery style, of course, circumvented the taint of promiscuity by asking male surrogates to deliver speeches for them. The Grimkés, however, adopted an entirely different strategy, appropriating masculine privileges of public speech and addressing mixed-sex audiences directly themselves, distinguishing markers of the masculine delivery style.

Antebellum women also violated gender conventions when they publicly discussed political or civic issues, which were perceived as masculine topics. Rhetors employing the feminine style negotiated this constraint by "domesticating" and thereby exonerating their discussion of sensitive subjects (an example, discussed in endnote 3, is Emma Willard's argument that woman's domestic sphere encompasses her children's school district). The Grimkés declined to use such tactics. They spoke directly and unapologetically about slavery and again assumed masculine prerogatives of public engagement. In addition to claiming the right to discuss civic affairs, the sisters also advocated women's direct political involvement, Angelina's *Appeal to the Christian Women of the Southern States* (1836), for instance, urging southern women to circulate antislavery petitions. Similarly, when the Grimké sisters attended the 1837 national convention of antislavery women, "the first public political meeting of women in the United States" (Sterling 44), Angelina introduced a resolution proclaiming a woman's right and obligation to address issues like slavery:

> Resolved, That as certain rights and duties are common to all moral beings, the time has come for woman to move in that sphere which Providence has assigned her, and no longer remain satisfied in the circumscribed limits with which corrupt custom and a perverted application of Scripture have encircled her; therefore that it is the duty of woman, and the province of woman, to plead the cause of the oppressed in our land, and to do all that she can by her voice, and her pen, and her purse, and the influence of her example, to overthrow the horrible system of American slavery. (qtd. in Sterling 49)

Rather than domesticating slavery by connecting it to feminized spaces, Grimké critiques the circumference of woman's province, distinguishing between the plans of Providence and the effects of "corrupt custom" and "perverted applications of Scripture." Both Grimké sisters proclaimed woman's moral obligation to advance antislavery through her voice, pen, purse, and example, and both enacted that duty by engaging directly in public political discourse, yet another characteristic of the masculine delivery style.

In addition to addressing proscribed topics, the Grimkés employed masculine genres, a practice that began inadvertently with their move from private to public spaces. The change in setting affected the public's perception of the sisters' discourse, as Angelina notes in a letter to Jane Smith:

> Thou mayest remark I speak of our *talks* as *lectures*. Well, this is the name that *others* have given our poor effort. . . . How little! How *very little* I supposed, when I used to say, "I wish I was a *man*, that I might go out and lecture," that *I* would ever do such a thing. The idea never crossed my mind that *as a woman* such work could possibly be assigned me. (Ceplair 115–16)

The vocabulary shift from talks to lectures reflects the changed setting of the sisters' meetings and their consequent movement from feminized genres like reading and conversation to more masculinized modes of public address. Indeed, the first recorded public debate between a man and a woman occurred in July 1837 when Angelina Grimké and John Page argued the Bible's stance on slavery. Although most agreed that Grimké successfully deconstructed Page's pro-slavery argument, response to the event was mixed. The Amesbury *Morning Courier* found the engagement "too indelicate" to merit coverage while William Lloyd Garrison's antislavery newspaper, the *Liberator,* applauded Grimké's "calm, modest, and dignified" comportment (qtd. in Lerner 179–80).

After experimenting with such masculine genres as lectures, conventions, and debates, Angelina Grimké tried her hand at legislative address. In February 1838, she delivered an antislavery speech as well as petitions bearing the signatures of twenty thousand women to the Massachusetts Legislative Committee (Japp 211). The unprecedented event attracted so many interested spectators that hundreds had to be turned away, and Grimké relates that she and her party had trouble entering the hearing room at all: "[T]he hall was jambed to such excess that it was with great difficulty we were squeezed in, and then were compelled to walk over the seats in order to reach the place assigned us. As soon as we entered we were received by clapping." She describes the audience's response to her address:

> After the bustle was over I rose to speak and was greeted by *hisses* from the doorway, tho' profound silence reigned thro' the crowd within. The noise in that direction increased and I was requested by the Chairman to suspend my remarks until at last order could be restored. Three times was I thus interrupted,

> until at last one of the Committee came to me and requested I would stand near
> the Speaker's desk. . . . I had just fixed my papers on two gentlemen's hats when
> at last I was invited to stand *in* the Speaker's desk. This was in the middle, more
> elevated and far more convenient in every respect. (Barnes and Dumond 2:
> 572–73)

Grimké defies gendered discursive constraints by appearing in a legislative
assembly, by delivering her own speech to legislators, and by standing and
speaking rather than sitting and reading her address. Furthermore, thanks to
the quirkiness of fate, she eventually addresses lawmakers from the room's center of symbolic power, the speaker's desk.

Thus, in their efforts to advance antislavery, Sarah and Angelina Grimké
claimed audiences, privileges, genres, topics, and spaces previously reserved
for men. Through their rhetorical innovations, they helped to develop an alternative delivery style and to extend the boundaries of women's discourse.

Attack

Although the Grimkés attracted large and enthusiastic audiences, their delivery generated controversy as well. By the summer of 1837, they began to draw
fire from critics questioning the propriety of women's public speech and
political activism. Typical in this regard is minister Hubbard Winslow's complaint, inspired by the Grimkés' reform efforts:

> [W]hen females undertake to assume the place of public teachers, whether
> to both sexes or only to their own; when they form societies for the purpose
> of sitting in judgment and acting upon the affairs of the church and state;
> when they travel about from place to place as lecturers, teachers, and guides
> to public sentiment; when they assemble in conventions to discuss questions,
> pass resolutions, make speeches, and vote upon civil, political, moral, and
> religious matters . . . it is then no longer a question whether they have
> stretched themselves beyond their measure and violated the inspired
> injunction which saith, "Let the woman learn in silence with all subjection;
> but I suffer not a woman to teach, nor to usurp authority over the man, but
> to be in silence." (30–31)

Joining the chorus of protesting voices was that of educator Catharine
Beecher, a member of the prominent Beecher clan. Eldest child of Calvinist
minister Lyman Beecher and sister to novelist Harriet Beecher Stowe, minister Henry Ward Beecher, and suffragist Isabella Beecher Hooker, Catharine
initially made her own mark in women's education, founding the Hartford
Female Seminary in 1823 and the Western Female Institute in 1832 (see fig. 3.5).

Fig. 3.5. Catharine Beecher, 1860. Courtesy of the
Schlesinger Library, Radcliffe Institute, Harvard University.

During the mid-1830s, Beecher conducted lecture tours throughout the
East, soliciting funds to train and settle women teachers on the western frontier (Sklar, *Catharine* 113). Unlike the Grimkés, however, the educator crafted
an ethos that harmonized with rather than opposed dominant gender ideals.
A practitioner of the circumspect feminine style, Beecher lectured to women
but relied upon male surrogates to address promiscuous assemblies. The most
detailed account of her rhetorical practice concerns her lecture tours of the
1840s when either brother Thomas Beecher or brother-in-law Calvin Stowe
accompanied her. While they delivered her addresses, she sat in "womanly
and demure silence on the platform" beside them, her conduct endorsing
"larger, unarticulated cultural prescriptions about women's limited participation in public life" (Tonkovich 121). Understanding that gender and rhetorical performance were intimately connected, Beecher upheld norms of feminine comportment while promoting her educational goals.

The educator objected vehemently to the Grimkés' suggestion that women exercise their voices, pens, and pocketbooks to advance the cause of abolition, and she explained why in *An Essay on Slavery and Abolition, with Reference to the Duty of American Females* (1837). Beecher embeds her account of women's proper roles, responsibilities, and realm within a critique of their public, persuasive efforts. She views hierarchy as divinely ordained and argues that women are subordinate to men in the same way that children are to their parents. It follows, then, that men and women have distinct spheres of action: Men are to move in the social realm, women in the domestic; men are to use force, intellect, and debate to shape civic life, women to exert a gentle, peaceful, and indirect influence on men, above all avoiding "the promptings of ambition, or the thirst for power" (100–1). By eschewing the public realm, women become ascendant in the domestic sphere and—through their roles as mothers, wives, and teachers—sway the nation.

From these premises arise Beecher's criticisms of woman's direct involvement in public reform. Each woman should avoid "whatever, in any measure, throws [her] into the attitude of a combatant, either for herself or others—whatever binds her in a party conflict—whatever obliges her in any way to exert coercive influences, [for it] throws her out of her appropriate sphere" (*Essay* 102). Women, therefore, have no place in the antislavery movement, which encourages strife between North and South, men and women, abolitionists and slaveholders; furthermore, they have no right to petition, for it, too, removes them from their appropriate sphere and promotes dissension (*Essay* 102–4). Women can best advance reform through indirect means, by privately (and subtly) exerting their moral influence and thereby shaping men's public, political actions.[5]

If women have no direct role to play in promoting social and political change, it follows that they have no place as public speakers (certainly an odd position to advance given Beecher's own rhetorical career). The educator had earlier identified the dangers that public address posed to woman's character in *Letters on the Difficulties of Religion* (1836), in which she contrasts a "genuine" woman with her antithesis Frances Wright, the pioneering woman rhetor who first addressed political topics and promiscuous audiences in the late 1820s:

> The ap[p]ropriate character of a woman demands delicacy of appearance and manners, refinement of sentiment, gentleness of speech, modesty in feeling and action, a shrinking from notoriety and public gaze, a love of dependence, and protection, aversion to all that is coarse and rude, and an instinctive abhorrence of all that tends to indelicacy and impurity, either in principles or actions. . . .

> With this standard of feeling and of taste, who can look without disgust and abhorrence upon such an one as Fanny Wright, with her great masculine person, her loud voice, her untasteful attire, going about unprotected, and feeling no need of protection, mingling with men in stormy debate, and standing up with barefaced impudence, to lecture to a public assembly. (23)

Appropriately enough, given her ideas on gender, Beecher emphasizes Wright's masculinity, depicting it as either the cause or effect of her departure from woman's sphere. What is more, the descriptors of Wright's delivery—her vocal and physical public presence, her willingness to argue with men and address promiscuous audiences, her independence, her unapologetic civic engagement—apply equally to the Grimké sisters as well.

Like Willard, Beecher also feared that women's blatant defiance of feminine norms would delay the expansion of their educational and professional opportunities, a concern apparent in her plea that learned women willingly embrace a "subordinate station":

> [I]f females, as they approach the other sex, in intellectual elevation, begin to claim, or to exercise in any manner, the peculiar prerogatives of that sex, education will prove a doubtful and dangerous blessing. But this will never be the result. For the more intelligent a woman becomes, the more she can appreciate the wisdom of that ordinance that appointed her subordinate station, and the more her taste will conform to the graceful and dignified retirement and submission it involves. (*Essay* 107–8)

Beecher's feminine delivery style reflected her theories of gender, and her rhetorical presentation enacted her belief that women, paradoxically, acquire power through submission. Furthermore, her promotion of women's domestic retirement, her advocacy of women's private and indirect influence, and her conviction that gender and rhetorical performance were of a piece led Beecher to oppose the Grimkés' appropriations of men's "peculiar prerogatives" because of the potential dangers they posed to women's status and progress.

Counterattack

Both Catharine Beecher and Angelina Grimké appeared publicly during the 1830s to advance their respective causes; however, they held dramatically different views on gender and embodied those differences in distinct styles of delivery. Beecher's critique of women's public engagement in *An Essay on Slavery and Abolition* (1837) prompted Grimké to clarify her own assumptions regarding women's roles, realm, and rights in *Letters to Catherine E. Beecher, in Reply to 'An Essay on Slavery and Abolitionism'* (1837). It consists of thirteen letters defending abolitionist principles and women's reform efforts.

Grimké centers her defense of woman's public participation on the equal moral rights and responsibilities of the sexes, arguing that "whatever it is morally right for man to do, it is morally right for woman to do" (*Letters* 195). It is a simple premise with the power to unsettle foundational practices and precepts. The conventional distribution of moral and public duties according to "the mere circumstance of sex" has

> robbed woman of essential rights, the right to think and speak and act on all great moral questions, just as men think and speak and act; the right to share their responsibilities, perils and toils; the right to fulfill the great end of her being, as a moral, intellectual and immortal creature, and of glorifying God in her body and her spirit. (*Letters* 194–95)

Woman must help shape the system by which she is governed, necessitating her involvement in spaces private and public, in matters sacred and secular:

> If Ecclesiastical and Civil governments are ordained of God, *then* I contend that woman has just as much right to sit in solemn counsel in Conventions, Conferences, Associations and General Assemblies, as man—just as much right to sit upon the throne of England, or in the Presidential chair of the United States. (*Letters* 197)

Maintaining existing gender relations, she warns, will result in widespread harm, "inflicting upon woman outrageous wrongs, working mischief incalculable in the social circle, and in its influence on the world producing only evil, and that continually." Grimké thus eradicates the notion that spheres and duties devolve from sex and posits instead complete gender equality. Stephen Browne argues that her greatest accomplishment in *Letters to Catherine E. Beecher* is

> to uncouple the principle of rights—constitutive as they are of one's moral being—from the notion of spheres altogether. Rights, in short, cannot be reduced to their space of operation. They are universal, the property neither of spheres, of lawgivers, nor even of God; they are held exclusively by one's self and are inexplicable except as a condition of one's very identity. (107)

Sarah and Angelina Grimké defended their public speech and engagement on the basis of equal moral rights and responsibilities despite considerable pressure to take an easier route. Although delighted by the crowds flocking to hear the sisters, the American Anti-Slavery Society grew apprehensive over the controversy generated by their appearances, especially after the tandem

1837 publication of Beecher's *An Essay on Slavery and Abolition* and Congregational ministers' *Pastoral Letter: The General Association of Massachusetts to the Churches under Their Care*, both of which denounced women's public discourse.[6] Antislavery agent Theodore Weld, for example, urged the sisters to deflect criticism from the movement by attributing their unusual behavior to Quaker beliefs and traditions. After all, Quaker women had preached to promiscuous audiences and addressed spiritual, practical, and political matters for nearly two centuries. Their right to do so was grounded in the sect's belief in men and women's spiritual equality and in "the power of God to use any 'instrument,' however weak, for His purposes," tenets with far-reaching consequences:

> Quaker belief in universal access to the Inward Light dramatically altered traditional gender roles and spheres of activity. Virtuous women, traditionally silent in public and confined to the domestic sphere, gave public testimonies and traveled to spread the message of "Truth." The repercussions of these changes became obvious in the nineteenth century, as Quaker women, habituated to public speaking and influence, were prominent in social reform movements such as abolition, temperance, prison reform, and woman's rights. (Larson 302–3)

The Grimkés were simply among the first in a long line of nineteenth-century Quaker reformers—including Lucretia Mott, Abby Kelley, Susan B. Anthony, and Anna Dickinson—to speak publicly for social justice. They might easily have justified their rhetorical delivery by appealing to membership in the Society of Friends, thereby casting themselves as followers of an established, if unconventional, religious tradition rather than as rebels against women's socially prescribed roles.

The Grimkés did call upon Quaker principles and practices in their lectures. Their Quaker dress, for instance, was a compelling form of visual rhetoric, the simple gray garb announcing their religious affiliation and strengthening their ethical authority:

> [T]he identity associated with the religious Quakers through costume offered some measure of protection from and credibility with audiences. The usual aspersions cast at the characters of women who dared to seek public attention were somewhat assuaged because of their religiously significant clothing. (Mattingly, *Appropriate[ing]* 34)

Carol Mattingly adds that the moral and religious connotations of Quaker dress deflected attention from the Grimkés' bodies and sexuality, shielding them somewhat from standard "charges of lewdness" and limiting critics' objections to "the fact of their public speaking." In addition to employing religious apparel, the sisters relied on religious precedent to craft effective rhetorical performances. Angelina, in particular, developed a prophetic persona, a strategy that Browne argues both fortified her break with cultural precedent and exonerated her public truth telling. After all, if the prophet is defined by her ability to see as others do not, then she must also have a concomitant duty to share her vision, come what may (49–50). Grimké skillfully evoked prophetic right and insight during her rhetorical presentations, an ethical option available to few but Quaker or evangelical women.

Although the sisters' delivery benefited greatly from their association with the Society of Friends, they refused to use religion to justify their public activism, in part, because their beliefs departed significantly from Quaker tradition. Angelina, for instance, charged that Quakers acknowledged woman's spiritual equality yet denied her a formative role in church affairs, thus keeping her subservient to man: "Woman may *preach*; this is a *gift;* but woman must *not* make the discipline by which *she herself* is to be governed" (Ceplair 283). More important, however, the Grimkés felt that rights, not religion, offered the surest foundation from which to argue for women's public speech and political participation. They urged abolitionists to sustain women rhetors "on the high ground of MORAL RIGHT *not* of Quaker peculiarity. . . . What we claim for ourselves, we claim for *every* woman whom God has called & qualified with gifts & graces" (Ceplair 277). Justifying delivery on the grounds of "Quaker peculiarity" would not shield women rhetors who came from other religious backgrounds. Angelina cautioned that failure to defend women's delivery on the basis of moral principles would eventually reduce them to silence:

> Why, my dear brothers, can you not see the deep laid scheme of the clergy against us as lecturers? They know full well that if they can persuade the people it is a *shame* for us to speak in public, & that every time we open our mouths for the dumb we are breaking a divine command, that even if we spoke with the tongues of *men* or of angels, we should have *no hearers*. They are springing a deep mine beneath our feet and we shall *very* soon be compelled to retreat for we shall have *no* ground to stand on. If we surrender the right to *speak* to the public this year, we must surrender the right to petition next year and the right to *write* the year after and so on. What *then* can woman do for the slave when she is herself under the feet of man and shamed into *silence*? (Ceplair 283–84)

The Grimkés defended woman's right to participate directly in the political process—whether through speech, print, or petition—by appealing to higher principles. Not only did woman's equality with man warrant her use of rhetorical forms and spaces traditionally denied her but her public contributions also had the potential to revolutionize a corrupt moral, social, and sexual order.

Victory and Defeat

Both Catharine Beecher and Angelina Grimké recognized a direct relationship between gender ideology and women's public speech and activism. However, where Beecher upheld the established hierarchy, Grimké identified systemic inequity in need of reformation. Where Beecher adopted a feminine delivery style compatible with dominant gender norms, Grimké appropriated the masculine style, employing restricted genres, spaces, and practices in order to perform gender and rhetoric more equitably. The educator and the abolitionist's textual debate prompted them to articulate contrary theories of gender and of women's realm, "the one arguing publicly for domestic virtue, the other arguing virtuously for going public" (Browne 103). Beecher's feminine and Grimké's masculine delivery styles enacted these theories, their rhetorical presentations the vocal, physical, spatial, and strategic embodiments of their beliefs about gender.

In terms of the larger and long-term controversy over women's gender and rhetorical performance, who was the victor? The answer depends upon one's analytical time frame. Throughout much of the antebellum period, the feminine delivery style was often more effective than the masculine if only because it allowed women rhetors to present themselves in nonthreatening verbal and visual positions relative to the audience, thereby increasing the likelihood of their messages' positive reception and consideration. Practitioners of the feminine delivery style—such as Willard, Dix, and Beecher—typically espoused woman's social retirement and subordination even as they discreetly addressed political and civic issues, advancing educational options, professional opportunities, and social reform from behind womanly facades. Practitioners of the masculine delivery style—such as the Grimkés, Stewart, Wright, and Ernestine Rose—enacted woman's social, moral, and discursive equality, a radical stance that created controversy and often undermined speakers' effectiveness with audiences. Kathryn Kish Sklar, for example, suggests that Beecher's less drastic methods of asserting "female influence as a function of [women's] difference from men" were, at least initially,

> more successful, possibly because they prescribed less dramatic cultural changes, spoke to real American anxieties about the pace of change, and introduced important stabilizing factors into the national ideology. To attack

the [gender] problem as straightforwardly as the Grimkés did was to push the eighteenth-century ideology of natural rights into an area where American men had never applied it. (*Catharine* 137)

In the long run, however, women who employed the masculine delivery style triumphed, at least in terms of the historical record. Their practices not only provided women access to previously prohibited rhetorical spaces but also extended the range of performative options available to them. Furthermore, their delivery style complemented the assumptions of the traditional fifth canon regarding the speaker's direct address of an audience in a public forum. This correspondence proved important as the canon of American public speakers began to take shape during the late nineteenth and early twentieth centuries, established in such anthologies as Melville Landon's *Kings of the Platform and the Pulpit* (1900), Alexander McClure's *Famous American Statesmen and Orators* (1902), William Jennings Bryan's *World's Famous Orations* (1906), and William Brigance's *History and Criticism of American Pubic Address* (1943). These books concentrated chiefly upon men, acknowledging women rarely if at all (see Nan Johnson's *Gender and Rhetorical Space in American Life* for detailed analysis of gender's impact upon the formation of the public speaking canon). The few women who were recognized almost invariably used the masculine delivery style, leading to the inclusion of the Grimké sisters, Elizabeth Cady Stanton, and Susan B. Anthony and the exclusion of Willard, Dix, and Beecher.

The twentieth-century recovery of women's rhetoric produced a number of revisionist histories that resurrected long-neglected, nineteenth-century women speakers, including Lillian O'Connor's *Pioneer Women Orators: Rhetoric in the Ante-Bellum Reform Movement* (1954), Karlyn Kohrs Campbell's *Man Cannot Speak for Her: A Critical Study of Early Feminist Rhetoric* (1989) and *Women Public Speakers in the United States, 1800–1925: A Bio-Critical Sourcebook* (1993), Carol Mattingly's *Well-Tempered Women: Nineteenth-Century Temperance Rhetoric* (1998), and Shirley Wilson Logan's *"We Are Coming": The Persuasive Discourse of Nineteenth-Century Black Women* (1999). While these works acknowledge diverse forms of rhetoric—for example, Campbell's *Women Public Speakers* includes an entry for Willard— they, nevertheless, continue to privilege women who employed a masculine delivery style.

Therefore, somewhat ironically, the masculine delivery style, initially perceived as a marginal and controversial manner of rhetorical presentation for women, moved center stage because of its affinity to men's oratorical practices while the feminine style was relegated to the margins, where it gradually became unrecognizable as delivery at all. Although women's indirect methods of rhetorical performance neither look like conventional delivery nor correspond to its masculinist assumptions, the feminine style allowed antebellum women to subvert dominant gender norms and interject their views into the public milieu, arguably the key feature or outcome of delivery. It is time to acknowledge that antebellum women's innovative use of private platforms, gendered genres, and surrogate speakers allowed them to access the otherwise inaccessible public, political arena. It is also time to validate the feminine delivery style as a method of rhetorical presentation, incorporating its many practitioners into the discipline's histories and integrating its alternative means and strategies into the regendered fifth canon.

4

Delivering Discourse and Children
The Maternal Difficulty

I n a letter dated 24 January 1856, woman's rights rhetor Elizabeth Cady Stanton announced the birth of her sixth child to collaborator Susan B. Anthony:

> Well, another female child is born into the world! Last Sunday afternoon, Harriot Eaton Stanton—oh the little heretic thus to desecrate that holy day— opened her soft blue eyes on this mundane sphere. . . . I am very . . . happy that the terrible ordeal is passed and that the result is another daughter. But I feel disappointed and sad at the same time at this grievous interruption of my plans. I might have been born an orator before spring, you acting as midwife. However, I feel that it will not be in vain that I am held back. My latent fires shall sometime burst forth. (DuBois 59–60)

In richly conflated imagery, Cady Stanton addresses the interrelationships and incompatibilities between women's delivery of discourse and children (see fig. 4.1). She depicts herself as an infant orator in the process of being born and Anthony as the facilitating midwife. Daughter Harriot's literal birth, however, halts or delays the mother's figurative nativity as a public speaker. Cady Stanton suggests that the unborn orator continues in a state of prolonged gestation, indefinitely suspended, but expresses faith in her future delivery, at which time her "latent fires" will blaze out boldly.

The analogy captures the complexities confronting maternal rhetors who aspired to deliver both offspring and oratory. Although maternity's shaping force in the lives of nineteenth-century American women is well-traveled terrain in the disciplines of history, sociology, and literary studies, it has been bypassed as a significant factor in women's public discourse within rhetoric. This oversight results from masculinist biases still undergirding conventions

Fig. 4.1. Elizabeth Cady Stanton and Harriot Stanton, 1856. Courtesy of the Library of Congress, Prints and Photographs Division, LC-USZ62-48965.

of rhetorical analysis, biases that have directed scholarly attention to "questions about rhetoric that appear interesting to men from within the rhetorical experiences that are characteristic for men" (Wu 84). Over the past few decades, however, feminist scholars have begun to challenge and recast traditional research methodologies and analytical frameworks in order to examine women and their practices.

One means of incorporating women's experience into the rhetorical tradition is to broaden definitions of what counts as evidence in scholarly inquiry. Such expansion is essential because "the evidence traditionally used to value rhetors simply does not always apply well to women" (Mattingly, "Telling" 105). Feminist scholars of nineteenth-century women are examining new forms of rhetorical evidence and are producing fresh, original, and inclusive studies, for example, Nan Johnson's analysis of parlor rhetorics in *Gender and Rhetorical Space in American Life, 1866–1910*, Carol Mattingly's exploration of women's fashion in *Appropriate[ing] Dress: Women's Rhetorical Style in*

Nineteenth-Century America, Wendy Dasler Johnson's study of undergarments in "Cultural Rhetorics of Women's Corsets," Maureen Daly Goggin's discussion of needlepoint in "An *Essamplaire Essai* on the Rhetoricity of Needlework Sampler-Making," and Liz Rohan's examination of quilting in "I Remember Mamma: Material Rhetoric, Mnemonic Activity, and One Woman's Turn-of-the-Twentieth-Century Quilt." Like these subjects, maternity has for too long been disregarded within rhetorical studies although it is highly relevant to women's discourse and, therefore, merits serious scholarly investigation.

Antebellum maternal rhetors occupy an especially promising position from which to begin rethinking the fifth rhetorical canon through the lens of gender, first, because women are most clearly marked "feminine" in relation to mothering and, second, because at few other periods have the social strictures governing women's rhetorical delivery been so noticeably in flux. Maternal rhetors who mounted public platforms to address civic issues soon discovered that delivery posed decidedly different considerations and constraints for them than it did for men. Indeed, once the maternal rhetor displaces the prototypical male speaker at the center of the rhetorical tradition, a number of gender differences immediately become apparent, and the contours and connotations of delivery begin to shift. Delivery suddenly assumes both a sexual and textual sense, and far from being the most material of the canons, it becomes imbued with ideological concerns and ramifications.

To illustrate these points, I examine four gender differences emerging from the study of antebellum women's delivery. First, when women addressed mixed-sex audiences, they consistently confronted suspicions regarding their sexual drive, motivation, and identity, responses to rhetorical delivery *not* routinely encountered by men. Second, maternal speakers had to be highly sensitive to the rhetorical implications of pregnancy, so they developed strategies for negotiating that condition on public platforms, considerations that, for obvious reasons, never factored into men's delivery at all. Third, maternal speakers' rhetorical delivery inevitably raised questions concerning the adequacy of their domestic performances. The specter of home and family always accompanied the maternal rhetor onstage although it was not a regular component of delivery for paternal rhetors. Fourth, bearing and raising children often ended, interrupted, or deferred maternal speakers' rhetorical careers (which consist of a history or sequence of public performances). Consequently, maternal rhetors often developed to their full potential later in life and continued practicing their craft longer than their male counterparts, yet another instance of gender's impact upon rhetorical delivery. By examining the complexities and contradictions inherent to maternal rhetors' production of children and discourse, I begin to trace the outlines of a regendered fifth canon, one capable of acknowledging the constraints and compensating strategies of both women and men.[1]

Vixens, Virgins, and Viragos: Sex and the Speaker

Nineteenth-century gender ideology and social practice discouraged women's discursive delivery through a number of tactics: by valuing women's silence over their speech, by limiting their opportunities for rhetorical training and practice, by restricting their access to public forums, and by decrying their use of masculine genres like oratory and debate. Women were told that their inherent "submissiveness and domesticity" disqualified them for the contentious civic arena but that their "purity and piety" simultaneously made them men's moral superiors and guides (Welter 152). Ironically, it was a sense of moral duty that eventually compelled (or justified) women's movement from private to public locations:

> [W]hat women saw as moral questions—slavery, prostitution, the devastation wrought by alcohol abuse on families, and the inability of women to protect their maternal obligations through the courts and the ballot box—was at odds with woman's submissiveness and her confinement to the home. In the face of that conflict, women asserted their moral right, indeed, their moral imperative, to breach domestic boundaries in order to protect the home and to apply their greater moral sensitivity and religious piety to issues of great ethical moment. (Campbell, Introduction xii)

Not only did women fulfill their moral obligations by joining church, benevolent, and reform associations but they soon raised their voices to promote social justice and improvement as well.

While antebellum women's delivery to other women was perceived as relatively harmless, their delivery to mixed-sex or promiscuous audiences aroused alarm. Conservatives objected to women's public speaking for two reasons: They charged, first, that women's civic participation would inspire immoral thoughts in men and result in lewd conduct, and, second, they feared that women's rhetorical powers would influence men's votes and thus shape politics and policy (Zaeske, "Promiscuous" 193, 198). Men who criticized female rhetors, however, found themselves in an awkward position because gender conventions prohibited them from engaging "in rhetorical combat with women"; therefore, as "long as the women who challenged them remained women, [men] found themselves impotent. Their hands were tied" (Hoffert

99–100). However, if a woman rhetor's femininity came into question, if she could be positioned outside the bounds of true womanhood, then she no longer fell within a protected category demanding gentlemanly behavior and instead became fair critical game. Three of the most common devices for recategorizing women in this manner were to depict them as vixens, desperate virgins, or viragos.

To cast a woman as a vixen was to suggest that she violated standards of feminine comportment in order to satisfy a voracious sexual appetite, a charge leveled at Abby Kelley in 1840 (see fig. 4.2). The pretty, young, full-figured abolitionist had just returned to the town of Washington, Connecticut, to deliver a second series of lectures and decided to attend church before the engagement. At the conclusion of the sermon, minister Gordon Hayes announced that although he had been asked to give notice of Kelley's upcoming lecture, he refused to do so. He cited the Pauline dictum that "it was a sin and a shame for women to teach men" and then called Kelley a wanton woman, this time quoting from Revelation: "I have a few things against thee, because thou sufferest that woman Jezebel, which calleth herself a prophetess, to teach and to seduce my servants to commit fornication" (Sterling 117). Hayes supported his charges of Kelley's sexual misconduct by noting that she traveled throughout the state "by night and by day, always with men and never with women" and concluded by calling her "a servant of Satan in the garb of an angel of light" (qtd. in Sterling 118). Stunned, Kelley listened as the congregation voted to prohibit women lecturers from speaking in church, thereby canceling her engagement and protecting the community from Jezebels like her.

Another method for edging women toward the margins of femininity was applied chiefly to spinsters, whose public speaking was interpreted as a sign of sexual desperation and a last-ditch effort to snare a husband. When Sarah and Angelina Grimké delivered their antislavery orations to promiscuous audiences in the late 1830s, the plain-faced, plainly dressed Quaker sisters often drew hostile reviews from the popular press. The *New Hampshire Patriot*, for instance, questioned their true motivation for speech making: "Why are all the old hens abolitionists? Because not being able to obtain husbands they think they may stand some chance for a negro, if they can only make amalgamation fashionable" (qtd. in Lerner 146). Depicting the rhetors as old hens so desperate to attract husbands that they would violate norms of feminine and racial propriety opened the Grimkés and their lectures to ridicule and disparagement.

A final strategy for placing women beyond the pale was to charge that public speaking had gradually eroded their womanly nature and transformed them

Fig. 4.2. Abby Kelley Foster, 1846.
Courtesy of the American Antiquarian Society.

into ersatz men. Describing a woman rhetor as a she-male, Amazon, or virago effectively unsexed her and made her a viable target. As was noted in chapter 3, educator Catharine Beecher penned a vitriolic attack on Frances Wright, one of the earliest and most notorious female civic orators of the nineteenth century, all the while highlighting her masculine qualities:

> Who can look without disgust and abhorrence upon such an one as Fanny Wright, with her great masculine person, her loud voice, her untasteful attire, going about unprotected, and feeling no need of protection, mingling with men in stormy debate, and standing up with bare-faced impudence, to lecture to a public assembly. . . . There she stands, with brazen front and brawny arms, attacking the safeguards of all that is . . . pure and lovely in domestic virtue. . . . [She] has so thrown off all feminine attractions, that freedom from temptation is her only, and shameful palladium. I cannot conceive any thing in the shape of a woman, more intolerably offensive and disgusting. (*Letters* 23)

Beecher suggests that Wright has become both physically and psychologically manlike as a result of her public participation, and the rhetor's body, voice, movements, clothes, and gender undergo critical scrutiny and appraisal. Sexually evaluative remarks like Beecher's

> gave warning to women who might presume to speak publicly that they would be examined according to every stricture and expectation by which the ideal woman was measured—by size, by musculature, by voice, by attire—nearly every facet that determined their "womanliness." In "abandoning" her assigned place she forfeited the privilege of pretended unawareness of her physical details. (Mattingly, *Appropriate[ing]* 22)

Antislavery speaker and former slave Sojourner Truth underwent a more extreme form of scrutiny at an 1858 meeting in Silver Lake, Indiana. A proslavery faction circulated rumors that Truth was, in reality, a man masquerading as a woman, and one T. W. Strain directly confronted her, charging, "[Y]our voice is not the voice of a woman, it is the voice of a man, and we believe you are a man" (qtd. in Titus 138). Although Truth was encouraged to "prove" her sexual identity to other women, a report from the *Liberator* indicates that she chose to give bodily testimony to the entire audience instead:

> Sojourner told them that her breasts had suckled many a white babe, to the exclusion of her own offspring; that some of those white babies had grown to man's estate; that, although they had suckled her colored breasts, they were, in her estimation, far more manly than they (her persecutors) appeared to be; and she quietly asked them, as she disrobed her bosom, if they, too, wished to suck! In vindication of her truthfulness, she told them that she would show her breast to the whole congregation; that it was not to her shame that she uncovered her breast before them, but to their shame. (qtd. in Painter 139)

Nell Painter notes that, in addition to the shock value of Truth's breast baring, her invitation to suckle both "infantilized" and "unmanned" her critics (140).

Although both white and black women rhetors were accused of being men, the charge may well have been levied at African-American speakers more frequently. For example, Jarena Lee—an itinerant preacher—recalled such an incident occurring while she addressed a full house in 1822: "Here I found some very ill-behaved persons, who talked roughly and said among other things, 'I was not a woman, but a man dressed in female clothes'" (23). Even fame afforded no protection from the accusation. As Shirley Wilson Logan observes, Frances Watkins Harper was arguably the "most prominent, active, and productive black woman speaker of the nineteenth century" (44). Nevertheless, like Truth and Lee, the soft-spoken, graceful, and conventionally feminine Watkins Harper also faced doubts regarding her sex *and* her race, as she confided in a letter to William Still: "I don't know but that you would laugh if you were to hear some of the remarks which my lectures call forth. . . . 'She is a man,' again 'She is not colored, she is painted'" (Still 772). The charges and suspicions directed at Truth, Lee, and Harper illustrate how race intensified the gender issues confronting women rhetors.

When antebellum women spoke from public platforms, they risked being characterized as vixens, desperate virgins, or viragos, forms of critical scrutiny that constitute a first gender difference in the canon of delivery. Not only was the physical and vocal performance of the woman orator assessed but her sexuality and gender identity were as well, concerns *not* routinely encountered by male speakers of the day. Women rhetors faced suspicions of rampant sexuality, husband hunting, or manliness, suspicions they learned to allay by emphasizing their conventional roles as sisters, daughters, wives, and, especially, mothers. Maternity did not entirely shield a rhetor from misogynist criticisms, but it did undercut them. However, while eliminating the potency of certain lines of attack, motherhood created new rhetorical complications for speakers, as Mari Boor Tonn explains: "Because dominant maternal images often conflict with rhetorical purposes, the effectiveness of motherhood as a rhetorical strategy hinges, in part, on how successfully a speaker can both appropriate and contest those images" (16). Dominant maternal images were perhaps nowhere more intrusive or essential to negotiate than when antebellum women tried to reconcile pregnancy with public speaking, the subject to which I turn next.

Pregnancy and the Platform

To understand the maternal images appropriated and contested by antebellum women rhetors, it is necessary to review the profound shift in gender ideology that took place during the first half of the nineteenth century, one detailed in Mary Ryan's *Empire of the Mother* (1982). At the beginning of the century, families were father centered, extended, and community oriented. By midcentury, however, a dramatic economic and ideological transition had occurred, and families were mother centered, nuclear, and isolated (33–37). Fathers were relegated to the contentious, hard-scrabble world of work, and mothers displaced them as rulers of the hearth. Women were urged to devote themselves to tending their husbands, children, and homes, which were envisioned as islands of love and light in a dark and turbulent universe. Although increasingly secluded within the domestic realm, women were assured that they played a central social role because as went the home, so went the nation.

When maternal rhetors crossed domestic boundaries in order to speak publicly, they moved contrary to feminine gender codes and so confronted a variety of religious, biological, and ideological arguments opposing their public participation. One of the most prevalent and pernicious was that of the *maternal difficulty*, a line of reasoning holding that because "*some* women at *some* times could not conveniently perform the duties of Judge, Legislator, [or] military commander, because of the duties of the nursery . . . [then] *all* women should at *all* times be excluded from *all* political franchises" (Senex 20, emphasis added). A representative example of the argument appears in a *New York Herald* editorial of 12 September 1852, ridiculing the professional efforts of woman's rights activists because of their potential fertility:

> [Woman's rights women] want to fill all the . . . posts which men are ambitious to occupy, to be lawyers, doctors, captains of vessels, and generals in the field. How funny it would sound in the newspapers that Lucy Stone, pleading a cause, took suddenly ill in the pains of parturition and perhaps gave birth to a fine bouncing boy in court! Or that Reverend Antoinette Brown was arrested in the pulpit in the middle of her sermon from the same cause, and presented a "pledge" to her husband and the congregation; or that Dr. Harriot Hunt, while attending a gentleman patient in a fit of the gout or *fistula in ano* found it necessary to send for a doctor there and then, and to be delivered of a man or woman child—perhaps twins! A similar event might happen on the floor of Congress, in a storm at sea or in the raging tempest of battle, and then, what is to become of the woman legislator? (qtd. in Harper 1: 78–79)

The editorial depicts women's public activity as fundamentally incompatible with their childbearing capacity. Women's rhetorical and professional efforts— Stone's plea, Brown's sermon, Hunt's practice, the politician's debate—are interrupted midact by labor pains and the public delivery of offspring, suggesting that women are not only biologically handicapped but also lack propriety, modesty, and common sense.

The maternal-difficulty argument pervaded the culture, and to avoid lending it further credence, maternal rhetors became highly sensitive to the messages imparted by pregnancy and motherhood, as is apparent in the case of Elizabeth Cady Stanton. In June 1858, the forty-three-year-old wife and mother discovered herself pregnant for the seventh time. In early September, during her third month of pregnancy, she received an invitation to speak in Boston's Fraternity Lecture Course, a popular speakers' series featuring such notables as Ralph Waldo Emerson, Theodore Parker, Henry Ward Beecher, and Wendell Phillips. Cady Stanton was the first woman ever invited to participate in the prestigious course, an effort on the part of series' organizers to "recognize the equality of woman in the lecture-room" (Slack 9.140). Knowing full well the symbolic importance of her appearance, she accepted the mid-November engagement; however, by early October, a weak and exhausted Cady Stanton realized that her seventh pregnancy would prove far more difficult than the previous six. When rumors reached series' organizers that she might be unable to fulfill her commitment, a flurry of urgent letters issued from Boston, challenging her to prove herself "a woman of utmost reliability," threatening that cancellation would bring "mortification" to the entire female sex, and admonishing that only "Death—or the prison-bed of sickness" was an adequate excuse for not appearing (Severance 9.132; Thayer 9.141–42). Despite such pleas and strong-arm tactics, Cady Stanton ultimately missed her engagement, pointing to the theft of a trunk containing her speech and wardrobe as the culprit.

Furious at the damage caused by Cady Stanton's cancellation, collaborator Susan B. Anthony complained that "to lose such a golden moment to say the word, which Mrs. Stanton professes she so longs to utter, is wholly unaccountable to me" (Gordon, *Selected* 384). Publicly, and apparently even to Anthony, the maternal rhetor maintained that the theft of her trunk en route to Boston had caused the cancellation, but privately, in a letter to intimate friend Elizabeth Smith Miller, Cady Stanton confessed the real obstacle:

> I made the engagement in good faith and prepared myself, expecting fully to be there at the appointed date, which would have been in the fifth month—maternally, not quakerly, speaking—at which time I always have felt well and heroic. But my present experience differed from all its antecedents. I grew worse instead of better,—sick, nervous, timid, and so short-breathed that it was impossible for me to read one page aloud. You see I had a good excuse for not going. I selected the trunk episode as an excuse. I could not give the other to strangers. I knew that if I told Mrs. Severance [a series' organizer] my dilemma, she would have to repeat it, and as the maternal difficulty has always been one of the arguments against woman entering public life, I did not like the idea that I, who had a hundred times declared that difficulty to be absurd, should illustrate in my own person the contrary thesis. (Gordon, *Selected* 383)

To avoid reinforcing popular prejudices, Cady Stanton withheld the true cause of her cancellation, pregnancy, from the public and instead used the stolen trunk as an excuse. Paradoxically, her decision to erase her pregnancy both challenged and supported prevailing notions of woman's [in]capacity. By refusing to acknowledge the impact of the maternal body, Cady Stanton refuted gender conventions and arguments used to limit woman's access to the public realm. At the same time, her decision also permitted the masculine body to continue functioning as the unquestioned standard of social reliability, a standard making no provision for women's corporeal experience, which includes pregnancy and its side effects. Pregnancy, childbirth, and childrearing profoundly impacted the rhetorical delivery of maternal speakers like Cady Stanton. However, these influences, while acknowledged privately, were more often than not effaced publicly in an effort to present women as the corporeal equals of men.

Cady Stanton's public erasure of her pregnancy leads naturally to a related question: How did maternal rhetors handle visible pregnancy on the platform? In general, pregnant women may have circulated more widely and freely during the nineteenth century than twenty-first-century readers imagine. Jane Pease and William Pease, in their study of antebellum women in Charleston and Boston, observe, "Until the last weeks before their deliveries, most women were not only active as usual in their homes but, wearing loose gowns, pursued their customary routines, going out in public for errands and visiting—even attending parties" (*Ladies* 25). Evidence suggests that pregnant rhetors also continued to circulate and lecture publicly, at least until their condition became undeniable.

Maternal rhetors did not immediately retire from the public platform upon learning that they were pregnant. This much is apparent in a September 1858 letter from Anthony to the recently married Antoinette Brown Blackwell, in which Anthony discusses Cady Stanton's pregnancy and calculates her window of oratorical opportunity: "Mrs. Stanton!! is embarked on the rolling sea—three long months of terrible nausea are behind and what the future has in store—the deep only knows—She will be able to lecture however up to January—provided she will only make her surroundings bend to such a work" (Gordon, *Selected* 378). Anthony's analysis suggests that maternal rhetors typically sequestered themselves once pregnancy became apparent after the fifth or sixth month (which in Cady Stanton's case would occur in January). Similarly, antislavery lecturers Abby Kelley (Foster) and Lucy Stone both continued to speak publicly into their sixth month of pregnancy as well (Sterling 234–37; Kerr 101).[2]

Although propriety eventually required visibly pregnant rhetors to retire from the public stage, their willingness to "show" may have depended upon the composition of the audience itself. Maternal rhetors generally stopped appearing before mixed-sex audiences after the sixth month of pregnancy, but they continued to participate publicly far later when their audiences consisted chiefly of women, as is apparent in the case of Maria Weston Chapman. By

the late 1830s, controversy over women's roles within antislavery reform threatened to split the movement in two. Tensions between liberals who supported
and conservatives who opposed women's membership and equal participation in the parent organization, the American Anti-Slavery Society, arose in
the women's branches as well. At the April 1840 meeting of the Boston Female
Anti-Slavery Society (BFASS), conservatives attempted to dissolve the organization and thereby undermine the liberal faction. Chapman, a liberal leader
within the BFASS who also happened to be eight months' pregnant at the time,
foiled the conservatives by rising to her feet and announcing, "The Boston
Female Society is *not* dissolved but will hold a meeting to choose officers on
Saturday next at Marlborough Hall" (Sterling 100). Thanks to Chapman's
quick thinking, 120 women of the liberal faction met a few days later to elect
new officers, ensuring the continuation of an organization committed to
women's full participation in the fight against slavery. Chapman's presence at
the April meeting indicates that undeniably pregnant women did indeed appear and act publicly, at least when their audience consisted of other women.

Twenty-three years later, another visibly pregnant rhetor played a prominent role at the first convention of the Woman's National Loyal League, an
organization committed to doing "everything in [its] power to aid the Government" of the North during the Civil War and to furthering the cause of
freedom (Stanton, Anthony, and Gage 2: 54). The convention attracted an
"immense audience, mostly women" and included such woman's rights lu-
minaries as Anthony, Stone, Cady Stanton, Ernestine Rose, and Angelina
Grimké (Weld) (Stanton, Anthony, and Gage 2: 53). Antoinette Brown
Blackwell, who was seven months' pregnant, addressed the evening session,
delivering a speech urging the enfranchisement of black and white, male and
female, northern and southern Americans at the end of the war (Lasser and
Merrill, *Friends* 164). Maternal rhetors apparently selected venues carefully
during the last trimester of pregnancy, confident that the pregnant form would
be less of an ethical liability with same- than with mixed-sex audiences.[3]

Speakers' strategies for managing pregnancy on public platforms indicate how women's corporeal experiences shape their rhetorical delivery.
Antebellum women clearly were aware that "the body is not only an instrument of expression but is also itself expressive of meaning" (Mountford,
Gendered 7), capable of conveying multiple messages to the audience about
the speaker's performance of gender and rhetoric. Therefore, to counter prejudices holding that the maternal difficulty disqualified women from public
endeavors, speakers learned to anticipate and minimize pregnancy's potentially
negative impact onstage. Expectant rhetors adjusted schedules and selected

venues carefully to complement their pregnant forms, thereby helping to ensure a favorable reception by audiences. They consciously decided how, when, where, and whether to acknowledge and display the maternal body, rhetorical considerations that constitute a second noteworthy gender difference in delivery for men and women.

Justifying Delivery

In addition to negotiating pregnancy in public forums, speakers also contended with the adverse implications of rhetorical delivery itself, which suggested a woman's willingness to neglect domestic and maternal obligations for personal acclaim and glory. Antebellum society viewed a woman's rhetorical activity as fundamentally incompatible with her private, personal responsibilities, as this excerpt from the *New York Sun* (1853) indicates:

> The quiet duties of daughter, wife or mother are not congenial to those hermaphrodite spirits who thirst to win the title of champion of one sex and victor over another. What is the love and submission of one manly heart to the woman whose ambition it is to sway the minds of multitudes as did Demosthenes or Cicero? What are the tender affections and childish prattle of the family circle to women whose ears itch for the loud laugh and boisterous cheer of the public assembly? (qtd. in Chambers-Schiller 177)

To counter such perceptions, maternal rhetors felt obliged to reassure the audience that they were able housekeepers, loving wives, and dedicated mothers in addition to being public participants, assurances that Nan Johnson argues are commonplace in the biographies and autobiographies of nineteenth-century women speakers. The strategy of justifying women's public performances by highlighting their "domestic interests and conventional feminine dispositions" is also evident in the letters and memoirs examined in this chapter and provides important insights into the unique rhetorical constraints and compensating strategies of antebellum women rhetors (Johnson, *Gender* 112).

Pressure to demonstrate domestic competence began the moment women rhetors married, as Angelina Grimké could attest. She wed fellow abolitionist Theodore Weld at the conclusion of her highly successful New England speaking tour in 1838. Both Angelina and her sister Sarah (who immediately joined the newlyweds' household following the wedding) felt it imperative to perform their domestic duties expertly even though their upbringing in an aristocratic southern home meant that the sisters knew virtually nothing about housekeeping. Nevertheless, as representatives of a new and progressive type of woman, they knew their home would reflect well or poorly on other female lecturers, so the two committed themselves to learning the mysteries of cooking and cleaning. Grimké Weld explains:

> Now I verily believe that we are *thus* doing *as much* for the cause of woman as we did by public speaking. For it is absolutely necessary that we should show that we are *not* ruined as domestic characters, but so far from it, *as soon* as duty calls us home, we can & do rejoice in the release from public service, & are as anxious to make good bread as we ever were to deliver a good lecture. (Ceplair 326)

The sisters felt that their domestic talents could refute prejudices regarding women lecturers' unfitness for the private realm and benefit all who followed their public path.

In addition to feeling obliged to prove themselves able housekeepers, maternal rhetors encountered suspicions of having slighted their familial duties when they lectured, attended conventions, or participated in public events. An indignant Cady Stanton recounts an instance when her absent children overshadowed her oratory:

> On one occasion, after addressing the Legislature, some of the ladies in congratulating me, inquired in a deprecating tone, "What do you do with your children?" "Ladies," I said, "it takes me no longer to speak than you to listen; what have you done with your children the two hours you have been sitting here? But to answer your questions. I never leave my children to go to Saratoga, Washington, Newport, or Europe, nor even to come here. They are this moment with a faithful nurse at the Delavan House [a nearby hotel], and having accomplished my mission, we shall all return home together. (Stanton, Anthony, and Gage 1: 461)

In this narrative, women support the speaker by attending her address but then undercut her efforts by asking about her children's whereabouts. Although a radical in so many areas of her life, a defensive Cady Stanton does not challenge the women's assumption that children take precedence over all other interests and responsibilities. She instead presents herself as a rhetor who fulfills her maternal duties even as she delivers speeches, crafting an oddly reassuring figure who combines conventional and unconventional attributes, blending the old with the new.

Another method for justifying women's delivery was to recast the traditional forms and functions of motherhood itself. This alternative strategy is apparent in the memoirs of Zilpha Elaw, an itinerant African-American preacher who followed inner promptings to speak God's word following her husband's death in 1823. Elaw traveled and preached throughout the North and South, sometimes leaving her daughter in the care of others, sometimes journeying with the child beside her. Her unusual lifestyle—particularly, her rootlessness and frequent separations from her daughter—elicited "strong criticism of [her] seemingly unmaternal and hence unfeminine behavior" (Bollinger 359). Elaw responded by presenting herself as a woman who combined mothering and rhetoric for the highest purposes, as a Christian with "divinely inspired speaking obligations" that took precedence over her maternal duties, as a mother who first served God in order to then better serve her child (Bollinger 360). The power of the maternal word is apparent in Elaw's account of a crowded camp meeting that included her child in the audience. As she preached,

> It pleased God to capture my own daughter in the gospel net. . . . [She] cried out aloud, during the service, and exclaimed, "Oh, Lord! Have mercy upon me, for I can hold out no longer. . . ." This occurred in the midst of listening hundreds, and it produced a most thrilling sensation upon the congregation; for, said they, "It is her own daughter!" and that she was my only child. Many a mother strongly felt with me on that occasion; and though my position would not allow me to leave the pulpit, to go and pour the oil of consolation into her wounded spirit, yet, thank God, there were abundance of dear friends present who were ready for every good word and work. (103)

The daughter's conversion not only testifies to the mother's gifts as a preacher but also evokes the sympathy of other mothers in the congregation, this despite the fact that Elaw's public duties prevent her from leaving the pulpit to attend to her distressed child. Instead, an "abundance of dear friends" care for her, enabling Elaw to honor her mandate to preach. Elaw thus constructs an image of a maternal rhetor speaking from the pulpit and thereby touching the heart and soul of her listening child. By allowing the pulpit to separate her from her daughter and by serving as a conduit for God's message, the preacher fulfills the nineteenth-century mother's highest goal and responsibility, that of promoting the moral and spiritual welfare of her child. Elaw thus recasts the conventions of motherhood by depicting herself as a maternal rhetor who saves the soul of her child and congregation through public speech.

Both Cady Stanton and Elaw justified their public discourse by demonstrating their maternal competence. Their self-representations indicate that women's delivery was never simply assessed for the effective use of voice, gesture, and expression, the standard elements of the traditional fifth canon. Instead, when maternal rhetors entered public spaces, society's feminine ideal accompanied them like a shadow self, and they were evaluated as well for their fit with or divergence from the chimerical true woman. Audiences projected this ideal onto maternal rhetors, scrutinizing the adequacy of both their public and private performances, considerations not routinely imposed upon paternal rhetors. Nineteenth-century women were well aware of this critical inequity, as is apparent in Mrs. O. W. Scott's "The Model Woman" (1874):

> A woman, a *married* woman, we mean—may be a noted author, charming platform-speaker, a very Lady bountiful in her charities; but the inquisitive public, before which she stands, inquires: "Does she use soap at home?" "Is she a good wife, mother, and housekeeper?" ... A man is not thus criticized. He may have left his wife at home alone, with five small children; but who inquires about that? ... He may not have left her money enough to buy a postage-stamp; but bright eyes beam upon him from the galleries, and unstinted applause greets the "talented speaker." (qtd. in N. Johnson, *Gender* 120)

While the paternal rhetor is assessed solely for his oratorical abilities, the maternal rhetor must please as a speaker and as a "good wife, mother, and housekeeper." Gender ideology thus permeates women's delivery. The persistent overlay of domestic and maternal expectations onto women's rhetorical performances marks a third gender difference in the fifth canon for men and women.

Maternity and Rhetorical Career

Although antebellum women displayed remarkable ingenuity in coping with physical and ideological constraints, maternity shaped their ethos and performance in substantive ways. Maternity also affected the overall course of women's rhetorical careers, ending, disrupting, or postponing them for years or even decades. This section examines how bearing and rearing children impacted the rhetorical delivery of six maternal rhetors: Frances Wright, Angelina Grimké Weld, Abby Kelley Foster, Antoinette Brown Blackwell, Isabella Beecher Hooker, and Elizabeth Cady Stanton.[4]

Maternity's influence on delivery is apparent from the outset of women's public, political discourse in this country, a tradition that conventionally starts with Wright, "the first important female practitioner of [civic] rhetoric to be found in American culture" (Connors, "Frances" 32). In 1828, Wright addressed a promiscuous assembly at a Fourth of July celebration and embarked upon a remarkable two-year speaking campaign, during which she "sounded the themes of equality, rationality, tolerance, and peace" (Eckhardt 171). Wright's lectures attracted crowds numbering into the thousands, composed of the curious, the respectful, and the scandalized (see fig. 4.3). Not only did she deliver rhetoric viva voce but she also published her views in a newspaper coedited with Robert Dale Owen, the *Free Enquirer*. In 1830, however, the unmarried speaker discovered that she was pregnant. Because of the outcry that would ensue should her condition become known, Wright decided to leave the country for a time, announcing her departure at the conclusion of an address to three thousand New Yorkers:

> And now, my fellow citizens! After two years of public exertion in a work I have believed righteous, and called for by the accumulated corruptions and errors which had gathered in and around our social edifice, I feel warned, for a season, to retire. . . . I wish not my name to be made a scarecrow to the timid, or a stumbling-block to the innocently prejudiced, at a season when all should unite round the altar of their country, with its name only in their mouths, and its love in their hearts. For these motives, which I trust my fellow citizens will appreciate, I shall take the present season for attention to some more private interests of my own, and shortly leave this city and the country for a few months, not to return, until after the decision of the autumnal elections. (D'Arusmont 220)

Wright's farewell can be read on two levels, first, as a radical's temporary adieu to politics and, second, as an honest (if indirect) communication, coding rather than confessing her pregnancy. Although she masks her physical condition by discussing it in terms of private reasons for retirement, the public and the personal, politics and pregnancy intermingle throughout the good-bye. Wright concludes by predicting her return to America after the fall elections, but her absence would last five years, long enough for the zeitgeist to change and for interest in Wright to wane. After her return in 1835, she never managed to recapture her earlier momentum and soon retired permanently from lecturing. Wright's course illustrates maternity's ability to derail women's rhetorical careers.

Another prominent woman rhetor of the 1830s is, of course, Angelina Grimké Weld, who left the front lines of the antislavery movement shortly after marrying Theodore Weld despite the couple's joint commitment to her speaking career. Although the reasons for her withdrawal are multiple and complex—including economics, psychology, and changes within the antislavery movement itself—maternity was certainly one of the most significant. Grimké Weld bore four children within six years, undergoing difficult pregnancies each time and sustaining at least two childbirth-related injuries, a prolapsed uterus and a hernia (Lerner 290). Both are easily treatable conditions today, but they were sources of lifelong suffering in the nineteenth

Fig. 4.3. Frances Wright. Courtesy of the Library of Congress, Prints and Photographs Division, LC-USZ62-39344.

century. Grimké Weld never directly or publicly acknowledged these ailments as the cause of her retirement; however, her husband insisted that illness had ended her public-speaking career, an insistence that Gerda Lerner contends salved his sore conscience, which resisted admitting that his wife's "gifts had been stifled by anything as prosaic as childbearing and domesticity" (291). Although Grimké Weld occasionally appeared in public during the 1850s and 1860s to advance the antislavery cause, the physical, emotional, intellectual, and economic costs of being a wife and mother curtailed her trajectory as a public speaker. The mystery that continues to surround her early retirement indicates the generally unrecognized but, nevertheless, strong interconnections between women's delivery of children and discourse.

Wright's and Grimké Weld's histories illustrate how maternity could halt promising oratorical careers. For most women, however, motherhood interrupted their rhetorical commitments only for a time although the length of that interruption varied considerably, with some returning to public speaking within months of a child's birth and others waiting decades.

When antislavery lecturer Abby Kelley Foster gave birth to daughter Alla on 19 May 1847, she decided to resume public speaking within a year. In a 17

December 1847 letter to antislavery cohort Maria Weston Chapman, Kelley Foster announced her "intention . . . to wean [Alla] at nine months" instead of the customary twelve so as to begin a spring lecture tour with her husband, Stephen Foster (qtd. in Sterling 245). Her ambitions scandalized many in the abolition movement, as is evident in a 23 January 1848 letter to Kelley Foster from Lizzie Jones, who was herself with child:

> For the sake of millions of suffering children whose mothers have left them in the care of aunts & sisters or hired nurses, I am sorry. Your influence on the course of human freedom will be good but your influence on home duties and home virtues will be bad. If you would wait until your child is old enough to wean it would be less reprehensible. I shall set a better example. If the little stranger that we expect shall live I shall not feel like leaving it to lecture in ten months. (qtd. in Sterling 246)

Jones's letter expresses common assumptions of the day, namely, that a mother's primary responsibilities concerned "home duties and home virtues" rather than issues of human freedom and that the care of aunts, sisters, or nurses could not replace hers, even for a short time. Furthermore, Kelley Foster's decision to wean Alla early was apparently not simply a personal matter; instead, weaning functioned synecdochically for an entire cluster of beliefs surrounding motherhood, beliefs that Kelley Foster and other antebellum women confronted whenever maternal and rhetorical obligations collided.

Like Kelley Foster, Antoinette Brown Blackwell was also determined to combine marriage, motherhood, and reform. Following her 1853 ordination as a Congregational minister, she actively supported a number of reform movements, including temperance, antislavery, and woman's rights. Her dedication to public work was so strong that she initially foreswore marriage altogether, having observed the incompatibility of domesticity and reform for most women. That, however, was before she met Samuel Blackwell—brother of the first woman physician in America, Elizabeth Blackwell—and a full supporter of Brown's ministerial and reform efforts. The two wed in January 1856, and in early November, Brown Blackwell became a mother, giving birth to daughter Florence (see fig. 4.4).

Remaining true to her social commitments, Brown Blackwell discovered ways to maintain an active lecturing schedule throughout her first seven years of marriage and maternity. Although Florence's birth a few weeks before the 1856 National Woman's Rights Convention prevented Brown Blackwell's attendance, she, nevertheless, participated by sending a long letter on woman suffrage that was then read aloud to the convention audience (Cazden 116).

Fig. 4.4. Antoinette Brown Blackwell and
Florence Blackwell, 1857. Courtesy of the Schlesinger
Library, Radcliffe Institute, Harvard University.

The birth of a second daughter, Mabel, on 13 April 1858 did not keep Brown
Blackwell from attending and addressing the Ninth National Woman's Rights
Convention a month later. Furthermore, following the death of three-month-
old Mabel later that summer, the grieving mother "threw herself into platform
appearances, first on a temperance lecture tour, and then preaching weekly
at a New York City hall she hired for the purpose," the public work consol-
ing her somewhat for her loss (Lasser and Merrill, *Friends* 93).

Over time, however, Brown Blackwell found it increasingly difficult to balance domestic and maternal responsibilities with a rhetorical career despite
the assistance of a supportive husband and family. Each time she left home
for an extended period to preach or lecture, she returned to chaos. In a letter
to Anthony, she describes the shambles awaiting her at the conclusion of a
summer speaking tour:

The ordeal which I have passed through! . . . Remember that a little three year old is capable of growing out of every thing it wears once in three month—just the time of my absence—and fancy me set down in a <u>very</u> dirty house just on the outside edge of cold weather with a child minus one decent or comfortable winter suit, a husband whose garments, as well as himself, have been deserted the whole season, and ones own wardrobe the worse for wear. Then there is a winter store of coal, provisions, &c to be taken in, a garden to be covered up from the frost; seeds to save, label & put up for spring; bulbs to store away, shrubs to transplant; &c &c. . . . This, Susan, is woman's sphere! In addition fancy me spending four mortal days from morning till night tramping up and down NY streets & stairs; interspersed with omnibus rides; in search of a suitable hall to preach in; then fancy me setting down in the midst of it all to write an appropriate introductory sermon, going in by the Sunday afternoon boat, preaching it, and coming home to breakfast and to a dress maker next morning, and you have a fair history of my doings & surroundings since we parted, only if all the items were to be enumerated I suppose all the letter paper in the house would not contain them. (Gordon, *Selected* 397–98)

The letter interweaves such domestic concerns as clothing, cleaning, and provisioning with public endeavors like finding and renting a hall, writing and delivering sermons. Brown Blackwell's easy transitions from gardening to preaching to family breakfasts suggest the seamlessness of private and public spaces, the commingled details revealing the adroit juggling demanded of maternal rhetors, who were expected to perform well in not one but all areas of life.

The difficulty of reconciling discursive and domestic obligations increased with the birth of additional children—Edith in 1860, Grace in 1863, a stillborn boy in 1865, Agnes in 1866, and Ethel in 1869 (Cazden 127–43). Brown Blackwell eventually found it impossible to attend to both, and her 1863 speech to the Woman's National Loyal League, delivered when she was seven months' pregnant, marked her last public appearance until the end of the decade. She did not, however, relinquish her intellectual interests altogether during this retirement. Instead, she turned to research and writing, devoting three hours a day to "brain work," and in 1869 published her first book, *Studies in General Science* (Lasser and Merrill, *Friends* 93–94). Brown Blackwell's hiatus from lecturing convinced her of the importance of the print medium for maternal rhetors. Not only did writing provide them with an alternative route for disseminating ideas but publication also reached far larger audiences than conventional methods of oral delivery could.[5]

As Kelley Foster's and Brown Blackwell's experiences suggest, maternity might suspend speakers' public involvement for months or years. While the length of the interruption varied, the interludes themselves had a dramatic impact on the arc of women's rhetorical careers. Because of multiple or sustained periods devoted to bearing and raising children, maternal rhetors were often older when they resumed (or even began) their public speaking careers, and they continued actively in those careers far longer than their male counterparts, frequently working well into their seventies, eighties, or nineties.

A case in point is Isabella Beecher, yet another member of the influential Beecher clan, which included educator Catharine Beecher, novelist Harriet Beecher Stowe, and minister Henry Ward Beecher. Isabella married John Hooker in 1841 and, over the course of fourteen years, bore four children, three of whom survived to adulthood. For nearly three decades, marriage and maternity were the central focus of her life although she did occasionally participate in social causes, for example, attending antislavery events with her husband, composing prosuffrage arguments, and joining the Sanitary Commission during the Civil War. Not until 1868, however, did Beecher Hooker fully commit herself to the reform issue that most engaged her, woman's rights. By that time, her eldest daughter had married, her second daughter was engaged, and her son had turned fourteen, thus freeing the forty-seven-year-old wife and mother "to seek a nonfamilial outlet for her pent-up energies, aspirations, and ideas" (Boydston, Kelley, and Margolis 81). Beecher Hooker's transformation from a relatively unknown housewife into a national leader in the woman's rights movement was rapid. In the late 1860s, she established the Connecticut Woman Suffrage Association; in the 1870s, she worked to enact laws promoting married women's equal property rights, became a lecturer for and leading organizer of the National Woman Suffrage Association, and published a book, *Womanhood: Its Sanctities and Fidelities*; in the 1880s, she organized and addressed the first International Convention of Women; and in the 1890s, well into her seventies, she continued to address legislators and audiences on woman's rights (Starr).

Reflecting on her own experiences, Beecher Hooker protested the vast pool of unrecognized and undeveloped talent among women. In "Shall Women Vote? A Matrimonial Dialogue" (1860), she makes the case that women—particularly mothers—are well suited for political life:

> [J]ust see what maturity of thought, real wisdom, there is in her, gained in this most motherly way of discriminating between her own children, adapting influence and government according to character and bringing out a harmonious

whole, from so many discordant or at least different elements. What a pity that such a disciplined mind should lie inactive, unfelt almost, in the very fullness of its power. (qtd. in Boydston, Kelley, and Margolis 109)

Beecher Hooker envisions "a very respectable Congress" composed of able mothers, widows, and spinsters.

Unlike Beecher Hooker, Cady Stanton did not postpone her rhetorical career until after her children had grown. In 1848, her frustrations as an isolated, homebound mother actually inspired her to help arrange the first Woman's Rights Convention at Seneca Falls, New York, and she subsequently struggled to remain involved in the movement despite the demands of a large household and eventual brood of seven children. Throughout the 1850s, her maternal obligations were such that she attended woman's rights conventions and delivered public addresses only with great difficulty. So wearying was the effort required to balance public and private endeavors that she occasionally threatened to withdraw from reform completely, as she announced in an 1853 letter to Anthony:

> I forbid you to ask me to send one thought or one line to any convention, any paper, or any individual; for I swear by all the saints that whilst I am nursing this baby I will not be tormented with suffering humanity. I am determined to make no effort to do anything beyond my imperative home duties until I can bring about the following conditions: 1st, Relieve myself of housekeeping altogether; 2nd, Secure some capable teacher for my children; 3rd, See my present baby on her feet. My ceaseless cares begin to wear upon my spirit. Therefore, I say adieu to the public for a time, for I must give all my moments and my thoughts to my children. (Stanton and Blatch 2: 51)

Cady Stanton's public profile increased as her children grew older and her maternal duties lessened in consequence. She emerged fully as a public speaker as she entered her early fifties. During the 1860s, she helped found the Woman's National Loyal League (which mounted a massive petition drive to ensure passage of the Thirteenth Amendment) and the American Equal Rights Association (which advocated suffrage for both African Americans and women following the war); crossed Kansas urging the enfranchisement of freedmen and of women; and established a woman's rights newspaper, *The Revolution*, with Susan Anthony. During the 1870s, she helped found the first national woman's rights organization, the National Woman Suffrage Association, and toured the country as a popular and well-paid lyceum lecturer. During the 1880s, she collaborated with Anthony and Matilda Gage to produce the first three volumes of *A History of Woman Suffrage*; and during the 1890s, she reinterpreted women's biblical role in the controversial best-seller *The Woman's Bible*. Cady Stanton worked steadily to promote woman's rights until her death at the age of eighty-seven (Griffith).

Antebellum women moderated maternity's disruptive impact on their rhetorical careers, the frequent interruptions and endless delays, with a stubborn faith in future usefulness. They held fiercely to the belief that long and productive careers lay ahead of them, confidence apparent in an 1857 letter from Cady Stanton to Anthony, who had complained that the woman's rights movement was languishing because its most accomplished speakers were at home birthing babies. Cady Stanton reassured Anthony that the present state of affairs would not last forever: "Courage Susan this is my last baby & she will be two years old in January. Two years more & & &, time will tell what.—You and I have a prospect of a good long life we shall not be in our prime before fifty & after that we shall be good for twenty years at least" (Gordon, *Selected* 351–52). Brown Blackwell expressed similar assurance of future accomplishments in "The Relation of Woman's Work in the Household to the Work Outside," an article composed during her own hiatus to raise five daughters: "Fifty or fifty-five should be but the prime—the very crown and summit of a woman's life. Thenceforward she should aim at vigorous personal achievements with a reach beyond the household" (qtd. in Cazden 181). A great many maternal rhetors did indeed enjoy unusually long careers, Beecher Hooker remaining active in public affairs until well into her seventies, Cady Stanton into her late eighties, and Brown Blackwell into her nineties.

Thus, as a consequence of maternal interludes, antebellum women often developed to their full abilities later and continued delivering rhetoric longer than was the norm for male speakers of the day. Clearly, corporeal, family, and social constraints limited women's opportunities to participate publicly and influenced the overall shape of their rhetorical careers. Maternity's power to halt, interrupt, or delay rhetors' public speaking efforts marks a fourth gender difference in the canon of delivery for women and men.

How, then, does the fifth canon change when the male speaker at the center of the rhetorical tradition is replaced with a woman? The four differences identified in this chapter—sexual suspicion, pregnancy, gender norms, and career pattern—suggest that when antebellum women delivered rhetoric, they were enmeshed within and cognizant of gender ideology in a way that their male counterparts were not. A woman rhetor underwent a different kind of critical scrutiny than a man. His delivery was evaluated chiefly for the effective use of voice, gesture, and expression, standard concerns of the traditional fifth canon, while hers was assessed for something extra. The woman rhetor was scrutinized for her private performance as well as her public presentation. The audience evaluated her sexuality, gender, body, and ethos for their correspondence to or divergence from an idealized true woman, and both the speaker's motivation for appearing in public and the state of her home and children became matters for speculation. Indeed, the audience's projection of a feminine ideal onto the "body, flesh, blood, and bones" of the maternal rhetor may finally constitute the most telling difference between men's and women's delivery (Selzer 10). Unfortunately, the traditional fifth canon, with its material focus on the orator's voice and body, is completely blind to the ideological inflections of delivery, thus underlining the importance of reconsidering rhetorical precepts from the vantage point of differently located speakers.

5

Forging and Firing Thunderbolts
Collaboration and Women's Delivery

One of the most fruitful collaborative partnerships of the nineteenth century was that of Elizabeth Cady Stanton and Susan B. Anthony, who, over the course of fifty years, devoted themselves to promoting woman's rights in all its forms (see fig. 5.1). The two met in 1851 and immediately recognized a shared passion for social reform. Cady Stanton was already an important figure in the woman's rights movement due to her involvement in the 1848 Woman's Rights Convention in Seneca Falls, New York, and Anthony had recently retired from a fifteen-year teaching career in order to promote temperance and abolition. The women's differences contributed as much as their similarities to the blossoming of a collaborative relationship that would last the rest of their lives.

At the time of their first encounter, Cady Stanton was already the mother of four boys, and she would give birth to three more children by the end of the decade. Her husband Henry was absent ten months out of the year pursuing legal and political ambitions and leaving Cady Stanton primary responsibility for their home and children (Griffith 80). Anthony, meanwhile, used her relative freedom as an unmarried woman to assume public roles unusual for women of the day. As a paid temperance and abolition agent, she met a wide assortment of people, traveled extensively, organized meetings, arranged speaking tours, planned publications, gathered petition signatures, managed finances, and delivered speeches. Indeed, throughout the early decades of their acquaintance, the two women's distinct domestic obligations and professional opportunities had a decisive impact on their collaborative endeavors, which Cady Stanton described in terms of lightning and explosives:

> [I]t has been said that I forged the thunderbolts and she fired them. Perhaps all this is in a measure true. With the cares of a large family, I might in time,

Fig. 5.1. Susan B. Anthony and Elizabeth Cady Stanton, 1870. Courtesy of the Schlesinger Library, Radcliffe Institute, Harvard University.

like too many women, have become wholly absorbed in a narrow family selfishness, had not my friend been continually exploring new fields for missionary labors. Her description of a body of men on any platform, complacently deciding questions in which women had an equal interest, without an equal voice, readily roused me to a determination to throw a firebrand in the midst of their assembly. Thus, whenever I saw that stately Quaker girl coming across my lawn, I knew that some happy convocation of the sons of Adam were to be set by the ears, by one of our appeals or resolutions. (Stanton, Anthony, and Gage 1: 458–59)

In contrasting the two women's realms, the matron in the home and the spinster in the wide world, Cady Stanton suggests their typical collaborative methods. She depicts Anthony as a nomadic investigator identifying women's woes, herself as the housebound composer of fiery "appeals" and "resolutions," and Anthony as the transmitter of these incendiary missives to the public. In addition to outlining the pair's typical division of rhetorical labor, the passage indicates another important but generally disregarded purpose of women's collaboration, namely, reconciling conflicting domestic, maternal, and discursive obligations.

As becomes apparent in the discussion of Anthony and Cady Stanton later in this chapter, collaboration's malleability made it indispensable to nineteenth-century women's rhetorical production and delivery. However, despite its prevalence, the discipline currently lacks a model of rhetorical collaboration that can account fully for its many forms and multiple functions. This chapter speaks to that problem by introducing a new framework for understanding collaboration. First, though, before describing that model, I must address the fact that collaboration is more often associated with the first canon of invention than with the fifth canon of delivery and explain why it should be considered in relation to women's rhetorical performance.

In recent decades, scholars in composition and rhetoric have chiefly examined collaboration in terms of the social construction of knowledge, studying how groups of students or writers talk and compose together in order to generate abundant material, identify alternative rhetorical options, consider diverse audiences, explore opposing viewpoints, and encourage dialogic exchange (Bruffee; LeFevre). While collaboration is certainly a useful tool for invention, it has more applications and fulfills more purposes than can be addressed via the first canon. To illustrate this point, antebellum women collaborated extensively with their friends, families, and servants in order to achieve two objectives, resolving gender and rhetorical conflicts and reaching public platforms. Both objectives involve issues of rhetorical access and performance and thus concern the fifth canon far more than they do the first. Nevertheless, collaboration has rarely been considered in relation to delivery. One reason for this oversight is the scope of the traditional fifth canon, which focuses exclusively on the vocal and physical presentation of the solitary speaker. However, I would argue that scholars must extend their analysis from the speaker onstage to the web of backstage relationships that made her rhetorical delivery possible in the first place if they are to appreciate fully the obstacles and strategies of the antebellum woman. Failure to recognize the collaborative network that surrounded and supported her impoverishes the discipline's knowledge not only of women's rhetoric but also, more broadly, of a crucial means by which marginalized groups gain access to the public forum and come to public voice. For these reasons, antebellum women's collaboration should be analyzed in terms of delivery and their delivery analyzed in terms of collaboration.

What exactly is collaboration? The term is highly contested and ambiguous, assuming markedly different referents according to one's field or theoretical perspective. In composition studies, collaboration generally refers to classroom practices promoting invention and student-centered learning, activities including "reader response, peer critiques, small writing groups, joint writing projects, and peer tutoring in writing centers and classrooms" (Trimbur 87). In literary studies, collaboration usually denotes coauthorship and the study of writers who share the roles of "verbal companion and author, writer and editor, with each other" (Laird 7). In feminist studies, collaboration has been valorized as a particularly feminine (i.e., cooperative and communal) form of interaction and opposed to traditionally masculine (or individualistic and competitive) modes of learning and production (Brody 214; Doane and Hodges 54; Belenky et al. xxv). In workplace studies, collaboration refers broadly to shared labor directed toward the completion of a task, such as the construction of a building or the design of a software program (see Cross; Ede and Lunsford). None of these definitions, however, adequately accounts for the ways that antebellum women collaborated in order to circumvent gender constraints and deliver public discourse.[1]

I define collaboration as a cooperative endeavor involving two or more people that results in a rhetorical product, performance, or event. This definition considers process fully as much as product, examining the shared social and rhetorical practices that lead to such discursive outcomes as books and articles, speeches and sermons, petition drives and conventions. While credit for the end result may go either to an individual or a collective, the product itself is constructed and completed through the direct and/or indirect contributions of others. Current models of collaboration do not adequately recognize both direct and indirect forms of assistance and thus disregard the entire range of cooperative activities essential to women rhetors. To address this shortcoming, I offer the following model of rhetorical collaboration, consisting of a continuum that includes direct as well as indirect collaborative forms and accounts fully for the power of this cooperative method (see fig. 5.2). Productive and supportive collaboration lie at either end of the spectrum, each possessing distinct purposes, rhetorical contributions, and types of assistance.

Productive collaborations are those in which two or more people contribute to the crafting and completion of a rhetorical product, such as a pamphlet, address, or public event. Productive collaborators make *direct* contributions to the end result, for example, by dividing up and taking individual responsibility for particular parts of the rhetorical process or by laboring together on

Productive	Productive/Supportive	Supportive
Purpose: rhetorical end product	Purpose: social accommodation	
Contributions: direct, conventional	Contributions: indirect, "invisible"	
Assistance: research, writing, delivery	Assistance: domestic, maternal, ethical	

Fig. 5.2. The collaborative continuum

some or all of its phases. Familiar productive tasks include researching, organizing, drafting, revising, and delivering a text as well as merging individual
voices and styles into a unified product (Alm 128, 132). Productive collaboration is the kind most frequently recognized and studied by scholars, a focus
that, unfortunately, elides other kinds of collaboration that play an equal, if not
more important, role in women's rhetoric.

Supportive collaborations are those in which one person's efforts contribute *indirectly* to another's rhetorical production and delivery. Into this category fall myriad forms of assistance that are indispensable to women rhetors,
including families caring for children, hired help supervising households, and
coworkers shouldering one's business responsibilities. These indirect and
frequently overlooked types of collaboration allow women rhetors to attend
to both practical concerns and ideological constraints, two of the greatest
obstacles to their public discourse. Although it is the least studied or recognized kind of cooperative endeavor, supportive collaboration is key to understanding women's unique rhetorical challenges and compensating strategies.

If productive collaboration helps rhetors to generate rhetorical texts and
supportive collaboration permits them to reconcile private and public obligations, then it is not surprising to learn that many cooperative ventures combine elements of the two. Such productive/supportive collaborations are remarkably flexible arrangements, capable of assuming diverse forms in response to
exigence, purpose, process, and context. Some productive/supportive collaborations change shape constantly, with participants exchanging supportive and
productive roles regularly, while others remain fairly stable in terms of collaborators' assigned tasks. Overall, productive/supportive collaboration provides
the most inventive options for creating and delivering discourse in resistant
surroundings, for it attends to the dual demands of textual production and
social accommodation.

The collaborative continuum is capable of acknowledging the varied cooperative forms and functions central to women's rhetorical production and delivery. To illustrate the explanatory power of this model, I examine antebellum

women's use of productive, supportive, and productive/supportive collaboration to fashion and present public discourse. Although these pioneering rhetors did indeed work with others to produce rhetorical texts, a form of productive collaboration, their cooperative practices were more often motivated by the need to fulfill feminine gender expectations at home, on the road, and onstage. Antebellum women who spoke publicly were often perceived as masculine or sexually suspect; to compensate, they had to project convincing feminine ethos and prove their domestic competence to audiences. Supportive collaboration allowed them to placate the ghostly ideal of true womanhood, providing them a way of concurrently fulfilling domestic and maternal obligations while accessing and succeeding on public platforms. Finally, collaboration permitted women to negotiate, challenge, and, ultimately, reshape feminine gender norms through the assumption of new discursive roles in the public forum. I conclude the chapter by examining the intersection of gender and collaboration and address whether or not collaboration is an inherently feminine mode of rhetorical production and delivery.

Productive Collaboration

Antebellum women used productive collaboration—associations formed chiefly for the sake of producing a text, speech, or event—less frequently than either supportive or productive/supportive collaboration. Nevertheless, productive collaboration was responsible not only for creating milestone events like the first Woman's Rights Convention in Seneca Falls but also for ensuring the textual delivery of women contending with educational and racial disadvantages. African-American women frequently collaborated with white abolitionists to ensure the recording or publication of their addresses and autobiographies. The impetus to collaborate was especially strong for women who could neither read nor write, as was the situation with Sojourner Truth (see fig. 5.3). Born into slavery in the 1790s and emancipated in 1827, Truth was a memorable speaker at antislavery, temperance, and woman's rights conventions during the 1850s. With her "use of the simple language of the uneducated, which she could weave into striking narrative and metaphors, her nearly six-foot frame that revealed the strength developed working as a farmhand and house maid, and her powerful low voice telling of her denied rights as a woman and an African-American," Truth's charismatic presence and delivery left a lasting impression on audiences unused to seeing authoritative black women onstage (Fitch 421). After observing the brisk sales of Frederick Douglass's autobiography, *Life of Frederick Douglass, an American Slave*, Truth collaborated with abolitionist Olive Gilbert to compose the *Narrative of Sojourner Truth* (1850), a text that gives evidence of the women's joint input. Truth's influence is apparent in the story's focus on religion, a central feature of her existence, while Gilbert's appears in numerous asides addressing such issues as the horrors of slavery and Truth's troubled relationship with her children (Fitch 422–23). After the narrative's completion, William Lloyd Garrison—leader of the American Anti-Slavery Society and editor of the abolitionist newspaper, the *Liberator*—referred Truth to his publisher George Yerrington, Garrison's support and connections undoubtedly playing an important role in the memoir's publication (Painter 110). Truth's association with Gilbert and Garrison displays the chief characteristics of productive collaboration, the cooperative efforts of all three contributing directly to the production and delivery of a rhetorical text.

I Sell the Shadow to Support the Substance.

SOJOURNER TRUTH.

Fig. 5.3. Sojourner Truth. Courtesy of the Library of Congress, Prints and Photographs Division, LC-USZC4-6165.

Productive collaboration is also responsible for preserving what remains of Truth's oratory, including the famed "Ar'n't I a Woman?" speech that she delivered to the 1851 Woman's Rights Convention in Akron, Ohio. Various accounts of the address exist: one by convention secretary Marius Robinson; embedded descriptions within articles printed in the *New York Tribune*, the *Anti-Slavery Bugle*, the *Liberator*, and the *Saturday Visiter*; and, most popular and controversial of all, the version later composed by Frances Gage. My argument that Gage's rendition of Truth's address exemplifies productive collaboration may initially appear questionable on several counts. For one, Truth did not intentionally cooperate with Gage (as she did with Gilbert) to preserve "A'rn't I a Woman?" Also, recent studies by Nell Painter, Carla Peterson, and Carleton Mabee dispute the accuracy of Gage's depiction of the rhetorical context and of Truth's language. Nevertheless, as I explain in the following analysis, I believe that scholars can access more useful ways of acknowledging both the shortcomings and strengths of this address when it is considered as a case of productive collaboration rather than outright appropriation.

All of those who recorded Truth's oratory left their imprints on the textual product: "Because Sojourner Truth was illiterate, her words have come down to us—if at all—as transcribed by others. The varied ways that her language has been rendered suggest the enormous influence of her transcribers in shaping the texts we have today" (Yellin 77). The ways in which Truth's transcribers distorted her language is particularly troubling. She undoubtedly spoke a marked idiolect of English (after all, Dutch was her first and English her second language). However, the first account of Truth's 1851 convention address, composed by convention secretary Robinson, depicts her speaking in standard English. Truth asks, for example, "[H]ow came Jesus into the world? Through God who created him and woman who bore him. Man, where is your part?" (qtd. in Painter 126). Subsequent versions of Truth's address render her speech in heavy dialect. When Gage crafted her own account of Truth's address to the Ohio convention, the contrast between Truth's speech (in dialect) and Gage's response (in standard English) could not be sharper. In the following excerpt, Truth reacts passionately to a minister's argument for women's inferiority while the admiring Gage looks on:

> "[D]at little man in black dar [the minister], he say women can't have as much rights as men, 'cause Christ wan't a woman! Whar did your Christ come from?" Rolling thunder couldn't have stilled that crowd, as did those deep, wonderful tones, as she stood there with outstretched arms and eyes of fire. Raising her voice still louder, she repeated, "Whar did your Christ come from? From God

and a woman! Man had nothin' to do wid Him." Oh, what a rebuke that was to that little man. (Stanton, Anthony, and Gage 1: 116)

Truth resented such representations of her language, feeling they were fundamentally inaccurate and unfair whether they were so composed in order to conform with popular notions of African-American speech or to make Truth's rhetoric less threatening. Given her complete dependence on others for her presentation in print, however, she had few options for remedying the situation.[2]

For well over a century, Gage's account stood as the definitive version of Truth's oration. Although suspect for a number of reasons (one being that Gage composed it twelve years *after* the event), I contend that "Ar'n't I a Woman?" is a collaborative document, first, because it records both Truth's and Gage's voices, actions, and reactions and, second, because it contains contributions by both women. Nell Painter, for example, argues that the speech's most famous line and the one with which Truth is most frequently identified—"Ar'n't I a woman?"—is actually of Gage's invention, for it appears in no other account of the address (171). Repeated four times in rapid succession, Gage's rhetorical question underscores the humanity of African-American women and the equality of the sexes:

> Dat man ober dar say dat womin needs to be helped into carriages, and lifted ober ditches, and to hab de best place everywhar. Nobody eber helps me into carriages, or ober mud-puddles, or gibs me any best place! . . . And a'n't I a woman? Look at me! Look at my arm! (and she bared her right arm to the shoulder, showing her tremendous muscular power). I have ploughed, and planted, and gathered into barns, and no man could head me! And a'n't I a woman? I could work as much and eat as much as a man—when I could get it—and bear de lash as well! And a'n't I a woman? I have borne thirteen chilern, and seen 'em mos' all sold off to slavery, and when I cried out with my mother's grief, none but Jesus heard me! And a'n't I a woman? (Stanton, Anthony, and Gage 1: 116)

Although historically unreliable, Gage's dramatic rendition of the setting and substance of Truth's address that long ago day in 1851 is largely responsible for the former slave's place in our cultural memory. Painter situates Gage's heroic portrait of Truth within "a company of 'invented greats'" that includes Jesus and Joan of Arc, figures who are likewise known "purely through the agency of others, who have constructed and maintained their legends" (285). I would argue, however, that Gage is not solely responsible for Truth's legend, which is, in fact, a collaborative endeavor. Truth's extraordinary storytelling and performative abilities combined with Gage's forceful writing to ensure the survival of "Ar'n't I a Woman?" and the creation of a cultural icon distinct from the historical woman herself. The speaker and writer contributed jointly to a textual product and social legacy composed in equal measure of fact and fiction, and in the end, their productive collaboration preserved Truth's spirit if not her literal words and actions. Karlyn Kohrs Campbell observes that although Gage's version of the speech is "constrained by debased language," it renders Truth's unshakable sense of agency, her "challenge to the classism and racism" around her, vividly, dramatically, and memorably, thus accomplishing what more accurate or scholarly accounts do not ("Agency" 24). In short, "Truth comes to life" (23). The final reason for regarding "Ar'n't I a Woman?" as a collaborative text is this: Truth included Gage's account in the 1878 edition of the *Narrative of Sojourner Truth* (an expanded edition completed with the assistance of yet another productive collaborator, Frances Titus). While the decision to include Gage's version was undoubtedly a practical move given its appeal and popularity, the gesture may also represent acknowledgment that the speech was, on some level, a shared text.

The manipulation of Truth's language and image by white cohorts, nevertheless, raises disturbing issues, the chief being that, despite the best of intentions, productive collaboration is inescapably treacherous when substantial inequities exist between partners. This dilemma is encoded in the polysemy of the term *collaboration*, which, as Holly Laird remarks, is forever "caught between the dual valences of working together with someone in common cause and colluding with an enemy." Such "dual valences" were unavoidable when African-American women collaborated with those "aligned (usually by race, gender, or class, but also by financial or emotional pressure) with the white supremacist, patriarchal system of [their] day" (Laird 58).[3] Although fraught with complex and conflicting alliances, productive collaboration between white abolitionists and African-American rhetors was extensive, from William Lloyd Garrison's publication of Maria Stewart's public addresses in the *Liberator* and Lydia Maria Child's editing of evangelist Julia Pell's and former slave Harriet Jacobs's narratives to the varied contributions of Gilbert, Gage, and Titus to Sojourner Truth's textual legacy (Peterson 57, 153, 30–54). Collectively, these collaborative efforts ensured the composition, publication, and survival of African-American women's perspectives, experiences, and performances and enriched subsequent generations' knowledge of nineteenth-century women.

Supportive Collaboration

Supportive collaboration occurs when the creation and completion of a text, speech, or event are made possible through the indirect contributions of others. This kind of collaboration underlies virtually every rhetorical performance and includes such efforts as a manager making touring arrangements for a speaker, a spouse assuming household duties in order to free a professionally active partner, or a nanny providing child care for a rhetor. Because women have afforded men these forms of assistance since time immemorial, a cultural misperception has ensued equating supportive collaboration with "women's work." Its feminine associations may explain why supportive collaboration typically remains invisible as a rhetorical contribution, but it is, nevertheless, essential to women's public discourse and accomplishments.

Antebellum women rhetors confronted the daunting problem of reconciling conflicting domestic and discursive commitments. Because their rhetorical delivery defied dominant gender norms, women speakers were obliged to convince the audience of their femininity, respectability, and competence in both the private and public realms. Supportive collaboration helped them to accomplish these ends by providing such fundamental (if devalued) forms of assistance as housekeeping, family care, and traveling companionship, thereby enabling women rhetors to access public platforms and construct feminine ethos, without which their words invariably failed or offended. Whether antebellum women were single or married, their supportive collaboration addressed key practical and ideological concerns, affording them a means of attending to the mundane and of accommodating feminine ideals while producing and delivering rhetoric.

Spinsters, Matrons, and Fellow Travelers

Many antebellum speakers began their rhetorical careers as single women: Frances Wright, Angelina Grimké, Sarah Grimké, Abby Kelley, Lucy Stone, Antoinette Brown, Sallie Holley, Mary Ann Shadd, Frances Watkins, and Susan B. Anthony. Although maidens and spinsters might address issues of education, abolition, woman's rights, temperance, social justice, and moral reform from the public platform, they occupied a complex and paradoxical position, at once free from the obligations of marriage and maternity yet still burdened by family obligations. Unmarried women were expected to be perennially "on call," willing and able to respond to the needs of family members, an expectation expressed in Horace Mann's 1853 lectures on womanly duty:

I hold the "Over-Thirties" to be a beneficent provision in the economy of nature. Not being mothers on their own account, they have leisure to be mothers for everybody else. What a blessing the circle of the families to which she belongs is an unmarried sister! She watches by the aged father or mother with a vestal's fidelity, while her sisters and brothers abandon the old homestead for Cupid, or cupidity. . . . How Protean her capabilities of usefulness, transforming herself by turns into friend, nurse, physician, or spiritual guide;— into the grave companion of the old, or the frolicsome playmate of the young, as ever-varying occasion may demand! (*Few* 35–36)

The single woman was to be all things to all people, a shape shifter (a "friend, nurse, physician, or spiritual guide") and an emotional chameleon ("grave" or "frolicsome") on demand. Spared motherly duties of her own, she became a universal mother, dedicated and nurturing to all.

Fulfilling these expectations sometimes required women to sacrifice their rhetorical commitments, as is apparent in the early career of Lucy Stone, one of the most successful lecturers of the period. In the late 1840s, Stone advocated abolition each weekend as a salaried agent for the American Anti-Slavery Society and then promoted woman's rights independently on the weekdays, charging listeners twelve-cents' admission. Her magnetism and eloquence drew such large crowds that she managed to save seven thousand dollars in her first three years of lecturing, a phenomenal sum (Kerr 54). Nevertheless, between 1850 and 1851, Stone spent eight months away from the lecture circuit because, as the only unmarried woman in her family, she felt obliged to cancel speaking engagements whenever siblings or parents requested her services. In June 1850, she left a speaking tour in order to travel to Illinois and tend her ailing brother Luther. Following his death, she escorted Luther's pregnant widow on a disastrous trip back East. En route, the widow miscarried, and Stone caught typhoid fever; in total, the episode consumed four months of Stone's time. Shortly after her recuperation and return to public speaking, Stone's sister Sarah requested assistance with the approaching birth of her first child, so the rhetor once again interrupted her work and gave four more months to her family (Kerr 59–61). Despite freedom from a home, husband, and child of her own, Stone felt obliged to sacrifice her rhetorical ambitions whenever they interfered with family duties.

More fortunate spinsters collaborated in order to reconcile conflicting personal and public obligations. Following their father's death in 1862, for example, Susan Anthony and her sister Mary, as the two remaining unmarried children in the family, became responsible for their mother and the family farm.

Anthony was an established public speaker by this time, having dedicated herself to promoting social justice for nearly a decade. Mary wholeheartedly supported her sister's public work, so she agreed to care for their mother and property, her indirect supportive collaboration thus freeing Anthony to continue her full-time commitment to reform (Gordon, *Selected* 47, 536). Nevertheless, in public, Anthony faced suspicions of neglecting family obligations for personal glory, suspicions she combated both in person and in print by presenting herself as a dutiful daughter and sibling. Nan Johnson observes that Ida Harper and Anthony's collaborative *Life and Work of Susan B. Anthony* repeatedly emphasizes the rhetor's "conventional femininity," a theme apparent in its account of her nursing brother Daniel back to health after a shooting accident: "Harper describes Anthony's attendance in detail, representing the nine weeks that Anthony nursed her brother and cared for his wife and her four-year-old niece and namesake, 'Susie B.,' as a saintly and loving act that proved beyond doubt the fundamental womanliness of Anthony's nature" (*Gender* 143). Women rhetors who failed to convince the audience of their "fundamental womanliness" could find their reception and effectiveness seriously impaired.

Like spinsters, matrons also contended with clashing domestic and rhetorical responsibilities that few could negotiate without the help of families, friends, and servants. Supportive collaboration often determined whether or not a woman continued to speak publicly after marriage and maternity, as is evident in the early domestic careers of Antoinette Brown Blackwell and Lucy Stone. The women's long association began at Oberlin College in the 1840s and developed with their efforts to advance social justice in the early 1850s, Stone touring as a popular, well-paid lecturer for abolition and woman's rights and Brown advancing reform as a Protestant minister and public speaker. Their friendship deepened into kinship when the two wed the Blackwell brothers, Antoinette marrying Sam and Lucy marrying Henry, and then contemporaneously became mothers in the late 1850s. Although both women were determined to combine marriage, motherhood, and reform, only Brown Blackwell initially succeeded in doing so, an accomplishment grounded in supportive collaboration.

From the outset, Sam Blackwell and Antoinette Brown agreed on two points, first, that her "public work would be as nearly uninterrupted as circumstances would allow" following their marriage and, second, that women could manage both a family and profession only if spouses renegotiated standard marital expectations (Brown Blackwell, qtd. in Cazden 106). Sam assumed unconventional roles and tasks in order to support his wife's rhetorical efforts, assistance she always acknowledged gratefully: "Mr. Blackwell, who was engaged in business and might have fewer hours to give to home occupations, declared himself more than willing to help me with home duties. This promise he generously more than redeemed for almost fifty years" (qtd. in Cazden 162). The rhetor also received valuable aid from the extended Blackwell and Brown clans: "Our families on both sides always came heartily to the rescue in any and every family emergency. This is a suggestive opening for the way in which women who take up public business may have the necessary help from interested and affectionate relatives" (qtd. in Cazden 134). Through her husband's and families' supportive collaboration, the young wife and mother managed to combine domesticity with reform, attending woman's rights conventions, conducting lecture tours, maintaining an active preaching schedule, and, following the outbreak of the Civil War, supporting the Woman's National Loyal League (Lasser and Merrill, *Friends*). Brown Blackwell, then, not only enjoyed the support of family members but she was also willing to accept their assistance in order to integrate public speaking with private duties.

Neither Stone's marriage nor her collaborative abilities fare well in comparison. During the first decade of their marriage, Henry Blackwell's business ventures kept him out West much of the time. Initially, Stone curtailed her lecturing commitments in order to accompany him, but after the birth of daughter Alice in 1857, the couple began to spend long periods apart (see Kerr). Therefore, when the maternal rhetor decided to resume lecturing, she initially relied on nursemaids to watch Alice; however, dissatisfied with the care they provided, she began to dread leaving the child to attend conventions or fulfill speaking engagements (see fig. 5.4). Stone confessed her conflict in a letter to Brown Blackwell:

> I wish I felt the old impulse and power to lecture, both for the sake of cherished principles and to help Harry with the heavy burden he has to bear; but I am afraid, and dare not trust Lucy Stone. I went to hear E. P. Whipple lecture on Joan of Arc. It was very inspiring, and for the hour I felt as though all things were possible to me. But when I came home and looked at Alice's sleeping face, and thought of the possible evil that might befall her if my guardian eye was turned away, I shrank like a snail into its shell, and saw that, for these years, I can be only a mother—no trivial thing, either. (qtd. in Blackwell 99)

Stone's remark that she "dare not trust Lucy Stone" indicates flagging faith in her own rhetorical abilities and persona, a sign of the recurrent depression and plummeting self-confidence that accompanied her retirement from public life (Kerr 109). Furthermore, Stone's reluctance to trust Alice's care to others, her fear that harm would befall the child if she turned away her "guardian eye," meant the loss of a large pool of potential supportive collaborators, hired help.[4]

Concerned by Stone's isolation and unhappiness, Brown Blackwell tried to reassure her sister-in-law that motherhood and lecturing were compatible endeavors. Certain that Stone's waning self-esteem and waxing anxiety stemmed from her seclusion, Brown Blackwell shared her own experience of initial fearfulness and then renewed confidence with a return to the platform. She also sought to allay Stone's separation anxiety by describing visits to her husband and daughter Florence during a lecture tour with Anthony:

> [T]he subject, political rights for woman is a grand one & has my fullest sympathies; & the change is for me a good one after being so long at home. I try to throw my whole soul into the movement & have certainly not lost in

Fig. 5.4. Lucy Stone and Alice Stone Blackwell, 1858. Courtesy of the Library of Congress, Prints and Photographs Division, LOT-13267-2, No. 26.

power as a speaker by the years of comparative rest. I shall accompany Susan only two or three months. Am to take a week for visiting home next month with Sam. Little Floey is doing nicely at Fathers. I went home after being out a few days, the dear little soul was delighted, & it made my heart ache to leave her again, though my reason tells me she will be as well off there as with me. (Lasser and Merrill, *Friends* 155–56)

The account suggests that just as Florence thrived during her mother's absence so, too, would Alice during Stone's. Furthermore, Brown Blackwell offered to care for Alice herself when Stone lectured or attended conventions, thereby encouraging her to return to public life and providing Stone another opportunity for supportive collaboration.

Stone, however, did not manage to combine maternity with public speaking during Alice's early years, first, because she lacked an available husband like Sam Blackwell and, second, because she could not bring herself to accept the help of either servants or sisters-in-law. Stone anguished over her choices but ultimately decided to relinquish public work in order to apply herself fully to homemaking and mothering, the consequence of being "almost too careful and self-sacrificing a mother," according to the normally circumspect Brown Blackwell (Lasser and Merrill, *Friends* 93). Stone's daughter Alice reflected in later years, "Neither mobs nor matrimony had been able to 'shut up the mouth of Lucy Stone,' but mother love did it, for a time" (Blackwell 199). Stone's public reemergence began when she joined the Woman's National Loyal League during the Civil War, and it was complete by 1867 when Alice turned ten, at which point Stone finally felt comfortable leaving her in the care of others (Blackwell 207). During this period, the speaker also discovered a productive collaborator in her husband Henry, whose improved finances permitted him to devote time to the couple's shared interest in promoting woman's rights.[5] The trajectory of Stone's career indicates that supportive collaboration was critical to maternal rhetors' public participation; without it, their involvement often ceased entirely, at least for a time.

In addition to helping them fulfill private obligations, supportive collaboration also allowed women to manage another challenging aspect of the lecturing life—travel. Women rhetors had to consider traveling arrangements carefully because the public scrutinized them for evidence of immorality and sexual misconduct. As was mentioned in chapter 4, minister Gordon Hayes accused lecturer Abby Kelley of being a wanton woman and pointed to her travels "by night and by day, always with men and never with women" as proof of reprehensible conduct (qtd. in Sterling 117–18). His charges convinced the congregation to ban women lecturers from the church, thereby effectively canceling Kelley's speaking engagement. In addition to imperiling their reputations, travel also exposed women to the dangers and inconveniences of the road, including wild animals, unpredictable weather, sinister men, unreliable transportation, and inadequate lodging. To reduce their vulnerability on all counts, women rhetors sought traveling companions, another crucial form of supportive collaboration.

The partnership of abolitionist lecturer Sallie Holley and her "lifelong companion" Caroline Putnam initially developed because of the speaker's need for support on the road (Pease and Pease, "Holley" 205). The two women first met at Oberlin College in 1848 where Holley's antislavery zeal dazzled Putnam. When Holley enrolled as a lecturer with the American Anti-Slavery Society following her 1851 graduation, Putnam abandoned her own studies to join the speaker on a six-month tour of Ohio and New York. She eventually forged a life for herself on the lecture circuit as Holley's traveling companion-manager and dedicated fourteen years to organizing tours, scheduling lectures, hiring halls, arranging transportation and lodging, and selling antislavery literature and subscriptions (Chambers-Schiller 151). Although Putnam advanced the antislavery cause through these behind-the-scenes efforts, she also functioned as Holley's supportive collaborator, her presence on the road defusing suspicions of the speaker's sexual promiscuity and thus contributing indirectly to the success of the lectures. However, despite the centrality of her assistance, Putnam remained a shadowy figure in the background of Holley's colorful public life, a predicament common to supportive collaborators.

Whether the post is filled by a friend, husband, sibling, or servant, the supportive partner plays a conventionally feminine and, therefore, largely unappreciated role, one that often goes unnoticed in life and in studies of collaboration. Furthermore, cooperative tasks traditionally considered ancillary—in the case of antebellum rhetors, such positions as traveling companion, nursemaid, and housekeeper—are denigrated (when recognized at all) even though they contribute substantially to women's rhetorical production and delivery (London 26). Scholars slight supportive contributions, in part, due to an inadequate model of rhetorical collaboration that fails to acknowledge the full range of cooperative settings, forms, and functions. The domestic, maternal, and ethical concerns so neatly addressed by supportive collaboration may frequently be overlooked, but they, nevertheless, often determine how, when, where, and whether women create and deliver public discourse at all.

Productive/Supportive Collaboration

Productive/supportive partnerships combine both kinds of collaboration and are capable of assuming countless forms. Participants can contribute to the rhetorical process and product either by adopting stable supportive or productive roles or by exchanging those roles fluidly and frequently. The following examples of antebellum women's productive/supportive collaborations with siblings, spouses, and friends illustrate the force of this cooperative method and its relevance to rhetorical delivery. I examine, in particular, the collaborative practices of rhetors Mary Ann Shadd, Lucretia Mott, Elizabeth Cady Stanton, and Susan B. Anthony.

Throughout her life, Mary Ann Shadd collaborated extensively with her brothers and sisters in order to reconcile her conflicting personal and professional obligations as an educator, journalist, and speaker. The eldest of thirteen children, Shadd was born in 1823 to a family of free blacks living in the slave state of Delaware (see fig. 5.5). Her father, Abraham Shadd, was a committed reformer, an activist in the antislavery movement, a participant in the Underground Railroad, and president of the National Convention for the Improvement of Free People of Color. Raised in a home that stressed the importance of education, politics, civic involvement, and racial uplift, Mary Ann Shadd responded decisively to passage of the Fugitive Slave Law in 1850, which she viewed as proof positive of the United States' enmity toward African Americans, and moved to Canada (Bearden and Butler 12–23).

In 1853, she launched the *Provincial Freeman*, an antislavery newspaper addressing the concerns of African-American emigrants in Canada, thereby becoming the first black woman newspaper editor in North America (Guy-Sheftall 17). From the beginning of the journalistic enterprise, the Shadd family's collaboration helped ensure the newspaper's survival. In 1854, sister Amelia arrived to help with the *Freeman*'s production. She ran the paper, a form of productive collaboration, while Mary Ann conducted lecture and subscription tours throughout Canada and the United States, raising necessary funds for the venture. However, as news spread that the *Provincial Freeman* was composed and edited by women, public outrage threatened to close the paper. Mary Ann reassured readers that she and Amelia, although "members of the unfortunate sex, . . . never in their most ambitious moments, aspired to the drudgery" of editing and that a "gentleman" editor would soon fill the post (qtd. in Rhodes 98). Brother Isaac would eventually share the editing position with a revolving cast of distinguished African-American men, their names on the masthead helping to calm subscribers and keep the struggling paper afloat.

Fig. 5.5. Mary Ann Shadd. Courtesy of Prints & Photographs Dept., Moorland-Spingarn Research Center, Howard University.

The Shadd family's productive collaboration ensured the *Freeman's* assembly and publication at home and freed Mary Ann to tour even more widely on its behalf. Her lectures stirred up subscribers, and her experiences on the road provided material for articles, but in the course of her travels, she regularly faced (and often overcame) gender barriers. For example, she attended the 1855 National Convention of Colored Men in Philadelphia and, by virtue of her presence, required the assembly to debate and decide whether women should be admitted as members. The convention voted 38 to 23 to accept her membership and then invited her to deliver an address on emigration (Logan 2). Shadd thus forced the issue of women's inclusion and participation at the prestigious event, her attendance and achievement made possible by collaborators at home.

In 1856, Shadd wed Toronto businessman Thomas Cary, with whom she enjoyed an unconventional companionate marriage. Shadd Cary continued with her journalistic work, and due to conflicting professional obligations in different cities, the husband and wife often resided apart from each other for extended periods. Nevertheless, Shadd Cary gave birth to two children within four years of marriage. When it came time to return to the subscription and lecture circuit, she collaborated with another sister, Sarah, who cared for the rhetor's babies and household. This arrangement marked the beginning of a supportive collaboration that would last for decades, one that became absolutely vital to Shadd Cary after her husband's death in 1860 left her with two children to support (Bearden and Butler 198, 231). Sarah's assumption of her sister's domestic and maternal obligations allowed the widow to embark on a remarkable series of jobs that, once again, defied existing gender and racial conventions. To note just a few of the high points, after closing the *Provincial Freeman* at the beginning of the Civil War, Shadd Cary enrolled as an agent for the United States government and recruited black soldiers for the Union army. Following the war, she administered a number of public schools for African-American children and adults in Washington, D.C.; wrote and toured for assorted African-American newspapers, including Frederick Douglass's *New National Era*; became active in the woman's suffrage and club movements; and earned her LLB (bachelor of laws) from Howard University in 1883, taking up the practice of law at age sixty (Bearden and Butler 202–26). Shadd Cary's extraordinary rhetorical career in journalism, education, lecturing, and law was characterized by impatience "with boundaries of all kinds" and by persistent efforts to "transcend, if not erase" them (Peterson 99). Throughout, it was sustained by her siblings' productive and supportive collaboration, from Amelia's and Isaac's productive help with the *Provincial Freeman* to Sarah's supportive assistance in domestic and maternal matters.

Like Shadd Cary, the pioneering preacher and public speaker Lucretia Mott also worked closely with family members, particularly with her husband of fifty-seven years, James Mott (see fig. 5.6). James collaborated both supportively and productively with Lucretia, and his efforts undergirded her groundbreaking achievements as an advocate for religious tolerance, antislavery, and woman's rights. Anna Hallowell, the Motts' granddaughter, observed of the couple that "although he was not so widely known as she, and his field of usefulness in consequence might seem more restricted, yet no one can contemplate [their] lives . . . without realizing that *his* life made *hers* a possibility" (89).

In 1821, the twenty-eight-year-old wife and mother became a Quaker minister officially invested with the authority to travel and preach to other Quaker communities (Bacon 37). Serving as a supportive collaborator, James usually accompanied Lucretia on her ministerial and reform travels, both nationally

Fig. 5.6. James and Lucretia Mott, 1842. Courtesy of the Friends
Historical Library of Swarthmore College.

and internationally. A typical regional tour unfolded at a grueling pace, requiring the pair to cover twenty-four hundred miles and Lucretia to address seventy Quaker meetings in as many days (Hallowell 123). James also journeyed
to London when Lucretia was selected as a delegate to the 1840 World's Anti-
Slavery Convention. Amid great controversy, the convention refused to recognize women delegates, whose outrage at being excluded on the basis of sex found
expression eight years later in the first Woman's Rights Convention, an event
to which I will return in a moment. James's presence and emotional support
during this and other trials were vital to Lucretia, especially in the increasingly
hostile church climate that developed once she began to address such contentious issues as the Hicksite–Orthodox Quaker divide, abolition, and woman's
rights. A final example of their supportive collaboration was apparent when
Lucretia had the opportunity to travel with others; at such times, James would
remain at home, tend his business and their five children, and thus substitute

for her in the domestic scene. Serving as his wife's traveling companion, providing her emotional sustenance, and caring for their home and family constitute forms of supportive collaboration, and all were crucial to Lucretia's rhetorical production and delivery.

Although James usually functioned in a supportive capacity, he assumed a productive role when necessary, for example, at the 1848 Woman's Rights Convention in Seneca Falls. The event's organizers—which included Lucretia, her sister Martha Coffin Wright, Jane C. Hunt, Mary Ann McClintock, and Elizabeth Cady Stanton—anticipated attracting an audience composed chiefly of women; however, on the convention's opening day, they discovered both men and women in attendance. Unwilling to turn away anyone and unused to facilitating events before promiscuous audiences, the women asked James to open the convention and chair its sessions, and his efforts contributed directly to the success of the rhetorical event (a characteristic of productive collaboration) (Bacon 126–28). James's movement from a supportive to a productive role in response to exigence demonstrates the flexibility of productive/supportive collaboration.[6]

In addition to collaborating with family members, antebellum women also worked closely with friends in order to sustain their rhetorical production and delivery. To return to the friendship that opened this chapter, Elizabeth Cady Stanton and Susan B. Anthony exchanged productive and supportive roles fluidly and frequently over the course of their fifty-year partnership. In many ways, the relationship grew out of their complementary rhetorical strengths and weaknesses, as Cady Stanton explains:

> We were at once fast friends, in thought and sympathy we were one, and in the division of labor we exactly complemented each other. In writing we did better work together than either could alone. While she is slow and analytical in composition, I am rapid and synthetic. I am the better writer, she the better critic. She supplied the facts and statistics, I the philosophy and rhetoric, and together we have made arguments that have stood unshaken.... Our speeches may be considered the united product of our two brains. (Stanton, Anthony, and Gage 1: 458–59)

Cady Stanton describes the collaboration as a blending of the two women's talents and contributions into a unified and seamless product. To illustrate their use of productive/supportive collaboration, I examine Anthony and Cady Stanton's "division of [rhetorical] labor" in more depth, exploring their typical methods of topic selection, research, writing, and delivery during the 1850s, the first decade of their friendship.

Because the unmarried Anthony enjoyed greater mobility throughout this period, she often selected topics and occasions for the women's rhetorical efforts, thereby playing a productive role in the collaboration. For instance, after agreeing to address the New York State Teachers' Convention in August 1856, she appealed to Cady Stanton for help with the speech:

> I cant get up a decent document, so for the love of me, & for the saving of the reputation of womanhood, I beg you with one baby on your knee & another at your feet & four boys whistling buzzing hallooing Ma Ma set your self about the work—it is of small moment who writes the Address, but of vast moment that it be well done. (Gordon, *Selected* 321–22)

Anthony knew that she wanted to argue for the equal education of the sexes, and she included an outline of her major points with the letter, detailing the lack of funding and endowments for women's institutions, girls' exclusion from declamatory exercises, and the need for "like motives" in obtaining an education (women, after all, had few professional venues in which to apply their hard-won knowledge following graduation). Her requests for assistance were like manna to the housebound mother, who battled claustrophobia and frustration constantly, both the struggle and relief audible in her reply: "I pace up and down these two chambers of mine like a caged lioness, longing to bring nursing and housekeeping cares to a close. . . . Come here and I will do what I can to help you with your address, if you will hold the baby and make the puddings" (Gordon, *Selected* 325).

Once a topic or occasion was selected, finding time for research and writing often proved difficult for Cady Stanton. Fortunately for her, Anthony was an inveterate collector of evidence, gathering newspaper clippings, convention minutes, magazine articles, letters, and speeches into voluminous scrapbooks. She shared her riches during visits to Cady Stanton's home in Seneca Falls, an experience the matron described as an open-sesame moment: "That little portmanteau stuffed with facts was opened, and there we had what the Rev. John Smith and the Hon. Richard Roe had said, false interpretations of bible texts, the statistics of women robbed of their property, shut out of some college, half paid for their work, the reports of some disgraceful trial, injustice enough to turn any woman's thoughts from stockings and puddings" (Stanton, Anthony, and Gage 1: 458–59). Anthony's facts, statistics, testimonies, and narratives were indispensable to the maternal rhetor, who rarely had the luxury of time alone. She describes her dilemma in a letter to Anthony:

> I can generalize and philosophize by myself, but I have not time to look up statistics. While I am about the house, surrounded by my children, washing

> dishes, baking, sewing, I can think up many points, but I cannot search books, for my hands, as well as my brains, would be necessary for that work. . . . [P]repare yourself to be disappointed in [the address's] merits, for I seldom have one hour to sit down and write undisturbed. Men who can shut themselves up for days with their books and thoughts know little of what difficulties a woman must surmount. (Gordon, *Selected* 237–38)

Cady Stanton apparently knew how to multitask, concurrently thinking up rhetorical strategies while performing intellectually undemanding tasks. However, her letter also identifies crucial differences in women's and men's research and writing processes. Women, their hands busy with domestic tasks, construct arguments while surrounded by others; men create in solitude and quiet. Women compose in short bursts and contend with constant interruption; men compose in concentrated, continuous sessions, writing "undisturbed" and shutting "themselves up for days with their books and thoughts." Gender thus creates inequities in the rhetorical process itself, a situation unacknowledged by men and society.

Collaboration helped Cady Stanton overcome both of these obstacles. First, thanks to Anthony's productive collaboration, the maternal rhetor obtained research materials she would otherwise have had great difficulty collecting. Then, when it came time to compose a text, Anthony would often visit Cady Stanton's home, where the two would jointly negotiate the children and household while planning and organizing their project. Once it was ready for drafting, Anthony became Cady Stanton's domestic and maternal substitute, thereby providing her partner with uninterrupted writing time:

> Mrs. Stanton would seek the quietest spot in the house and begin writing, while Miss Anthony would give the children their breakfast, start the older ones to school, make the dessert for dinner and trundle the babies up and down the walk, rushing in occasionally to help the writer out of a vortex. Many an article which will be read with delight by future generations was thus prepared. (Harper 1: 187–88)

Even when Anthony functioned in a supportive capacity, her domestic efforts contributing indirectly to Cady Stanton's rhetorical output, she could transform at a moment's notice into a productive collaborator in order to help the writer "out of a vortex." The pair's rapid-fire exchange of productive and supportive roles demonstrates collaboration's ability to address both personal and rhetorical concerns.

Domesticity shaped not only antebellum women's creation of reform rhetoric but also their delivery of it. Cady Stanton was a gifted speaker, her wit and passion rarely failing to impress an audience, so Anthony constantly urged her to "waive <u>household</u> & <u>baby</u> cares" and use her talents to advocate woman's rights (Gordon, *Selected* 231); however, home duties often kept the matron from fulfilling these requests. For example, a child's illness prevented her attendance at the 1853 New York State Woman's Rights Convention, and an accident very nearly kept her away the following year as well, as she relates in a letter to Anthony: "[M]ake no arrangements with reference to my coming to Rochester, for I cannot say when I can come, if even I may come at all. Yesterday one of the boys shot an arrow into my baby's eye. The eye is safe, but oh! ... Imagine if I had been in Rochester when this happened!" (DuBois 58). Fortunately, Anthony was willing to deliver Cady Stanton's lectures and addresses for her, a service she provided for other maternal rhetors as well, including Stone and Brown Blackwell. To do so, Anthony had to confront debilitating self-doubts regarding her effectiveness as a public speaker, a struggle she confessed candidly to her journal: "Crowded house at Port Byron. I tried to say a few words at opening, but soon curled up like a sensitive plant. It is a terrible martyrdom for me to speak" (qtd. in Harper 1: 198). Anthony's commitment to woman's rights steeled her to move from the background into the spotlight and fill the vacancy left by the marriage, motherhood, and temporary retirement of the movement's most eloquent speakers. Furthermore, her surrogate delivery, a form of productive collaboration, directly promoted three rhetorical ends: the circulation of her cohorts' texts, the success of such discursive events as reform meetings and conventions, and the continuing vibrancy of the ongoing debate on woman's rights.[7]

Although I am focusing primarily on Anthony and Cady Stanton's division of rhetorical labor in this section, the two women's collaborative efforts extended well beyond simple textual production and delivery. To illustrate, in late 1853, Cady Stanton researched and wrote an address on married women's legal disabilities while Anthony canvassed the state and collected ten thousand petition signatures requesting changes to women's property, earning, and custodial rights in New York (Lutz, *Anthony* 41). In February 1854, Cady Stanton delivered her speech to the New York State Woman's Rights Convention, which then voted to print and distribute copies of the address to every member of the state legislature (Gordon, *Selected* 240). Anthony's petition and Cady Stanton's printed address were then presented to and considered by the New York assembly; unfortunately, it made only minor revisions to existing state laws concerning married women. The incident, nevertheless, illustrates the complexity of the two women's productive collaboration and their interlacing of text, oratory, and discursive events to improve women's legal status.

Productive/supportive collaboration permitted pioneering women rhetors to accommodate gender ideology, satisfy domestic obligations, uphold professional responsibilities, and produce and present public discourse in an unaccommodating time and place. Indeed, once the framework surrounding the public speaker is extended even slightly, the intricate system of collaborative alliances that surrounded and sustained her delivery becomes evident. Both productive and supportive collaboration are woven throughout the fabric of antebellum women's private lives and public discourse, sometimes apparent, sometimes barely perceptible, always indispensable.

Gender and Collaboration

The traditional fifth canon centers its attention on the speaker's use of voice, body, and expression, a focus that is simply too narrow to do justice to the complexities of women's delivery. This chapter argues that the fifth canon's scope must be expanded to include both the social context surrounding the speaker and the network of collaborative relationships that makes her rhetorical performance possible in the first place. Once the rhetor, context, and network are available for analysis, the collaborative con-tinuum can provide a useful model for examining the varied cooperative practices—both direct and indirect, productive and supportive—that undergird women's discourse and delivery. The continuum reveals that productive and supportive collaboration provided antebellum women with a highly effective means not only for creating and presenting texts but also for negotiating the ideological construct of true womanhood. Women rhetors needed to account for their private duties each time they stepped onto public platforms, and collaboration allowed them to reassure the audience that home fires were still burning (fueled by a supportive husband, servant, or friend), that families were being fed and cared for (again, thanks to supportive collaborators), and that women whose circuit extended beyond the home could be chaste and moral, too (their reputations preserved by traveling companions, yet another important form of supportive collaboration). Without recourse to collaboration, antebellum women would have had great difficulty either accessing the public platform or establishing feminine ethos. Men, by way of contrast, did not need to assure an audience of their manliness or prove they were fulfilling their duties as husbands, fathers, sons, or brothers. Masculine gender conventions simply did not necessitate collaboration in the same way that feminine conventions did.

The patterns of difference emerging from this analysis lead inevitably to the question of gender's role in collaboration. Scholars and writers have debated this point, arguing variously that a distinctly feminine variant of collaboration exists or that collaboration itself is a quintessentially feminine method of rhetorical production. Lisa Ede and Andrea Lunsford, for example, take the first position and posit two types of collaboration: a hierarchical (masculine) mode in which a leader directs group effort toward the goal of producing a unified, univocal text and a dialogical (feminine) mode favoring mutuality, negotiation, and a polyvocal text (133). Others, however, envision collaboration as an inherently feminine process. In her study of gender and composition, for instance, Miriam Brody contrasts a traditional masculine model of writing, which casts the author as solitary and combative, with a feminine model emphasizing collaboration and community. Brody enumerates the qualities that make collaborative writing particularly congenial for women: It promotes cooperation and compromise rather than argument and agonistic debate; it presents knowledge and writing as collective and social rather than individual products; it expresses multiple viewpoints rather than a single perspective (214). Brody thus identifies oppositional concepts of writing and links them to gender, suggesting that collaboration's communal and cooperative aspects reflect a feminine orientation. Like Brody, coauthors Janice Doane and Devon Hodges view collaboration as a distinctly feminine form necessitated by social context and ideology:

> Our writing practice was defined by interruption, by domesticity as it is constructed as a woman's sphere. Men in our same social and economic class (white, middle-class professionals) have not been pressured to redefine the way they do work; most often they do not feel conflict over domestic and professional duties to the same extent that women do. (54)

Collaborative writing provides Doane and Hodges a means for managing contrary domestic and professional obligations, a conflict culturally coded as feminine and, therefore, eliciting feminine modes of adaptation, collaboration being a prime example. (See Kaplan and Rose; Ellerby and Waxman; and Belenky et al. for other studies that present collaboration as a feminine process.)

While I agree with Doane and Hodges that particular contexts and ideologies encourage particular groups to employ particular rhetorical methods (in this case, promoting women's use of collaboration), I resist connecting particular rhetorical methods to particular groups in any necessary fashion (for instance, by identifying collaboration as a feminine process). Women may well collaborate, cooperate, coordinate, and form communities more often than men, but they do so because of the material, economic, social, and ideological conditions around them. Culture creates and constrains feminine gender performance and thus provides the major impetus for women's collaboration. Change the culture, and women's reliance on collaboration changes, too. A contextual grounding allows scholars to stop considering collaboration in simple binary terms, forever attributing cooperative, communal processes to women and competitive, individualistic practices to men. Collaboration is more usefully viewed as a rhetorical option available to and used by both men and women. Granted, as result of their cultural conditioning, women and men may collaborate for different reasons, in different settings, and with different types of people, but they both enjoy full access to the collaborative continuum.

If all rhetors, then, employ and have recourse to collaboration, antebellum women's cooperative efforts are not especially noteworthy. What is significant, however, is what their practices reveal about the process by which marginalized groups come to public voice. Collaboration permitted pioneering women rhetors to access and speak from public platforms in hostile surroundings, and their discourse and delivery, in turn, advanced changes in gender and power relations. Furthermore, the ever-shifting patterns and purposes of their cooperative relationships indicate that collaboration may well be the most effective means of rhetorical production and delivery available to nonprivileged groups. Indeed, without collaboration's rich malleability, diverse forms, and multiple functions, it is virtually impossible to imagine antebellum women even reaching the public platform, much less using voice, gesture, and expression to advocate reform and renovate society.

Conclusion
Regendering the Fifth Canon

Throughout these chapters, I have made the case that the traditional fifth canon suffers from a number of blind spots. First, it makes the assumption that rhetors are male, privileged, and authorized to speak publicly, thus ignoring the concerns and constraints of those who are not. Second, it focuses solely upon the speaker's vocal and physical presentation of discourse, which is too narrow a framework to allow for a full exploration of delivery's complexities for disenfranchised rhetors. Third, it defines delivery in corporeal terms (the speaker standing and addressing the audience directly) that are off limits to many rhetors, particularly those from marginalized groups, and, therefore, elides alternative forms of rhetorical presentation. Fourth, it completely overlooks the fact that rhetorical performance is grounded in social context, which exerts itself subtly but insistently in everything leading up to and expressed at the moment of delivery. Regendering the fifth canon—and thereby redefining, retheorizing, and reinvigorating it—promises to make the study of delivery more comprehensive, relevant, and productive.

A regendered fifth canon envisions delivery as a dynamic rhetorical performance occurring in a particular time and place and acknowledges the reciprocal influences of society upon speakers and speakers upon society. It thus historicizes delivery by situating it in a specific cultural and ideological setting and then tracing how that setting affects the delivery of particular groups and vice versa. Rhetorical presentations are interpreted simultaneously as an embodiment of and response to the surrounding social milieu. Although analysis begins and ends with the speaker, it also travels offstage in order to identify and evaluate the social factors shaping and informing delivery. The speaker's performance is considered in relation not only to an immediate audience but also to an enveloping context. The movement from stage to social setting and back again becomes a defining feature of the regendered fifth canon, expanding and contracting the boundaries of delivery but not erasing them. Cumulatively, these moves transform the fifth canon from a set of abstract, timeless, and presumably universal precepts about voice, gesture, and expression into analysis of an individual's or group's delivery in contingent social surroundings.

Adding the social to a canon that has traditionally focused exclusively on the individual both enriches and complicates it. A regendered fifth canon addresses far more than the speaker's manipulation of voice and body on a public platform and instead views rhetorical performance as the moment when dominant cultural values are enacted and, sometimes, are resisted and revised. Delivery thus becomes a site for investigating the intersection of variables like gender, sexuality, race, religion, nationality, ethnicity, age, class, or disability with power and discourse in particular settings, for what transpires on the public platform is simply a microcosm of larger social and ideological forces. In this study, I have demonstrated a method for examining how gender affected women's delivery in antebellum America and have considered speakers' onstage performances as well as offstage factors that obstructed or facilitated them. Six topoi have emerged from this analysis—education, access, space, genre, body, and rhetorical career—topoi that provide useful sites for tracing gender's impact upon delivery. Both context and ideology saturate each of these elements.

The first topos is education: Social context determines not only whether but also how particular groups are educated for public speaking. Chapter 1 details how late-eighteenth- and early-nineteenth-century women were denied opportunities for higher education, which centered on preparing male students for public life, but did encounter precepts of elocution and models of civic discourse in reading classes. Although their elocutionary instruction was intended strictly for private consumption, antebellum women appropriated the knowledge acquired in school settings and applied it to addressing public issues in public spaces. As they did so, pedagogy and educational materials changed in response, resulting in a backlash that eventually restricted the elocutionary coverage and oratorical content of textbooks likely to be read by young women. Thus, a reciprocal relationship is suggested between women's rhetorical delivery in public spaces and their rhetorical instruction in educational settings, a relationship that receives attention in a regendered fifth canon.

The second topos concerns access to public platforms: Social context grants or denies particular groups recourse to public forums in which to deliver rhetoric. As chapter 2 explains, when college women at Oberlin and

Antioch were denied access to academic platforms, venues where they could hone their presentation skills and practice addressing real audiences, many not only protested institutional policy but also founded extracurricular literary and debate clubs, thereby creating alternative platforms and circumventing restrictions. Furthermore, as chapters 4 and 5 detail, feminine gender ideals and expectations posed serious obstacles to women rhetors, who had to fulfill responsibilities to home, children, and family before even attempting to reach public platforms. Speakers managed to reconcile the two through collaboration, which proved indispensable for concurrently attending to private duties while entering public spaces. Thus, issues of access often determined how, where, and whether antebellum women delivered rhetoric, a connection that is recognized in a regendered fifth canon.

There is some overlap between the second and third topoi. The second topos of access concerns a rhetor's ability to reach a suitable platform from which to deliver (or practice delivering) public discourse. The issue of access is closely related to, but nevertheless distinct from, the third topos of space, which examines how a rhetor is perceived once she stands and speaks onstage. Thus, the second topos explores how a rhetor reaches the public forum while the third traces what transpires once she arrives there.

The third topos, then, examines space: Social context determines whether or not particular groups are perceived to "belong" in public settings. Because public space was gendered as masculine and private space as feminine during the eighteenth and nineteenth centuries, women who stepped onto public platforms were automatically perceived as being unnatural or out of place. One strategy for addressing the problem of fit, outlined in chapter 3, was to deliver discourse in feminized settings. Emma Willard and Dorothea Dix, for example, persuaded politicians in parlors rather than legislative halls and thereby circumvented the negative connotations clinging to women in public spaces. Another strategy for exonerating women's presence in masculine spaces was to argue that moral and religious obligations mandated their public participation, justification perfected by the Grimké sisters. Spatial issues like these constrained antebellum women's delivery, and they are acknowledged in a regendered fifth canon.[1]

The fourth topos explores discursive genre: Social context determines which forms of physical and vocal performance are deemed appropriate for particular groups. Antebellum women were strongly discouraged from directly addressing promiscuous audiences, a genre of delivery coded as masculine, and this restriction exerted pressure on speakers to devise alternative methods of rhetorical presentation. As chapter 3 details, pioneering rhetors developed a feminine delivery style that employed such feminized genres as conversation, letter writing, and reading and substituted male surrogates in situations requiring promiscuous address. This indirect, muted manner of rhetorical performance harmonized with conventional ideals of feminine comportment. Women rhetors' downcast eyes, seated position, reading and conversing, and occasional ventriloquism packaged public discourse into socially acceptable forms. The impact of genre on rhetorical presentation—in particular, which delivery options are [un]available to women rhetors—is addressed in a regendered fifth canon.

The fifth topos concerns the body: Social context determines how variables like sex and gender are typically practiced or enacted physically and thereby influences speakers' rhetorical delivery. Chapter 4 explains that visible pregnancy was considered unsightly and unseemly in certain public settings and that maternal rhetors arranged their speaking schedules carefully so as to accommodate gender norms surrounding the female body. Typically, antebellum women addressed mixed-sex audiences into the second trimester of pregnancy and thereafter restricted their appearances to same-sex audiences. Thus, the surrounding context established parameters for the public pregnant body and prompted women to devise inventive strategies of rhetorical presentation, corporeal concerns that are recognized in a regendered fifth canon.

The sixth topos examines rhetorical career: Social context influences the overall shape of speaking careers (which consist of a history or sequence of public performances) by encouraging particular groups to embrace particular life patterns. Antebellum women, whether single or married, were assigned primary responsibility for attending to family needs, an obligation that had an enormous impact on their rhetorical delivery over time. As chapters 4 and 5 describe, single women routinely abandoned speaking tours when siblings or parents called, and maternal rhetors interrupted or delayed their careers for extended periods in order to bear and raise children. Because private duties so frequently disrupted public involvement, women speakers often developed to their full potential later in life and continued their rhetorical careers longer than their male contemporaries, sometimes continuing to lecture well into their seventies, eighties, and nineties. The correlation between gender ideology and women's rhetorical careers is acknowledged in a regendered fifth canon.

The six topoi of education, access, space, genre, body, and career overlap at points, but they, nevertheless, provide generative sites for exploring the nexus of gender, power, and delivery and for identifying social and ideological currents at play on public platforms. The topoi indicate that pioneering women speakers attended to very different concerns and constraints when delivering public discourse than did men. Antebellum women struggled to obtain adequate educational preparation for and access to the public platform; negotiated distinct spatial, generic, and bodily issues onstage; and tolerated frequent interruptions to their rhetorical careers in order to accommodate feminine gender norms. Although I have focused on the impact of gender on families and antebellum women's delivery, the topoi are equally useful for examining the rhetorical performances of differently located women or other nonprivileged groups. After all, delivery occurs in a particular social setting and entails the speaker's enactment of identity, rhetoric, and ideology on a public platform; therefore, a cluster of concerns intersect and become apparent at the moment of performance. The regendered fifth canon can provide scholars with a window or framing device through which to view and study these elements in all of their richness and complexity.

At the conclusion of *The Gendered Pulpit*, Roxanne Mountford speculates that feminist rhetoricians may well find a new theoretical home in the "neglected" fifth canon (152). The regendered fifth canon does indeed provide a home in which to trace the differences that arise when good women (rather than good men) speak well on public platforms, but I would add that it welcomes not only feminists but all who study marginalized rhetors. While my own efforts center on women's practices and experiences, further studies of the distinct constraints and compensating strategies of disenfranchised speakers—however they are identified or defined—are likely to reveal additional topoi and further reinvigorate a canon that has for too long been undertheorized and understudied. Therefore, I throw open the doors and invite all interested scholars to enter the theoretical home afforded by the regendered fifth canon, confident that our examinations of delivery from multiple perspectives and through multiple lenses will ultimately make the classical canons, the rhetorical tradition, and the discipline itself more inclusive, pluralistic, and compelling.

Notes

Works Cited

Index

Notes

Introduction: Gender and Rhetorical Delivery

1. Feminist historiography has also spawned a number of critical controversies. One concerns whether interjecting women rhetors into standard rhetorical histories constitutes "female tokenism" and thus propagates a system valorizing men and their accomplishments (Biesecker 141). Although many, including Karlyn Kohrs Campbell, argue that adding *Great Women* to the established canon of *Great Men* is a necessary first step toward creating gender equity in the rhetorical tradition, most concede that the entire discipline must be revised before it can become truly inclusive. A novel strategy for accomplishing this end was discussed at the 2003 Alliance of Rhetoric Societies Conference, where participants explored the notion that the field might be better served if scholars abandoned the idea of a single, unified rhetorical tradition and instead thought in terms of multiple and concurrent rhetorical traditions.

Another critical controversy among feminist historiographers concerns the necessity and potential dangers of revising traditional research methods. Given that very little of the historical record concerning women has survived, scholars have argued the need for (and have enacted) creative research methodologies in order to locate "invisible and silenced women" and restore "them and their voices to rhetorical history" (Glenn, *Rhetoric* 2). To justify the innovative approaches needed to recover women's discursive practices and accomplishments, feminist scholars have questioned established research assumptions and conventions, for instance, by redefining what counts as rhetoric and as rhetorical evidence (see Mattingly's "Telling Evidence"). Many, inspired by Joan Wallach Scott's groundbreaking work in *Gender and the Politics of History* (1989), have rejected the notion of empirical or historical truth altogether and have instead embraced a postmodern vision of history, exchanging an objective, neutral stance for a positioned, passionate, and overtly political one. Postmodern historiographers also challenge conventions regarding acceptable and unacceptable methods of scholarly inquiry, proclaiming the value, for example, of the personal, the narrative, the emotional, and the interpretive in the construction of history.

Such moves have inspired concern and critique. In the controversial "Historical Studies and Postmodernism: Rereading Aspasia of Miletus" (2000), Xin Liu Gale examines the paradox confronting feminist historiographers, who simultaneously challenge "traditional masculine assumptions about women and women's ways of thinking and writing" and seek "colleagues' acceptance of the legitimacy and credibility" of their work. Gale cautions that reaching the second goal may prove impossible if scholars reject rather than revise established research methodology (363), and her analysis of potential grounds for dismissing such efforts as Cheryl Glenn's and Susan Jarratt and Rory Ong's recoveries of the classical rhetorician Aspasia has inspired thoughtful reexaminations of feminists' research methodologies. See, for example, Glenn and Jarratt's responses to Gale in *College English* 62 (2000) and the winter 2002 special issue of *Rhetoric Society Quarterly* (32:1), which is devoted to methods of feminist historiography.

2. Clearly, Michel Foucault's formulation of power relations informs my analysis. In *The History of Sexuality*, Foucault envisions power as the result of discursive formations, which promote distinct sets of values that in turn produce particular normative behaviors. These normative behaviors are then enacted (and perhaps resisted) by subjects who thus reinforce (or possibly modify) discursive formations. Regarding gender, Foucault speculates that unified masculine and feminine ideals began to emerge during the Enlightenment and replace previously contradictory and ambiguous notions regarding the inherent nature of the sexes. These "gender fictions" coalesced into a causal or foundational force that was then used to explain identity, human behavior, and society. As culturally constructed and speculative as notions of sex and gender may be, individuals, nevertheless, create identities for themselves by conforming to, revising, or defying society's normative standards, a process enforced through institutional and technological regulations as well as subjects' own self-disciplining.

Foucault's paradigm results in a dramatically different conception of the nature and direction of power. It posits that "(1) Power is exercised rather than possessed; (2) Power is not primarily repressive, but productive; [and] (3) Power is analyzed as coming from the bottom up" (Sawicki 21). Thinking of power as a bottom-up rather than a top-down phenomenon has an enormous impact on research methodology. First, power/subject relations become reciprocal and dynamic, with power formations determining the range of possible subject positions and subjects then enacting or resisting power formations. Additionally, Foucault analyzes power matrixes through local centers of power and knowledge, in other words, through focused examinations of the ways in which situated subjects enact discursive formations on a daily, practical level. I adopt the Foucauldian strategy of identifying feminine gender norms produced by nineteenth-century discursive formations and then examining how those norms were performed or resisted on a practical level by women rhetors, the subjects of those formations.

1. Readers and Rhetors: Schoolgirls' Formal Elocutionary Instruction

1. Although I primarily examine northern children's schooling in this chapter, it is important to note that opportunities for and forms of education varied widely throughout the colonies during the seventeenth and eighteenth centuries. The region in which girls resided often determined the kind of schooling available to them:

> Emphasis on literacy varied over the colonial period and depended to a large extent on which of the colonies one lived in and on the prevailing religious beliefs and practices. In New England, Puritan beliefs regarding salvation influenced parents to teach all their children to read so that they could understand the Bible. In the middle colonies, there appears to have been a more equitable attitude toward the education of girls. . . . [Quaker, German, Moravian, and Dutch Reformed settlers] maintained elementary schools for both boys and girls long before their contemporaries in New

England. . . . The system of formal education in the south also differed from that of the north; the population was more spread out, towns were not as readily accessible, and the wealthier families established a system of tutorial education for their children in which live-in tutors were often part of the family entourage. In this situation, girls sometimes were taught along with their brothers, and sometimes given educational attention when the boys were otherwise occupied. (McMelland 54–55)

2. To give some idea of the progression and oral emphasis of colonial reading instruction, lessons initially focused upon children's mastery of the alphabet, moving sequentially from naming and pronouncing individual letters, to syllables, and, eventually, to words of one or more syllables. This excerpt from Thomas Lye's *Reading and Spelling Made Easie* (1673) presents a typical exchange between a teacher and student, the teacher spelling syllables that the student then pronounces:

> QU. What sound *a-n*?
> ANS. *An.*
> QU. What sound *g-e-l*?
> ANS. *gel.*
> QU. Put it together.
> ANS. *Angel.*
>
> (qtd. in Michael 73)

Today, spelling is closely associated with writing, but this was not the case in the colonial classroom, where spelling and reading were taught as interrelated skills. After learning the alphabet, the syllabury (vowel and consonant clusters, such as ab/ eb/ ib/ ob/ ub and ba/ be/ bi/ bo/ bu), and word lists, students advanced to spelling and then saying every word in a reading passage. Only after accomplishing each of these steps would students be judged ready to read the passage itself. Students then memorized and eventually recited their reading passages aloud to the class, thus demonstrating their reading ability.

3. Frederick Haberman divides the interests of the British elocutionists into four major categories: (1) gesture, an area concerned with "bodily actions, such as the sweep of the arm, the pointing of the finger" as well as "the gesture of emotional expression," an area concerned with how affect is conveyed through expression, stance, and motion; (2) voice management, an area concerned with "vocal flexibility, buoyancy, responsiveness to meaning and innuendo, [and] control"; (3) pronunciation, an area concerned·with promoting a standard of English pronunciation and a notational system to indicate that standard; and (4) vocal production, an area concerned with "the identification of English sounds, the manner in which those sounds were produced, and the impediments which might interfere with the production of those sounds" (110–11). Although the elocutionary movement can be studied in terms of these four broad areas, my analysis in this chapter focuses on the instructional methods and texts used to teach elocution to children, particularly those emphasizing the connection between reading and public speaking.

4. Thomas Woody illustrates the progress of schoolgirls' education during the late eighteenth and early nineteenth centuries through the example of one New England township:

> In 1766, the town of Medford [Massachusetts] gave its committee "power to agree with their schoolmaster to instruct girls two hours in a day after the boys are dismissed,"

while in 1787 it was arranged that girls attend "one hour in the forenoon and one in the afternoon for four months." Three years later we learn "that girls have liberty to attend the master's school the three summer months." In 1794 they stipulated that the two sexes should attend school to the first of October. The schoolday was to be eight hours long and equally divided between boys and girls. Nevertheless, not before 1834 did the town vote "that the school committee be directed so to arrange the town schools that the girls may enjoy equal privileges therein with the boys throughout the year." (1: 144–45)

That girls' education was considered less important than boys' was reflected not only in their limited access to school but also in the salaries of their teachers. Summer schools typically received only a fraction of the funds provided winter schools. The township of Lexington, Massachusetts, one of the earliest to support women's education, paid ninety pounds a year plus board to its grammar school master but only five pounds a year each to the five women who taught summer sessions. They, unlike the grammar school master, also had to pay for their own board out of their meager salaries (Sklar, "Schooling" 538). Furthermore, despite improved educational opportunities, young women's schooling was in general not very thorough or rigorous, which has prompted Cathy Davidson to charge that early national schools provided women with a "second-class education" (63). Justified though her indignation may be, American girls' increased access to learning nevertheless represents a substantial improvement to women's status although the equitable education of the sexes would take far longer to achieve.

5. Two landmark books about delivery—one British and one American—were published early in the nineteenth century. Gilbert Austin's *Chironomia* (1806) is dedicated entirely to *actio*. It provides an exhaustive account of gesture and introduces a sophisticated notational system indicating the positioning of the speaker's foot, hand, arm, and body. His system is designed both to instruct and preserve the delivery of effective public performers, thus attempting "what is accomplished today with sophisticated video and audio equipment" (Stewart 156). *Chironomia* contains 122 sketches, illustrating stances and gestures for various types of public speakers, including lawyers, politicians, ministers, and actors. The first important American treatment of elocution appeared in 1827, namely, James Rush's *Philosophy of the Human Voice*. Rush ignored gesture to focus exclusively on *pronuntiatio*, grounding his study in science and human physiology. His scientific approach to vocal production allowed him to develop a clear, functional vocabulary and explanation of phonetic units, syllabication, inflection, vocal quality, and vocal elements, such as quality, force, time, abruptness, and pitch. Austin and Rush greatly influenced nineteenth-century textbooks' treatment of gesture and voice, and it was common to find one or both men acknowledged in title pages, prefaces, or introductions.

6. Nineteenth-century publishers developed graded reading series for common-school and academy use that contained substantial elocutionary material. The most popular were those associated with William McGuffey, David Tower, Charles Sanders, and Salem Town. Typically, reading series consisted of five or six books, the first four targeting what would now be considered the primary grades and the final books reserved for high school or advanced academy study. Elocution was introduced in increasing doses over the course

of the series. Typically, the first and second readers covered the phonics of letters, syllables, and words; the third and fourth readers introduced elementary principles of elocution; and the fifth and sixth books allocated between forty and sixty pages to the subject (Nietz 103–4).

7. I decided to study Sanders's schoolbooks for two reasons. First, I could find no other antebellum-period author or series boasting a general reader, a young ladies' reader, and a speaker. Second, Thomas Woody's research shows that nineteenth-century ladies' academies used "Sanders: Readers" to teach reading and "Sanders: Series" to teach elocution, indicating that young women read his textbooks but, unfortunately, not specifying which particular titles (1: 561).

To assess the relative popularity of Sanders's textbooks, I consulted the Online Computer Library Center (OCLC) catalogue and the National Union Catalog (NUC) and tallied the total number of printings. Because I have not examined the actual texts described in the OCLC and NUC entries, I cannot verify whether each listed entry consists of distinct editions or of impressions; therefore, I estimate the number of printings listed for each textbook, venturing information concerning editions only when the OCLC or NUC entries indicate a revised, revised and enlarged, or new edition of the textbook.

First published in 1848, *The School Reader, Fifth Book* had an impressive shelf life, undergoing thirty-eight printings and twenty-one editions by 1875: 1848, 1848, 1848 (revised edition), 1848, 185- (revised edition), 1852, 1854, 1854, 1855, 1855, 1855 (revised edition), 1855 (revised edition), 1856, 1859 (revised and enlarged), 1859 (revised edition), 1859, 1860 (revised and enlarged), 1861 (revised and enlarged), 1861, 1861, 1862, 1863, 1863 (revised and enlarged), 1864, 1864, 1864 (revised and enlarged), 1864 (revised and enlarged), 1865, 1866, 1866 (revised and enlarged edition), 1867 (revised and enlarged), 1867 (revised and enlarged), 1867 (revised and enlarged), 1868 (revised and enlarged), 1871? (revised and enlarged), 1872 (revised and enlarged), 1873 (revised edition), 1875 (revised and enlarged).

First published in 1855, *Sanders' Young Ladies' Reader* underwent ten printings with no indication of revision: 1855, 1855, 1855, 1856, 1858, 1860, 1863, 1864, 1865, 1866. *Sanders' School Speaker* did not enjoy the sales of the other two textbooks. First published in 1857, it was printed only two additional times (1860 and 1863) with no indication of revision.

8. The total number of selections indicated in table 1 do not always match the total number of selections listed in the textbooks' table of contents. This discrepancy results from two causes: First, Sanders occasionally divides long pieces into two or more separate listings or, second, groups multiple extracts together under one listing. Therefore, in order to ascertain the distribution of genres among practice selections, I count each extract as one selection regardless of Sanders's listings in the table of contents. For example, although *The School Reader, Fifth Book* lists Byron's "The Prisoner of Chillon" twice (reading selections 146 and 147), I count it only once in the poetry genre.

2. Practicing Delivery: Young Ladies on the Academic Platform

1. Educational historians have devoted considerable attention to exhibitions, examinations, and commencements, their observations generally embedded within broader studies of women's education or the academy movement. See Christie Farnham's *Education*

of the Southern Belle: Higher Education and Student Socialization in the Antebellum South (1994); Lori Ginzberg's "The 'Joint Education of the Sexes': Oberlin's Original Vision" (1987); Ann Gordon's "The Young Ladies Academy of Philadelphia" (1979); Nancy Green's "Female Education and School Competition: 1820–1850" (1978); Margaret Nash's "'Cultivating the Powers of *Human Beings*': Gendered Perspectives on Curricula and Pedagogy in Academies of the New Republic" (2001); John Rury and Glenn Harper's "The Trouble with Coeducation: Mann and Women at Antioch, 1853–1860" (1986); Marion Savin and Harold Abrahams's "The Young Ladies' Academy of Philadelphia" (1957); Barbara Solomon's *In the Company of Educated Women: A History of Women and Higher Education in America* (1985); Kim Tolley's "Science for Ladies, Classics for Gentlemen: A Comparative Analysis of Scientific Subjects in the Curricula of Boys' and Girls' Secondary Schools in the United States, 1794–1850" (1996); and Thomas Woody's *A History of Women's Education in the United States*, Vol. 2 (1929).

Additionally, a number of rhetorical studies examine nineteenth-century women's experiences on academic platforms in the course of larger works on college women, rhetoric, and composition, the majority concentrating on the postbellum period. See Kathryn Conway's "Woman Suffrage and the History of Rhetoric at the Seven Sisters Colleges, 1865–1919" (1995); Sandra Harmon's "'Voice, Pen, and Influence of Our Women Are Abroad in the Land': Women and the Illinois State Normal University, 1857–1899" (1995); Susan Kates's *Activist Rhetorics and American Higher Education 1885–1937* (2001); Lisa Mastrangelo's "Learning from the Past: Rhetoric, Composition, and Debate at Mount Holyoke College" (1999); Jacqueline Royster's *Traces of a Stream: Literacy and Social Change among African-American Women* (2000); and Heidemarie Weidner's "Silks, Congress Gaiters, and Rhetoric: A Butler University Graduate of 1860 Tells Her Story" (1995).

2. All excerpts from letters and journals include the writer's original punctuation, spelling, capitalization, and distinguishing orthographic marks, such as underlining and dashes. I do not label unorthodox practices *sic*.

3. In addition to public exhibitions, some ladies' academies published exhibition-day proceedings. For example, when the Young Ladies' Academy of Philadelphia released its institutional history, *The Rise and Progress of the Young-Ladies' Academy of Philadelphia: Containing an Account of a Number of Public Examinations and Commencements* (1794), it included Molly Wallace's and Priscilla Mason's commencement orations. In 1811, Susanna Rowson published *A Present for Young Ladies, Containing Poems, Dialogues, Addresses, etc, as Recited by the Pupils of Mrs. Rowson's Academy at the Annual Exhibitions*, composed entirely of pieces written by the headmistress herself. The book included poems; introductory and concluding addresses; recitation pieces drawing upon history, female biography, and navigation; and dialogues examining such issues as women's education, morality, and domestic duty.

Although Rowson's exhibition pieces are overtly didactic, they also contain flashes of wit and color. "A Dialogue Spoken by Two Little Misses," for instance, promotes female duty, industry, and service in its exchanges between two students, the earnest Lucretia and the irrepressible Mary. As the dialogue begins, Lucretia is hurrying to school, determined to win the prize for habitual promptness, when she is detained by her rebellious classmate Mary, who derides Lucretia's aspirations:

What's the prize of a book? such nonsensical stuff.
If I want new books aunt can give me enough.
I abominate reading, it makes one so dumpish.
And as to our governess; la, she's so frumpish.

(Rowson 22)

Dismissing Mary as a "giddy" girl, Lucretia details her own industry and devotion to duty, describing how she sews, cooks, and cleans for her aunt before and after school. Lucretia warns Mary that those "Who lead indolent lives/Are indifferent daughters and make wretched wives," a platitude to which Mary responds with scorn:

Wives! well, 'twere worth while to be married indeed,
Were one forced to do nothing but work, write and read.
Why, dear, when one's married the principle merit
Is dancing with elegance, betting with spirit,
At whist or at loo; . . .
And d'ye think when I'm married that I'll be confined,
At home to make pies, or the servants to mind?
No, child, I shall marry to live at my ease,
Eat, drink, dance and dress, and do just as I please;
But la, we're fine folks to be prating away
About marriage indeed, come, let's go out to play.

(Rowson 23–24)

Mary questions the advantages of being a proper young woman and instead praises dancing, gaming, drinking, eating, and doing just as she pleases. Mary's defiance, however, is soon quelled. In the course of two additional exchanges with Lucretia, Mary suddenly undergoes a conversion experience, forswears frivolity, and dedicates herself to serving the poor. Although Rowson's dialogues officially endorse "good" girls like Lucretia who promote benevolence, self-sacrifice, and industry, "naughty" girls like Mary give the pieces life and continuing interest. Given the novelty of young women's appearance on academic platforms at this time, exhibition pieces were scripted to be safe and inoffensive so as to avoid exacerbating an already delicate situation. Rowson's method of sounding the voice of rebellion briefly before vanquishing it with the voice of convention was a sound, sensible, and cautious strategy given these rhetorical constraints.

4. The Troy Female Seminary was by no means alone in providing schoolgirls with training in elocution and rhetoric. Although educators "did not expect women to make public orations . . . they did want women to have proper diction, tone, and pronunciation" for the purposes of reading aloud to and conversing with their own families (Nash 244). Girls might not have received direct instruction in oratory, but by 1800, rhetoric had become a common course offering. Thomas Woody's analysis of 162 ladies' academy catalogues published between 1742 and 1871 indicates that the five most frequently listed courses were English grammar (139 courses), arithmetic (132), natural philosophy (123), rhetoric (121), and reading (119) (1: 563–65). Two of the five courses, reading and rhetoric, had substantial oral components and thus required schoolgirls' instruction in elocution.

5. Brown told few people of her ambition to become an ordained Congregational minister because her desire was unprecedented. Even Stone, who was convinced of the church's misogyny, reacted with dismay when Brown confessed her aspirations:

I told her of my intention to become a minister. Her protest was most emphatic. She said, "You will never be allowed to do this. You will never be allowed to stand in a pulpit, nor to preach in a church, and certainly you can never be ordained." It was a long talk but we were no nearer to an agreement at the end than at the beginning. My final answer could only be, "I am going to do it." (qtd. in Cazden 31)

6. Brown displayed remarkable faith, patience, and forgiveness throughout her studies at Oberlin. She believed that Providence would provide for her needs and alter others' minds and hearts if she simply persisted in her path. Her very presence, she felt, raised issues that forced others to confront their own prejudices and faulty assumptions:

I have a grand chance to bring the subject [of women's ministry] in in some form, almost every time I meet an old friend or a stranger, for generally the first question after finding out what I am studying is "Are you going to preach—be a minister—a public lecturer," &c &c or else such remarks as "You can write sermons for your husband" or something else of the sort & so the subject comes in without dragging. Sometimes they warn me not to be a Fanny Wright man, sometimes believe I am joking sometimes stare at me with amacement & sometimes seem to start back with a kind of horror. Men & women are about equal & seem to have their eyes opened & tongues loosed to about the same extent. (Lasser and Merrill, *Soul* 33–34)

Brown believed that her embodiment of and willingness to discuss "the subject" advanced women's educational and professional progress, giving others the opportunity to express and reevaluate their positions through interaction with her. Rather than becoming bitter over responses of "amacement" and "horror," she habitually concentrated on communication, progress, and resolution in her dealings with others.

7. Brown's health and longevity brought her additional satisfactions as well. She lived long enough to witness ratification of the Woman Suffrage Amendment in 1920 and voted in the first national election open to women. Brown died the following year at the age of ninety-six, having witnessed and contributed to remarkable transformations in American women's political, professional, religious, and educational opportunities over the course of her long life.

8. Mann consistently minimized opportunities for intimacy between the sexes, and his principal method for doing so was strict supervision of students outside the classroom:

[Students] were not permitted to ride or walk together off the campus unless accompanied by a faculty member. The college Glen was open to males and females on alternate days to prevent them from meeting there. In the chapel and at other public exercises, men and women students sat on opposite sides of the aisle. (Rury and Harper 489)

Additionally, student marriages were prohibited, and undergraduates who wed prior to graduation risked expulsion (Vallance 485–86). Mann's notions of propriety are reflected in many faculty decisions involving student conduct and extracurricular literary societies.

9. Janet Carey Eldred and Peter Mortensen identify another possible contributor to educational backlash, namely, women's diminishing authority in female academies:

[T]he late eighteenth and early nineteenth centuries [were] likely the zenith of women's authority over the institutionalized schooling of women. What would follow by the mid-nineteenth century was a decline in that authority, even as women's educational "opportunities increased numerically." And as women's leadership in academy life narrowed, so did the horizons of academy graduates. Academies continued to ready girls to participate in civic affairs, but the opportunities for actual participation grew fewer and more tightly regulated. (25)

Paradoxically, then, despite large numbers of women in the teaching profession by the mid-nineteenth century, their control over the direction of women's education actually weakened. Female educators' reduced influence may have left them with few options for combating restrictions impeding schoolgirls' access to and performance on academic platforms.

10. Feminist scholars have produced a number of important works examining British and American women's religious rhetoric. For example, Vicki Collins details Methodist women's preaching during and after John Wesley's lifetime in "The Speaker Respoken: Rhetoric as Feminist Methodology" (1999) and "Walking in Light, Walking in Darkness: The Story of Women's Changing Rhetorical Space in Early Methodism" (1996); Rebecca Larson profiles the transatlantic ministry of eighteenth-century Quaker women in *Daughters of Light: Quaker Women Preaching and Prophesying in the Colonies and Abroad, 1700–1775* (1999); Carol Mattingly explores the rhetoric of Quaker women's dress and its signification on the reform platform in *Appropriate[ing] Dress: Women's Rhetorical Style in Nineteenth-Century America* (2002); Roxanne Mountford identifies masculinist assumptions embedded within nineteenth-century homiletics and the challenges they posed to women preachers in *The Gendered Pulpit: Preaching in American Protestant Spaces* (2003); Carla Peterson studies the spiritual justifications used by African-American orators like Maria Stewart and Jarena Lee in *"Doers of the Word": African American Women Speakers and Writers in the North* (1995); and Susan Zaeske analyzes antebellum women's use of the Book of Esther in public address in "Unveiling Esther as a Pragmatic Radical Rhetoric" (2000).

3. Performing Gender and Rhetoric: "Feminine" and "Masculine" Delivery Styles

1. In her study of nineteenth-century women speakers, *Man Cannot Speak for Her* (1989), Karlyn Kohrs Campbell identifies a feminine style of rhetoric characterized by personal tone (relying heavily upon first-person experience, stories, and examples), inductive structure, and appeals for audience participation and identification with the speaker (13). My work extends Campbell's analysis by suggesting that nineteenth-century women employed a feminine delivery style as well, a manner of rhetorical performance uniquely adapted to the period's gender norms that enabled women rhetors to address public issues and audiences discreetly.

2. For more on women's methods of appropriating and recasting rhetorical theory, see Jane Donawerth's "The Politics of Renaissance Rhetorical Theory by Women" (1995); "Textbooks for New Audiences: Women's Revisions of Rhetorical Theory at the Turn of the Century" (1997); "Conversation and the Boundaries of Public Discourse in Rhetorical Theory by Renaissance Women" (1998); "Hannah More, Lydia Sigourney, and the Creation of a Women's Tradition of Rhetoric" (1999); and "Poaching on Men's Philosophies of Rhetoric: Eighteenth- and Nineteenth-Century Rhetorical Theory by

Women" (2000). Additionally, Donawerth has collected women's rhetorical texts span-ning the classical period through the nineteenth century in the anthology *Rhetorical Theory by Women Before 1900* (2002).

3. Willard consistently used her leadership position in the common-school movement to promote women's involvement in educational affairs, arguing that the domestic sphere rightfully included all matters pertaining to children's learning. Making the case to school superintendents (all of whom were men), she acknowledged that her sentiments might initially "sound strange, as they foreshadow a new shade of things":

> I do not wish women to act out of their sphere; but it is time that modern improvement should reach their case and enlarge their sphere, from the walls of their own houses to the limits of the school district. In the use of the pen, women have entered the arena ... but, in the use of the living voice, women are generally considered as being properly restricted to conversation. St. Paul has said they must not speak in churches, but he has nowhere said they must not speak in school houses. (qtd. in Lutz, *Emma Willard: Pioneer* 112)

While Willard calls for men and women to discuss and decide school issues together, she characteristically makes a conciliatory move, assuring her male audience that "educated women" who participate in school matters will feel "honored" to serve "under the su-perintendents," in other words, will remain subordinate rather than assuming leadership positions themselves.

4. Emma Willard was also inconsistent regarding promiscuous speech. When the New York superintendents of common schools invited her to address their 1845 convention, Willard journeyed to Syracuse, but "instead of speaking at the convention, she followed the more ladylike way of allowing sixty of the gentlemen to call upon her and then read them an address which she had prepared for the occasion" (Lutz, *Emma Willard: Daugh-ter* 222). Although propriety apparently prohibited the educator from addressing a male or mixed-sex convention audience, Alma Lutz observes that during this same time pe-riod, Willard regularly instructed promiscuous groups of a hundred or more teachers during tours of teaching institutes. Presumably, she either found it acceptable to instruct (rather than address) promiscuous audiences or else felt comfortable speaking in school settings. Her somewhat contradictory behavior is yet another indication that women rhetors adjusted their delivery styles to suit particular contexts and occasions.

5. Elaborating on men's and women's respective political obligations, Beecher argues that women should play no direct role in petition drives,

> which seem, IN ALL CASES, to fall entirely without the sphere of female duty. Men are the proper persons to make appeals to the rulers whom they appoint, and if their female friends, by arguments and persuasions, can induce them to petition, all the good that can be done by such measure will be secured. But if females cannot influence their nearest friends, to urge forward a public measure in this way, they surely are out of their place, in attempting to do it themselves. (*Essay* 104–5)

Curiously enough, given her statement here, Beecher had involved her Hartford Female Seminary students in political analysis and petitioning during the 1820s:

> Under Catharine's leadership [the students] organized on behalf of the Cherokee Indians, who in 1827 were ordered to vacate their lands in the state of Georgia.

Throughout 1829 Catharine and her students were deeply involved in circulating petitions and circulars protesting this federal action. (Hedrick 58)

Furthermore, in 1854, she signed a petition opposing repeal of the Missouri Compromise (Zaeske, *Signatures* 166), and in 1870, she threatened to initiate a petition campaign against woman suffrage (Boydston, Kelley, and Margolis 229). Evidently, Beecher's official pronouncements sometimes conflicted with her actual practice, perhaps the inevitable consequence of attempting to propitiate nineteenth-century feminine gender ideals while actively engaging in public life.

6. While Angelina responded to Catharine Beecher's essay, Sarah parried Congregational ministers' *Pastoral Letter*, which warned flocks of imminent "dangers" threatening "the female character with wide spread and permanent injury":

> We cannot . . . but regret the mistaken conduct of those who encourage females to bear an obtrusive and ostentatious part in measures of reform, and countenance any of that sex who so far forget themselves as to itinerate in the character of public lecturers and teachers. We especially deplore the intimate acquaintance and promiscuous conversation of females with regard to things "which ought not to be named"; by which that modesty and delicacy which is the charm of domestic life, and which constitutes the true influence of woman in society, is consumed, and the way opened, as we apprehend, for degeneracy and ruin. (*Pastoral* 211)

The ministers caution that because women's public speech defies Scripture, it will ultimately produce domestic and social chaos.

Sarah Grimké countered with *Letters on the Equality of the Sexes and the Condition of Woman* (1838). Detailing misinterpretations and false translations of the Bible, especially the troublesome Pauline strictures prohibiting women's speech, Sarah comes to conclusions similar to those drawn by Angelina in *Letters to Catherine E. Beecher*. Because God created man and woman as moral equals, biblical sanctions and injunctions apply equally to them as well:

> WHATSOEVER IT IS MORALLY RIGHT FOR A MAN TO DO, IT IS MORALLY RIGHT FOR A WOMAN TO DO; and . . . confusion must exist in the moral world, until woman takes her stand on the same platform with man, and feels that she is clothed by her Maker with the *same rights*, and, of course, that upon her devolve the *same duties*. (269)

Sarah's apologia, rather than Angelina's, endures as the definitive defense of nineteenth-century women's public, political discourse.

4. Delivering Discourse and Children: The Maternal Difficulty

1. Most (but not all) of the women examined in this chapter participated in the anti-slavery or woman's rights movement prior to the Civil War. Some—including Angelina Grimké, Abby Kelley, Elizabeth Cady Stanton, Lucy Stone, and Antoinette Brown—left behind abundant and now easily accessible letters and journals that provide valuable insights into their negotiations of conflicting rhetorical and maternal obligations. Unfortunately, few of the personal effects of African-American maternal rhetors—such as Sojourner Truth, Mary Ann Shadd, and Frances Watkins—have survived, making it difficult to discuss their experiences in much detail.

To illustrate this point, Watkins toured and lectured extensively for the Maine and Pennsylvania antislavery societies up to the time of her 1860 marriage to Fenton Harper and subsequent relocation to an Ohio farm. Watkins Harper initially managed to maintain her public work on a part-time basis following marriage, as her friend William Still observed: "Notwithstanding her family cares, consequent upon married life, she only ceased from her literary and Anti-slavery labors, when compelled to do so by other duties," other duties likely referring to the birth of her daughter Mary (793). Watkins Harper's semiretirement ended with her husband's death in 1864, at which point she resumed lecturing to support herself and her daughter. However, no extant letters or diaries indicate what effect "motherhood had upon her career or how [Watkins] Harper dealt with the problems of childcare" once she resumed public speaking (Foster 18), leaving us with unanswered questions concerning the intersections of maternity and rhetoric in her career.

2. The rumor, much less the fact, of pregnancy had the potential to impair a speaker's ethos and so had to be handled very carefully. For example, shortly after their 1846 marriage, Abby Kelley Foster and her husband Stephen toured together as antislavery lecturers, and speculation regarding her possible pregnancy plagued the newlyweds at every stop along the way. Just prior to an engagement at Oberlin College, Kelley Foster confided her frustrations regarding the rumors to Lucy Stone, then an unmarried college student:

> I am no more going to have a baby than you are. And as I have not heard you were, I take it for granted you are not, though should I hear such a report I would not believe it, if you were an anti-slavery lecturer. No, in Heaven's name, I implore you to deny these malicious slanders. (qtd. in Sterling 232)

A pregnant speaker was an anathema to antebellum audiences, first, because she violated standards of feminine modesty and, second, because she risked the health of her unborn child in order to deliver rhetoric, thereby casting doubt upon on her womanliness. Kelley Foster charged antislavery opponents with intentionally spreading "malicious slanders" regarding her pregnancy in order "to destroy my influence for saving my sisters from chains."

3. Although antebellum women were willing to display their pregnant forms to same-sex audiences, I have found no instances of a visibly pregnant speaker deliberately employing the rhetoric of the body to complement her verbal message, say, by discussing issues in terms of motherhood or gestation. This is unsurprising, according to Sylvia Hoffert, who argues that woman's rights speakers exchanged conventionally feminine metaphors "alluding to conceiving, giving birth, nursing the sick, nurturing children, or assisting the poor and downtrodden" for those typically associated with masculine spaces, in that way attempting linguistically to "place women in contexts previously dominated by men" (54–55). Perhaps a general avoidance of such figures as well as the likelihood that allusions to their physical condition would be considered indelicate contributed to women's hesitation to exploit the visual rhetoric of pregnancy.

4. My understanding of maternity and rhetorical career has been greatly influenced by Tillie Olsen's analysis of women writers in *Silences* (1978). Examining mothering's impact on creative production, Olsen identifies a pattern of "[w]ork interrupted, deferred, [or] postponed" in the lives of maternal writers:

> In motherhood, as it is structured, circumstances for sustained creation are almost impossible. Not because the capacities to create no longer exist, or the need . . . [but because] the need cannot be first. It can have at best only part self, part time . . . Motherhood means being instantly interruptible, responsive, responsible. Children need one now (and remember, in our society, the family must often try to be the center for love and health the outside world is not). The very fact that these are needs of love, not duty, that one feels them as one's self; that there is no one else to be responsible for these needs, gives them primacy. (33)

In consequence, few women with children have writing careers of "unbroken productivity, or leave behind a 'body of work.' Early beginnings, then silence; or clogged late ones (foreground silences); long periods between books (hidden silences); characterize most of us" (Olsen 38).

The patterns that Olsen observes in mothers' writing careers apply equally to their rhetorical careers. Thankfully, like Olsen herself, many antebellum women had the resources and ingenuity necessary to combine mothering with rhetorical productivity, at least in the long run. However, while recognizing and celebrating their persistence, I also acknowledge the terrible cost that the institution of motherhood routinely imposed (and still imposes) on creative women, often resulting in their silencing and hampering their efforts to reach their highest potential. I end with Olsen's moving description of her own experience as a writer and mother:

> As for myself, who did not publish a book until I was fifty, who raised children without household help or the help of the "technological sublime" (the atom bomb was in manufacture before the first automatic washing machine); who worked outside the house on everyday jobs as well (as nearly half of all women do now, though a woman with a paid job, except as a maid or prostitute, is still rarest of any in literature); who could not kill the essential [household] angel (there was no one else to do her work); would not—if I could—have killed the caring part of [motherhood], as distant from the world of literature most of my life as literature is distant (in content too) from my world. . . .
>
> . . . The habits of a lifetime when everything else had to come before writing are not easily broken, even when circumstances now often make it possible for writing to be first; habits of years—response to others, distractibility, responsibility for daily matters—stay with you, mark you, become you. The cost of "discontinuity" (that pattern still imposed on women) is such a weight of things unsaid, an accumulation of material so great, that everything starts up something else in me; what should take weeks, takes me sometimes months to write; what should take months, years.
>
> I speak of myself to bring here the sense of those others to whom this is in the process of happening (unnecessarily happening, for it need not, must not continue to be) and to remind us of those (I so nearly was one) who never come to writing at all. (38–39)

5. Publication provided a venue for other maternal rhetors as well, offering them an alternative to the public platform and ensuring their continuing engagement with reform issues at times when they had difficulty leaving home. During the 1850s, for example, Elizabeth Cady Stanton was often housebound due to multiple pregnancies, a houseful

of young children, and an absent husband. However, she contributed to the ongoing conversation on woman's rights, temperance, antislavery, and other reform issues by writing letters, articles, and columns for such periodicals as *Una, Lily, Semi-Weekly Tribune, Rochester Tribune, Frederick Douglass's Paper,* and *Women's Advocate.* She also participated long distance at conventions she could not attend by sending letters and addresses subsequently delivered by surrogates. Thus, print was a crucial system of delivery for homebound maternal rhetors, offering them a means for articulating and circulating their ideas provided they could find time to write.

5. Forging and Firing Thunderbolts: Collaboration and Women's Delivery

1. Collaboration has been explored from many different perspectives in recent years. For examinations of collaboration in composition studies, see Kenneth Bruffee, "Collaborative Learning and the 'Conversation of Mankind'" (1984); Lisa Ede and Andrea Lunsford, *Singular Texts/Plural Authors: Perspectives on Collaborative Writing* (1990); Janis Forman, *New Visions of Collaborative Writing* (1992); Anne Ruggles Gere, *Writing Groups: History, Theory, and Implications* (1987); Karen LeFevre, *Invention as a Social Act* (1987); and Andrea Lunsford and Lisa Ede, "Rhetoric in a New Key: Women and Collaboration" (1990). For examinations of collaboration in literary studies, see Wayne Koestenbaum, *Double Talk: The Erotics of Male Literary Collaboration* (1989); Holly Laird, *Women Coauthors* (2000); Bette London, *Writing Double: Women's Literary Partnerships* (1999); and Jack Stillinger, *Multiple Authorship and the Myth of Solitary Genius* (1991). For examinations of collaboration in feminist studies, see Miriam Brody, *Manly Writing: Gender, Rhetoric, and the Rise of Composition* (1993); Carey Kaplan and Ellen Cronan Rose, "Strange Bedfellows: Feminist Collaboration" (1993); Elizabeth Peck and Jo Anna Mink, *Common Ground: Feminist Collaboration in the Academy* (1998); and special issues 13 and 14 of *Tulsa Studies in Women's Literature* (1994–1995). Finally, for examinations of collaboration in the workplace, see Geoffrey Cross, *Forming the Collective Mind: A Contextual Exploration of Large-Scale Collaborative Writing in Industry* (2001); and Lisa Ede and Andrea Lunsford, *Singular Texts/Plural Authors: Perspectives on Collaborative Writing* (1990).

2. Further complicating debate over the accuracy of various versions of Truth's 1851 address is the fact that additional distortions occurred when "original" accounts were later reprinted. To illustrate, when Frances Gage's rendition of Truth's speech first appeared in the New York *Independent* on 23 April 1863, it phrased the signature question as "Ar'n't I a woman?" This account was later reprinted in *The History of Woman Suffrage* (1881), and editors heightened Truth's dialect by changing "ar'n't" to "a'n't," producing the more vernacular "A'n't I a woman?" With each additional reprinting, Truth's words inched farther from standard edited English until, by the twentieth century, the address was commonly known as "Ain't I a Woman?" Thus, the difficulty of recovering Truth's "genuine" voice is further compounded; researchers must recognize not only that original transcribers influenced the text but also that subsequent editors introduced modifications of their own.

For extensive analysis of different renderings of this speech, including full texts of Marius Robinson's and Frances Gage's versions, see Nell Painter's biography *Sojourner Truth: A Life, A Symbol* (1996). Contemporaneous periodical accounts of Truth's address are collected in Suzanne Fitch and Roseann Mandziuk's *Sojourner Truth as Orator: Wit, Story, and Song* (1997).

3. Collaboration's "dual valences" are also apparent in the reception accorded Harriet Jacobs's memoir *Incidents in the Life of a Slave Girl, Written by Herself* (1861). When Jacobs decided to record her experiences as a slave, woman, and mother, she knew she had little chance of interesting publishers without the support of prominent white abolitionists. She initially approached Harriet Beecher Stowe as a possible collaborator but eventually decided to work with writer and editor Lydia Maria Child instead. Child's contributions included penning an introduction to Jacobs's memoir in an effort to placate publishers who demanded a preface "by some one known to the public—to effect the sale of the Book" (Jacobs, qtd. in Peterson 150–51). Child also edited Jacobs's narrative although she insisted that her work in that capacity had been minimal:

> [S]uch changes as I have made have been mainly for purposes of condensation and orderly arrangement. I have not added any thing to the incidents, or changed the import of her very pertinent remarks. With trifling exceptions, both the ideas and the language are her own. (Introduction xi)

However, despite editorial assurances and the title's insistence on sole authorship, uncertainty over the extent of Child's collaboration led to the dismissal of Jacobs's narrative as "inauthentic" and to its neglect for well over a century. The book's reception again demonstrates that white and black women's productive collaboration possessed unexpected perils due to suspicions surrounding collaborative texts and power differentials inherent to cross-race relationships.

4. Trusted servants often acted as supportive collaborators, especially for women rhetors who lacked encouraging husbands and families. Elizabeth Cady Stanton, for example, developed a strong and long-lasting partnership with her housekeeper Amelia Willard, whom the maternal rhetor variously described as a "treasure," "friend," "comforter," and "second mother" to her seven children. Willard joined the household in the early 1850s, a decade when Cady Stanton's husband was away much of the time, leaving her primary responsibility for the home and children. Willard's domestic abilities freed Cady Stanton to pursue reform interests during her home confinement in the 1850s and, later, during her reform and lyceum travels in the 1860s and 1870s. Cady Stanton acknowledged Willard's thirty years of support repeatedly in her autobiography, declaring, "But for this noble, self-sacrificing woman, much of my public work would have been quite impossible" (*Eighty* 204).

5. Andrea Kerr, Stone's most recent biographer, paints a dark picture of the Stone-Blackwell marriage. Vain, insecure, and competitive, Henry Blackwell felt threatened by his wife's success, and he cleverly manipulated her to his own emotional and financial advantage. Stone's undoing, according to Kerr, was her dual dedication to proving that "woman's rights would not be man's wrongs" and to embodying the public speaker as a true woman, commitments that left her vulnerable to Blackwell's criticism and maneuvering (Kerr 86–118).

Collaboration may well have salvaged the troubled marriage, which was marred by conflict and separation throughout its first decade. Collaboration provided Blackwell a means for subsuming his competitiveness with Stone into shared projects and common goals. Their cooperative partnership began in earnest in 1867 when the couple toured

Kansas together, encouraging voters to enfranchise both women and freedmen, and continued with a series of collaborative projects centered on woman suffrage:

> [I]n later years [Stone and Blackwell] traveled around the country, lecturing and participating in suffrage meetings and conventions. In 1869 they were instrumental in the formation of the American Woman Suffrage Association, remaining active in this organization throughout their lives. They also collaborated on *The Woman's Journal*, the longest-lived of all the suffrage papers. Established in 1870, the *Journal* was published until 1917, first under their editorship and then under that of their daughter, Alice Stone Blackwell. (Wheeler 5)

Clearly, collaboration ran in the family. Daughter Alice first worked alongside her parents but eventually assumed complete responsibility for *The Woman's Journal*. She also delivered speeches for her mother when ill health prevented Stone's public appearances, an example of intergenerational productive collaboration.

6. Like Lucretia Mott, Abby Kelley Foster also discovered a productive/supportive collaborator in her husband, Stephen Foster. The two antislavery lecturers met in the early 1840s, and following their 1845 marriage, both continued their public work, sometimes touring together, sometimes apart. Stephen Foster always considered his wife to be the better speaker:

> Your great success throws me entirely into the shade, and might awaken my envy, if it were not, after all, my own [i.e., a victory for antislavery]. As it is, I can only congratulate myself on the exercise of that good sense & sound discrimination which made you my first choice among all the women of my acquaintance . . . (qtd. in Sterling 255)

Foster's pride in his wife's oratorical abilities and his need to supplement their paltry lecturing income had two consequences: Abby continued to tour extensively while Stephen spent significant periods at home, tending the couple's farm and raising their daughter, an indispensable form of supportive collaboration for the maternal rhetor. Furthermore, whenever Abby's tireless touring schedule impaired her health, Stephen would step forward to fulfill her speaking engagements and provide her time for rest and recovery, his surrogate delivery a form of productive collaboration (Sterling 299). Throughout their long marriage, the Fosters worked together beautifully as collaborators, exchanging productive and supportive roles in response to changing personal needs and rhetorical goals.

7. Even Anthony's best collaborative efforts could not overcome the dearth of available woman's rights speakers at certain points in the 1850s. Anthony was forced to cancel the 1857 National Woman's Rights Convention because so many of the movement's leading lights—including Cady Stanton, Brown Blackwell, and Stone—had either just delivered or were about to deliver babies. Anthony humorously bewailed her predicament in a letter to Cady Stanton: "[T]hose of you who have the talent to do honor to poor oh how poor womanhood, have all given yourselves over to baby making, & left poor brainless me to battle alone—It is a shame,—such a body as I might be spared to rock cradles, but it is a crime for you & Lucy & Nette" (Gordon, *Selected* 322). Eventually, however, Anthony's patience wore thin, and she took to admonishing the "married sheep of the flock" to reproduce sparingly, keep domestic obligations to a minimum, and return

promptly to the field. In an 1858 letter to Brown Blackwell, for instance, Anthony scolds the letter's recipient as well as her sister-in-law:

> Now Nette not another baby, is my peremptory command—two will solve the problem, whether a woman can be any thing more than a wife and mother better than a half dozen, or Ten even—I am provoked at Lucy—just to think that she will attempt to speak in a course with such intellects as Brady, Curtis and Chapin, and then as her special preparation, take upon herself in addition to baby cares, quite too absorbing for careful close & continued intellectual effort—the entire work of her house.... What man would dream of going before the public on such an occasion . . . tired & worn from such a multitude of engrossing cares . . . Nette, I dont really want to be a downright scolder, but I can't help looking after the married sheep of the flock—a wee bit—I am sure it is folly for any human being to attempt to follow too many professions at the same time. (Gordon, *Selected* 360)

As Anthony knew only too well, even collaboration had its limits when it came to reconciling women's private and public obligations.

Conclusion: Regendering the Fifth Canon

1. Although my conception of space differs from hers, I want to review Roxanne Mountford's definition of rhetorical space, which she envisions as consisting of both the material and cultural elements that surround an oratorical performance. The material elements include the architectural setting and physical props employed by a speaker; in the case of a woman minister, these might include the church building, altar, pews, and pulpit. Culture also inhabits rhetorical spaces, which "carry the residue of history within them . . . [and thus are] a physical representation of relationships and ideas" (*Gendered* 17). The woman minister, for example, speaks in a church setting that has, until recently, precluded her sex from positions of authority. In some sense, she must confront, defy, and renovate this exclusionary history and tradition each time she delivers a sermon. Thus, culture inhabits rhetorical space and shapes speakers' performances as much as material settings and props do.

Works Cited

Alm, Mary. "The Role of Talk in the Writing Process of Intimate Collaboration." Peck and Mink 123–40.

Austin, Gilbert. *Chironomia; or, a Treatise on Rhetorical Delivery.* 1806. Ed. Mary Robb and Lester Thonssen. Carbondale: Southern Illinois UP, 1966.

Bacon, Margaret. *Valiant Friend: The Life of Lucretia Mott.* New York: Walker, 1980.

Bahn, Eugene, and Margaret Bahn. *A History of Oral Interpretation.* Minneapolis: Burgess, 1970.

Bailey, Ebenezer. *The Young Ladies' Class Book: A Selection of Lessons for Reading: In Prose and Verse.* Boston: Gould, 1837.

Barnes, Gilbert, and Dwight Dumond, eds. *Letters of Theodore Dwight Weld, Angelina Grimké Weld, and Sarah Grimké, 1822–1844.* Vol. 2. Gloucester, MA: Smith, 1965.

Bearden, Jim, and Linda Jean Butler. *Shadd: The Life and Times of Mary Shadd Cary.* Toronto: NC, 1977.

Beecher, Catharine. *An Essay on Slavery and Abolition, with Reference to the Duty of American Females.* Philadelphia: Perkins, 1837.

———. *Letters on the Difficulties of Religion.* Hartford, CT: Belknap, 1836.

———. *The True Remedy for the Wrongs of Woman with a History of an Enterprise Having That for Its Object.* Boston: Phillips, 1851.

Belenky, Mary, Blythe Clinchy, Nancy Goldberger, and Jill Tarule. Preface to the First Edition. *Women's Ways of Knowing.* New York: Basic, 1997. xxv.

Berlin, James. *Writing Instruction in Nineteenth-Century American Colleges.* Carbondale: Southern Illinois UP, 1984.

Biesecker, Barbara. "Coming to Terms with Recent Attempts to Write Women into the History of Rhetoric." *Philosophy and Rhetoric* 25 (1992): 140–61.

Bingham, Caleb. *American Preceptor; Being a New Selection of Lessons for Reading and Speaking.* Boston: Manning, 1794.

———. *Columbian Orator.* Boston: Frost, 1832. *Nietz Old Textbook Collection.* Digital Research Lib., U of Pittsburgh. 16 Dec. 2001. <http://digital.library.pitt.edu/cgi-bin/nietz.pl?type=browse>.

Blackwell, Alice Stone. *Lucy Stone: Pioneer of Woman's Rights.* 1930. Detroit: Grand River, 1971.

Blair, Hugh. *Lectures on Rhetoric and Belles Lettres.* 2nd ed. 1785. New York: Garland, 1970.

Bohman, George. "The Colonial Period." *A History and Criticism of American Public Address.* Ed. William Brigance. Vol. 1. New York: McGraw, 1943. 3–54.

Bollinger, Laurel. "'A Mother in the Deity': Maternity and Authority in the Nineteenth-Century African-American Spiritual Narrative." *Women's Studies* 29 (2000): 357–82.

Bordelon, Suzanne. "Challenging Nineteenth-Century Feminization Narratives: Mary Yost of Vassar College." *Peitho* 6.1 (2002): 2–5.

Boydston, Jeanne, Mary Kelley, and Anne Margolis. *The Limits of Sisterhood: The Beecher Sisters on Women's Rights and Woman's Sphere.* Chapel Hill: U of North Carolina P, 1988.

Boylan, Anne. "Timid Girls, Venerable Widows, and Dignified Matrons: Life Cycle Patterns among Organized Women in New York and Boston, 1797–1840." *American Quarterly* 38 (1986): 779–97.

———. "Women and Politics in the Era Before Seneca Falls." *Journal of the Early Republic* 10 (1990): 363–82.

Brekus, Catherine. *Female Preaching in America, Strangers, and Pilgrims, 1740–1845.* Chapel Hill: U of North Carolina P, 1998.

Brickley, Lynne. *Sarah Pierce's Litchfield Female Academy, 1792–1833.* Diss. Harvard U, 1985. Ann Arbor: UMI, 1985. 8523349.

Brigance, William, and Marie Hochmuth, eds. *A History and Criticism of American Public Address.* Vol. 1. New York: Russell, 1960.

Brody, Miriam. *Manly Writing: Gender, Rhetoric, and the Rise of Composition.* Carbondale: Southern Illinois UP, 1993.

Bronson, C. P. *Elocution; or, Mental and Vocal Philosophy.* New York: Barnes, 1845.

Brown, Thomas. *Dorothea Dix: New England Reformer.* Cambridge: Harvard UP, 1998.

Browne, Stephen. *Angelina Grimké: Rhetoric, Identity, and the Radical Imagination.* East Lansing: Michigan State UP, 1999.

Bruffee, Kenneth. "Collaborative Learning and the 'Conversation of Mankind.'" *College English* 46 (1984): 635–52.

Burgh, James. *The Art of Speaking.* 1761. Philadelphia: Aitken, 1775.

Caldwell, Merritt. *A Practical Manual of Elocution: Embracing Voice and Gesture.* 1845. 8th ed. Philadelphia: Lippincott, 1856.

Campbell, Karlyn Kohrs. "Agency: Promiscuous and Protean." *Alliance of Rhetoric Societies.* 3 Nov. 2003. <http://www.rhetoricalliance.org/>.

———. "Consciousness-Raising: Linking Theory, Criticism, and Practice." *Rhetoric Society Quarterly* 32 (2002): 45–64.

———. Introduction. Campbell, *Women Public Speakers* xi–xxii.

———. *Man Cannot Speak for Her: A Critical Study of Early Feminist Rhetoric.* Vol. 1. New York: Greenwood, 1989.

———, ed. *Women Public Speakers in the United States, 1800–1925: A Bio-Critical Sourcebook.* Westport: Greenwood, 1993.

Campbell, Karlyn Kohrs, and E. Claire Jerry. "Woman and Speaker: A Conflict in Roles." *Seeing Female: Social Roles and Personal Lives.* Ed. Sharon Brehm. New York: Greenwood, 1988. 123–33.

Cazden, Elizabeth. *Antoinette Brown Blackwell.* Old Westbury, NY: Feminist, 1983.

Ceplair, Larry, ed. *The Public Years of Sarah and Angelina Grimké, Selected Writing, 1835–1839.* New York: Columbia UP, 1989.

Chambers-Schiller, Lee. *Liberty, a Better Husband: Single Women in America.* New Haven: Yale UP, 1984.

Child, Lydia M. Introduction. *Incidents in the Life of a Slave Girl, Written by Herself.* By Linda Brent (aka Harriet Jacobs). 1861. New York: Harcourt, 1973.

Collins, Patricia Hill. "Shifting the Center: Race, Class, and Feminist Theorizing about Motherhood." *Representations of Motherhood.* Ed. Donna Bassin, Margaret Honey, and Meryle Kaplan. New Haven: Yale UP, 1994. 56–74.

Collins, Vicki. "The Speaker Respoken: Rhetoric as Feminist Methodology." *College English* 61 (1999): 545–71.

——. "Walking in Light, Walking in Darkness: The Story of Women's Changing Rhetorical Space in Early Methodism." *Rhetoric Review* 14 (1996): 336–54.

Connors, Robert. "*Adversus Haereses*: Robert J. Connors Responds to Roxanne Mountford." *Journal of Advanced Composition* 19 (1999): n. pag. 2 Sept. 2003. <http://jac.gsu.edu/jac/Reviewsreviewed/connors.htm>.

——. *Composition-Rhetoric: Backgrounds, Theory, and Pedagogy.* Pittsburgh: U of Pittsburgh P, 1997.

——. "Frances Wright: First Female Civic Rhetor in America." *College English* 62 (1999): 30–57.

Conway, Jill. "Perspectives on the History of Women's Education in the United States." *History of Education Quarterly* 14 (1974): 1–12.

Conway, Kathryn. "Woman Suffrage and the History of Rhetoric at the Seven Sisters Colleges, 1865–1919." Lunsford 203–26.

Cremin, Lawrence. *American Education: The Colonial Experience, 1607–1783.* New York: Harper, 1970.

Cross, Geoffrey. *Forming the Collective Mind: A Contextual Exploration of Large-Scale Collaborative Writing in Industry.* Cresskill, NJ: Hampton, 2001.

Crowley, Sharon. Review of *Composition-Rhetoric: Backgrounds, Theory, and Pedagogy,* by Robert Connors. *Rhetoric Review* 16 (1998): 340–43.

D'Arusmont, Frances Wright. *Life, Letters and Lectures, 1834–1844.* New York: Arno, 1972.

Davidson, Cathy. *Revolution and the Word: The Rise of the Novel in America.* New York: Oxford UP, 1986.

Dei, Sharon. "Emma Hart Willard." Campbell, *Women Public Speakers* 242–53.

Doane, Janice, and Devon Hodges. "Writing from the Trenches: Women's Work and Collaborative Writing." *Tulsa Studies in Women's Literature* 14 (1995): 51–57.

Donawerth, Jane. "Conversation and the Boundaries of Public Discourse in Rhetorical Theory by Renaissance Women." *Rhetorica* 16 (1998): 181–99.

——. "Hannah More, Lydia Sigourney, and the Creation of a Women's Tradition of Rhetoric." *Rhetoric, the Polis, and the Global Village.* Ed. C. Jan Swearingen. Mahwah, NJ: Erlbaum, 1999. 155–61.

——. "Poaching on Men's Philosophies of Rhetoric: Eighteenth- and Nineteenth-Century Rhetorical Theory by Women." *Philosophy and Rhetoric* 33 (2000): 243–57.

——. "The Politics of Renaissance Rhetorical Theory by Women." *Political Rhetoric, Power, and Renaissance Women.* Ed. Carole Levin and Patricia Sullivan. Albany: State U of New York P, 1995. 256–72.

——, ed. *Rhetorical Theory by Women Before 1900.* New York: Rowman, 2002.

——. "Textbooks for New Audiences: Women's Revisions of Rhetorical Theory at the Turn of the Century." Wertheimer 337–56.

Douglas, Ann. *The Feminization of American Culture.* New York: Knopf, 1977.

DuBois, Ellen, ed. *The Elizabeth Cady Stanton–Susan B. Anthony Reader.* Boston: Northeastern UP, 1992.

Eckhardt, Celia. *Fanny Wright: Rebel in America.* Cambridge: Harvard UP, 1984.

Ede, Lisa, and Andrea Lunsford. *Singular Texts/Plural Authors: Perspectives on Collaborative Writing.* Carbondale: Southern Illinois UP, 1990.

Ede, Lisa, Cheryl Glenn, and Andrea Lunsford. "Border Crossings: Intersections of Rhetoric and Feminism." *Rhetorica* 13 (1995): 401–41.

Elaw, Zilpha. *Memoirs of the Life, Religious Experience, Ministerial Travels and Labours of Mrs. Zilpha Elaw, an American Female of Colour.* 1846. *Sisters of the Spirit: Three Black Women's Autobiographies of the Nineteenth Century.* Ed. William Andrews. Bloomington: Indiana UP, 1986.

Eldred, Janet Carey, and Peter Mortensen. *Imagining Rhetoric: Composing Women of the Early United States.* Pittsburgh: U of Pittsburgh P, 2002.

Ellerby, Janet, and Barbara Waxman. "Collaboration + Feminism = New Voices, New Truths, New Discourses." *Women's Studies* 26 (1997): 203–22.

Fairbanks, Mrs. A. W. *Emma Willard and Her Pupils, or Fifty Years of Troy Female Seminary, 1822–1872.* New York: Mrs. Russell Sage, 1898.

Farnham, Christie. *The Education of the Southern Belle: Higher Education and Student Socialization in the Antebellum South.* New York: New York UP, 1994.

Fitch, Suzanne. "Sojourner Truth." Campbell, *Women Public Speakers* 421–33.

Fitch, Suzanne, and Roseann Mandziuk. *Sojourner Truth as Orator: Wit, Story, and Song.* Westport: Greenwood, 1997.

Fletcher, Robert. *A History of Oberlin College: From Its Foundation Through the Civil War.* Vols. 1–2. Oberlin, OH: Oberlin College, 1943.

Forman, Janis, ed. *New Visions of Collaborative Writing.* Portsmouth: Boynton/Cook, 1992.

Foss, Sonja, Cindy Griffin, and Karen Foss. *Feminist Rhetorical Theories.* Thousand Oaks, CA: Sage, 1999.

Foster, Frances. Introduction. *A Brighter Coming Day: A Frances Ellen Watkins Harper Reader.* New York: Feminist, 1990. 3–40.

Foucault, Michel. *The History of Sexuality. Volume 1: An Introduction.* Trans. Robert Hurley. New York: Pantheon, 1978.

Gale, Xin Liu. "Historical Studies and Postmodernism: Rereading Aspasia of Miletus." *College English* 62 (2000): 361–86.

Garrison, Wendell Phillips, and Francis Garrison. *William Lloyd Garrison, 1805–1879: The Story of His Life Told by His Children.* Vol. 2. New York: Century, 1885.

Gere, Anne Ruggles. *Writing Groups: History, Theory, and Implications.* Carbondale: Southern Illinois UP, 1987.

Ginzberg, Lori. "The 'Joint Education of the Sexes': Oberlin's Original Vision." *Educating Men and Women Together: Coeducation in a Changing World.* Ed. Carol Lasser. Urbana: U of Illinois P, 1987. 67–80.

———. *Women and the Work of Benevolence.* New Haven: Yale UP, 1990.

———. *Women in Antebellum Reform.* Wheeling, IL: Davidson, 2000.

Glenn, Cheryl. "Regendering the Rhetorical Tradition." *Rhetoric Review* 16 (1997): 22–44.

———. *Rhetoric Retold: Regendering the Tradition from Antiquity Through the Renaissance.* Carbondale: Southern Illinois UP, 1997.

Glenn, Evelyn. "Social Constructions of Mothering: A Thematic Overview." *Mothering: Ideology, Experience, and Agency.* Ed. Glenn, Grace Change, and Linda Forcey. New York: Routledge, 1994. 1–29.

Goggin, Maureen Daly. "An *Essamplaire Essai* on the Rhetoricity of Needlework Sampler-Making: A Contribution to Theorizing and Historicizing Rhetorical Praxis." *Rhetoric Review* 21 (2002): 309–38.

Goodrich, Samuel. *The Third Reader: For the Use of Schools.* Louisville: Morton, 1839. *Nietz Old Textbook Collection.* Digital Research Lib., U of Pittsburgh. 16 Dec. 2001. <http://digital.library.pitt.edu/cgi-bin/nietz.pl?type=browse>.

Goodsell, Willystine, ed. *Pioneers of Women's Education in the United States.* New York: McGraw, 1931.

Gordon, Ann, ed. *The Selected Papers of Elizabeth Cady Stanton and Susan B. Anthony: In the School of Anti-Slavery 1840–1866.* Vol. 1. New Brunswick: Rutgers UP, 1997.

———. "The Young Ladies Academy of Philadelphia." *Women of America: A History.* Ed. Carol Berkin and Mary Beth Norton. Dallas: Houghton, 1979. 69–91.

Green, Nancy. "Female Education and School Competition: 1820–1850." *History of Education Quarterly* 18 (1978): 129–42.

Griffith, Elisabeth. *In Her Own Right: The Life of Elizabeth Cady Stanton.* New York: Oxford UP, 1984.

Grimké, Angelina. *Letters to Catherine E. Beecher, in Reply to 'An Essay on Slavery and Abolitionism,' Addressed to A. E. Grimké.* 1837. Ceplair 146–204.

Grimké, Sarah. *Letters on the Equality of the Sexes and the Condition of Woman, Addressed to Mary S. Parker, President of the Boston Female Anti-Slavery Society.* 1838. Ceplair 204–72.

Guthrie, Warren. "The Development of Rhetorical Theory in America, 1635–1850, V." *Speech Monographs* 18 (1951): 17–30.

Guy-Sheftall, Beverly. "African-American Publishing Outlets." *The Oxford Companion to Women's Writing.* Ed. Cathy Davidson and Linda Wagner-Martin. New York: Oxford UP, 1995. 16–20.

Haberman, Frederick. "English Sources of American Elocution." *History of Speech Education in America.* Ed. Karl Wallace. New York: Appleton, 1954. 105–26.

Hallowell, Anna, ed. *James and Lucretia Mott: Life and Letters.* New York: Houghton, 1884.

Harmon, Sandra. "'The Voice, Pen, and Influence of Our Women Are Abroad in the Land': Women and the Illinois State Normal University, 1857–1899." Hobbs 84–102.

Harper, Ida Husted. *Life and Work of Susan B. Anthony.* Vol. 1. 1898. New York: Arno, 1969.

Hedrick, Joan. *Harriet Beecher Stowe: A Life.* New York: Oxford UP, 1994.

Hobbs, Catherine, ed. *Nineteenth-Century Women Learn to Write.* Charlottesville: UP of Virginia, 1995.

Hoffert, Sylvia. *When Hens Crow: The Woman's Rights Movement in Antebellum America.* Bloomington: Indiana UP, 1995.

Holland, Patricia, and Ann Gordon, eds. *The Papers of Elizabeth Cady Stanton and Susan B. Anthony.* Wilmington, DE: Scholarly, 1991. Microfilm.

Hosford, Frances. *Father Shipherd's Magna Charta: A Century of Coeducation in Oberlin College*. Boston: Jones, 1937.

Howell, Wilbur. *Eighteenth-Century British Logic and Rhetoric*. Princeton: Princeton UP, 1971.

Jacobs, Harriet. *Incidents in the Life of a Slave Girl, Written by Herself*. 1861. New York: Harcourt, 1973.

Japp, Phyllis. "Angelina Grimké Weld." Campbell, *Women Public Speakers* 206–15.

Johnson, Nan. *Gender and Rhetorical Space in American Life, 1866–1910*. Carbondale: Southern Illinois UP, 2002.

———. *Nineteenth-Century Rhetoric in North America*. Carbondale: Southern Illinois UP, 1991.

———. "The Popularization of Nineteenth-Century Rhetoric: Elocution and the Private Learner." *Oratorical Culture in Nineteenth-Century America*. Ed. Gregory Clark and S. Michael Halloran. Carbondale: Southern Illinois UP, 1993. 139–57.

Johnson, Wendy Dasler. "Cultural Rhetorics of Women's Corsets." *Rhetoric Review* 20 (2001): 203–33.

Kaplan, Carey, and Ellen Cronan Rose. "Strange Bedfellows: Feminist Collaboration." *Signs* 18 (1993): 547–61.

Kates, Susan. *Activist Rhetorics and American Higher Education 1885–1937*. Carbondale: Southern Illinois UP, 2001.

Keller-Cohen, Deborah. "The Web of Literacy: Speaking, Reading, and Writing in Seventeenth- and Eighteenth-Century America." *Literacy: Interdisciplinary Conversations*. Ed. Deborah Keller-Cohen. Cresskill, NJ: Hampton, 1994. 155–76.

Kerber, Linda. *Women of the Republic: Intellect and Ideology in Revolutionary America*. Chapel Hill: U of North Carolina P, 1980.

Kerr, Andrea. *Lucy Stone: Speaking Out for Equality*. New Brunswick: Rutgers UP, 1992.

Kitzhaber, Albert. "Rhetoric in American Colleges 1850–1900." Diss. U of Washington, 1953.

Koestenbaum, Wayne. *Double Talk: The Erotics of Male Literary Collaboration*. New York: Routledge, 1989.

Lach, Edward. "Horace Mann." *American National Biography*. Vol. 14. Ed. John Garraty and Mark Carnes. New York: Oxford UP, 1999. 424–27.

Laird, Holly. *Women Coauthors*. Urbana: U of Illinois P, 2000.

Larson, Rebecca. *Daughters of Light: Quaker Women Preaching and Prophesying in the Colonies and Abroad, 1700–1775*. Chapel Hill: U of North Carolina P, 1999.

Lasser, Carol, and Marlene Merrill, eds. *Friends and Sisters: Letters Between Lucy Stone and Antoinette Brown Blackwell, 1846–1893*. Urbana: U of Illinois P, 1987.

———, eds. *Soul Mates: The Oberlin Correspondence of Lucy Stone and Antoinette Brown, 1846–1850*. Oberlin, OH: Oberlin College, 1983.

Lee, Jarena. *Religious Experience and Journal of Mrs. Jarena Lee*. 1849. *Spiritual Narratives*. Ed. Henry Louis Gates. New York: Oxford UP, 1988.

LeFevre, Karen. *Invention as a Social Act*. Carbondale: Southern Illinois UP, 1987.

Lerner, Gerda. *The Grimké Sisters from South Carolina: Rebels Against Slavery*. Boston: Houghton, 1967.

Logan, Shirley Wilson. *"We Are Coming": The Persuasive Discourse of Nineteenth-Century Black Women*. Carbondale: Southern Illinois UP, 1999.

London, Bette. *Writing Double: Women's Literary Partnerships*. Ithaca, NY: Cornell UP, 1999.

Lord, John. *The Life of Emma Willard*. New York: Appleton, 1873.

Lunsford, Andrea, ed. *Reclaiming Rhetorica: Women in the Rhetorical Tradition*. Pittsburgh: U of Pittsburgh P, 1995.

Lunsford, Andrea, and Lisa Ede. "Rhetoric in a New Key: Women and Collaboration." *Rhetoric Review* 8 (1990): 234–41.

Lutz, Alma. *Emma Willard: Daughter of Democracy*. 1929. Washington: Zenger, 1975.

——. *Emma Willard: Pioneer Educator of American Women*. Boston: Beacon, 1964.

——. *Susan B. Anthony: Rebel, Crusader, Humanitarian*. Boston: Beacon, 1959.

Mann, Horace. *Dedication of Antioch College, and Inaugural Address of Its President, Hon. Horace Mann*. Boston: Crosby, 1854.

——. *A Few Thoughts on the Powers and Duties of Women: Two Lectures*. Syracuse, NY: Hall, 1853.

Mann, Mary. *Life of Horace Mann*. 1865. Washington: NEA, 1937.

Marshall, Helen. "Dorothea Dix." *Notable American Women, 1607–1950*. Ed. Edward James et al. Vol. 1. Cambridge: Belknap, 1971. 486–89.

——. *Dorothea Dix: Forgotten Samaritan*. New York: Russell, 1937.

Mastrangelo, Lisa. "Learning from the Past: Rhetoric, Composition, and Debate at Mount Holyoke College." *Rhetoric Review* 18 (1999): 46–64.

Mattingly, Carol. *Appropriate[ing] Dress: Women's Rhetorical Style in Nineteenth-Century America*. Carbondale: Southern Illinois UP, 2002.

——. "Telling Evidence: Rethinking What Counts in Rhetoric." *Rhetoric Society Quarterly* 32 (2002): 99–108.

——. *Well-Tempered Women: Nineteenth-Century Temperance Rhetoric*. Carbondale: Southern Illinois UP, 1998.

McGuffey, William Holmes. *McGuffey's New Fifth Eclectic Reader: Selected and Original Exercises for Schools*. Cincinnati: Sargent, 1857. *Nietz Old Textbook Collection*. Digital Research Lib., U of Pittsburgh. 16 Dec. 2001. <http://digital.library.pitt.edu/cgi-bin/nietz.pl?type=browse>.

——. *McGuffey's New Sixth Eclectic Reader: Exercises in Rhetorical Reading, with Introductory Rules and Examples*. Cincinnati: Sargent, 1857. *Nietz Old Textbook Collection*. Digital Research Lib., U of Pittsburgh. 16 Dec. 2001. <http://digital.library.pitt.edu/cgi-bin/nietz.pl?type=browse>.

McMelland, Averil. *The Education of Women in the United States: A Guide to Theory, Teaching, and Research*. New York: Garland, 1992.

Messerli, Jonathan. *Horace Mann: A Biography*. New York: Knopf, 1972.

Michael, Ian. *The Teaching of English from the Sixteenth Century to 1870*. New York: Cambridge UP, 1987.

Monaghan, Charles. *The Murrays of Murray Hill*. Brooklyn, NY: Urban, 1998.

Monaghan, E. Jennifer. *A Common Heritage: Noah Webster's Blue-Back Speller*. Hamden, CT: Archon, 1983.

——. "Literacy Instruction and Gender in Colonial New England." *Reading in America: Literature and Social History*. Ed. Cathy Davidson. Baltimore: Johns Hopkins UP, 1989. 53–80.

Mountford, Roxanne. "Feminization of Rhetoric?" *Journal of Advanced Composition* 19 (1999): n. pag. 2 Sept. 2003. <http://jac.gsu.edu/jac/19.3/Reviews/1.htm>.

———. *The Gendered Pulpit: Preaching in American Protestant Spaces.* Carbondale: Southern Illinois UP, 2003.

Murray, Lindley. *The English Reader.* Utica: Hastings, 1827. *Nietz Old Textbook Collection.* Digital Research Lib., U of Pittsburgh. 25 Sept. 2001. <http://digital.library.pitt.edu/cgi-bin/nietz.pl?type=browse>.

Nash, Margaret. "'Cultivating the Powers of *Human Beings*': Gendered Perspectives on Curricula and Pedagogy in Academies of the New Republic." *History of Education Quarterly* 41 (2001): 239–50.

Nason, Elias. *A Memoir of Mrs. Susanna Rowson with Elegant and Illustrative Extracts from Her Writings in Prose and Poetry.* Albany: Munsell, 1870.

Nietz, John. *Old Textbooks.* Pittsburgh: U of Pittsburgh P, 1961.

Norton, Mary Beth. *Liberty's Daughters: The Revolutionary Experience of American Women, 1750–1800.* Boston: Little, 1980.

O'Connor, Lillian. *Pioneer Women Orators: Rhetoric in the Ante-Bellum Reform Movement.* New York: Columbia UP, 1954.

Olsen, Tillie. *Silences.* New York: Delacorte, 1978.

Osgood, Lucius. *Osgood's Progressive Fifth Reader.* Pittsburgh: English, 1858. *Nietz Old Textbook Collection.* Digital Research Lib., U of Pittsburgh. 16 Dec. 2001. <http://digital.library.pitt.edu/cgi-bin/nietz.pl?type=browse>.

Painter, Nell. *Sojourner Truth: A Life, a Symbol.* New York: Norton, 1996.

Pastoral Letter: The General Association of Massachusetts to the Churches under Their Care. 1837. Ceplair 211–12.

Pease, Jane, and William Pease. *Ladies, Women, and Wenches: Choice and Constraint in Antebellum Charleston and Boston.* Chapel Hill: U of North Carolina P, 1990.

Pease, William, and Jane Pease. "Sallie Holley." *Notable American Women, 1607–1950.* Ed. Edward James et al. Vol. 2. Cambridge: Belknap, 1971. 205–6.

Peck, Elizabeth, and Jo Anna Mink, eds. *Common Ground: Feminist Collaboration in the Academy.* Albany: State U of New York P, 1998.

Perlmann, Joel, Silvana Siddali, and Keith Whitescarver. "Literacy, Schooling, and Teaching among New England Women, 1730–1820." *History of Education Quarterly* 37 (1997): 117–39.

Peterson, Carla. *"Doers of the Word": African American Women Speakers and Writers in the North (1830–1880).* New York: Oxford UP, 1995.

Pierpont, John. *The American First Class Book, or, Exercises in Reading and Recitation.* Boston: Bowen, 1836. *Nietz Old Textbook Collection.* Digital Research Lib., U of Pittsburgh. 16 Dec. 2001. <http://digital.library.pitt.edu/cgi-bin/nietz.pl?type=browse>.

Pinneo, T. S. *The Hemans Reader for Female Schools.* New York: Clark, 1847. *Nietz Old Textbook Collection.* Digital Research Lib., U of Pittsburgh. 16 Dec. 2001. <http://digital.library.pitt.edu/cgi-bin/nietz.pl?type=browse>.

Porter, Ebenezer. *Analysis of the Principles of Rhetorical Delivery as Applied in Reading and Speaking.* Andover, MA: Newman, 1827.

———. *The Rhetorical Reader.* New York: Newman, 1835.

Rhodes, Jane. *Mary Ann Shadd Cary: The Black Press and Protest in the Nineteenth Century.* Bloomington: Indiana UP, 1998.

Ricker, Lisa. "'*Ars* Stripped of Praxis': Robert J. Connors on Coeducation and the Demise of Agonistic Rhetoric." *Rhetoric Review* 23 (2004): 235–52.

Ritchie, Joy, and Kate Ronald. "A Gathering of Rhetorics." Introduction. *Available Means: An Anthology of Women's Rhetoric(s)*. Ed. Ritchie and Ronald. Pittsburgh: U of Pittsburgh P, 2001. xv–xxxi.

Rohan, Liz. "I Remember Mamma: Material Rhetoric, Mnemonic Activity, and One Woman's Turn-of-the-Twentieth-Century Quilt." *Rhetoric Review* 23 (2004): 368–87.

Rowson, Susanna. *A Present for Young Ladies, Containing Poems, Dialogues, Addresses, etc, as Recited by the Pupils of Mrs. Rowson's Academy at the Annual Exhibitions*. Boston: West, 1811.

Royster, Jacqueline. *Traces of a Stream: Literacy and Social Change among African-American Women*. Pittsburgh: U of Pittsburgh P, 2000.

Rury, John, and Glenn Harper. "The Trouble with Coeducation: Mann and Women at Antioch, 1853–1860." *History of Education Quarterly* 26 (1986): 481–502.

Rush, James. *The Philosophy of the Human Voice*. 1827. Philadelphia: Lippincott, 1867.

Russell, William. *The American Elocutionist*. 5th ed. Boston: Jenks, 1851.

Russell, William, and Anna Russell. *Introduction to the Young Ladies' Elocutionary Reader*. Boston: Munroe, 1845.

———. *The Young Ladies' Elocutionary Reader; Containing a Selection of Reading Lessons . . . with Introductory Rules and Exercises in Elocution, Adapted to Female Readers*. Boston: Munroe, 1846.

Ryan, Mary. *The Empire of the Mother: American Writing about Domesticity, 1830–1860*. New York: Haworth, 1982.

Sanders, Charles. *Sanders' School Speaker: A Comprehensive Course of Instruction in the Principles of Oratory; with Numerous Exercises for Practice in Declamation*. New York: Ivison, 1857.

———. *Sanders' Young Ladies' Reader: Embracing a Comprehensive Course of Instruction in the Principles of Rhetorical Reading*. Chicago: Griggs, 1855.

Sanders, Charles, and Joshua Sanders. *The School Reader, Fifth Book*. New York: Ivison, 1855.

———. *The School Reader, Fourth Book*. New York: Newman, 1852.

Savin, Marion, and Harold Abrahams. "The Young Ladies' Academy of Philadelphia." *History of Education Journal* 8 (1957): 58–67.

Sawicki, Jana. *Disciplining Foucault: Feminism, Power, and the Body*. New York: Routledge, 1991.

Schultz, Lucille. *The Young Composers: Composition's Beginnings in Nineteenth-Century Schools*. Carbondale: Southern Illinois UP, 1999.

Scott, Anne Firor. "What, Then, Is the American: This New Woman?" *Journal of American History* 65 (1978): 679–703.

Scott, Joan Wallach. *Gender and the Politics of History*. 1989. Rev. ed. New York: Columbia UP, 1999.

Scott, William. *Lessons in Elocution*. Montpelier, VT: Walton, 1820.

Selzer, Jack. "Habeas Corpus." *Rhetorical Bodies*. Ed. Selzer and Sharon Crowley. Madison: U of Wisconsin P, 1999. 3–16.

Senex. "Equality of Rights to Woman." Part 7. *Lily* March 1852: 20.

Severance, Caroline. Letter to Elizabeth Cady Stanton. 24 Oct. 1858. Holland and Gordon, microfilm 9, item 132.

Sheridan, Thomas. *A Course of Lectures on Elocution.* 1762. New York: Blom, 1968.

Sigourney, Lydia. *The Girl's Reading-Book: In Prose and Poetry, for Schools.* New York: Taylor, 1838. *Nietz Old Textbook Collection.* Digital Research Lib., U of Pittsburgh. 16 Dec. 2001. <http://digital.library.pitt.edu/cgi-bin/nietz.pl?type=browse>.

Sizer, Theodore. *The Age of the Academies.* New York: Columbia UP, 1964.

Sklar, Kathryn Kish. *Catharine Beecher: A Study in American Domesticity.* New Haven: Yale UP, 1973.

———. "The Schooling of Girls and Changing Community Values in Massachusetts Towns, 1750–1820." *History of Education Quarterly* 33 (1993): 511–42.

Slack, Charles. Letter to Elizabeth Cady Stanton. 2 Sept. 1858. Holland and Gordon, microfilm 9, item 140.

Smith, Nila. *American Reading Instruction.* 1934. Newark, DE: Intl. Reading Assn., 1970.

Solomon, Barbara. *In the Company of Educated Women: A History of Women and Higher Education in America.* New Haven: Yale UP, 1985.

———. "The Oberlin Model and Its Impact on Other Colleges." *Educating Men and Women Together: Coeducation in a Changing World.* Ed. Carol Lasser. Urbana: U of Illinois P, 1987. 81–90.

Stanton, Elizabeth Cady. *Eighty Years and More.* 1898. Boston: Northeastern UP, 1993.

Stanton, Elizabeth Cady, Susan B. Anthony, and Matilda Joslyn Gage, eds. *The History of Woman Suffrage.* Vols. 1–2. Rochester, NY: Mann, 1881.

Stanton, Theodore, and Harriot Stanton Blatch, eds. *Elizabeth Cady Stanton.* Vol. 2. New York: Arno, 1969.

Starr, Harris. "Isabella Beecher Hooker." *Biography Resource Center.* Farmington Hills, MI: Gale, 2001. 6 Feb. 2002. <http://galenet.galegroup.com/servlet/BioRC>.

Stein, Geoffrey. "Antioch's Literary Societies in the 1850s." Thesis. Antioch College, 1965.

Sterling, Dorothy. *Ahead of Her Time: Abby Kelley and the Politics of Anti-Slavery.* New York: Norton, 1991.

Stewart, Donald. "The Nineteenth Century." *The Present State of Scholarship in Historical and Contemporary Rhetoric.* Columbia: U of Missouri P, 1990. 151–85.

Still, William. *The Underground Railroad.* Philadelphia: Porter, 1872.

Stillinger, Jack. *Multiple Authorship and the Myth of Solitary Genius.* Oxford: Oxford UP, 1991.

Sutherland, Christine, and Rebecca Sutcliffe, eds. *The Changing Tradition: Women in the History of Rhetoric.* Calgary, Can.: U of Calgary P, 1999.

Thayer, Caroline. Letter to Elizabeth Cady Stanton. 11 Nov. 1858. Holland and Gordon, microfilm 9, item 141–42.

Titus, Frances. *Narrative of Sojourner Truth.* 1878. Salem, NH: Ayer, 1992.

Tolley, Kim. "The Rise of the Academies: Continuity or Change?" *History of Education Quarterly* 41 (2001): 225–39.

———. "Science for Ladies, Classics for Gentlemen: A Comparative Analysis of Scientific Subjects in the Curricula of Boys' and Girls' Secondary Schools in the United States, 1794–1850." *History of Education Quarterly* 36 (1996): 129–53.

Tonkovich, Nicole. *Domesticity with a Difference: The Nonfiction of Catharine Beecher, Sarah J. Hale, Fanny Fern, and Margaret Fuller.* Jackson: U of Mississippi P, 1997.

Tonn, Mari Boor. "Militant Motherhood: Labor's Mary Harris 'Mother' Jones." *Quarterly Journal of Speech* 82 (1996): 1–21.

Town, Salem, and Nelson Holbrook. *The Progressive Third Reader, for Public and Private Schools*. Boston: Bazin, 1857. *Nietz Old Textbook Collection*. Digital Research Lib., U of Pittsburgh. 16 Dec. 2001. <http://digital.library.pitt.edu/cgi-bin/nietz.pl?type=browse>.

Trimbur, John. "Collaborative Learning and Teaching Writing." *Perspectives on Research and Scholarship in Composition*. Ed. Ben McClelland and Timothy Donovan. New York: MLA, 1985. 87–109.

Vallance, Harvard. "A History of Antioch College." Diss. Ohio State U, 1936.

Venezky, Richard. "A History of the American Reading Textbook." *Elementary School Journal* 87 (1987): 247–65.

Watson, Shevaun. "Complicating the Classics: Neoclassical Rhetorics in Two Early American Schoolbooks." *Rhetoric Society Quarterly* 31 (2001): 45–65.

Webster, Noah. *An American Selection of Lessons in Reading and Speaking*. Rpt. of 1789 ed. New York: Arno, 1974.

Weidner, Heidemarie. "Silks, Congress Gaiters, and Rhetoric: A Butler University Graduate of 1860 Tells Her Story." Hobbs 248–63.

Welter, Barbara. "The Cult of True Womanhood: 1820–1860." *American Quarterly* 18 (1966): 151–74.

Wertheimer, Molly, ed. *Listening to Their Voices: The Rhetorical Activities of Historical Women*. Columbia: U of South Carolina P, 1997.

Wheeler, Leslie, ed. *Loving Warriors: Selected Letters of Lucy Stone and Henry B. Blackwell, 1853 to 1893*. New York: Dial, 1981.

Willard, Emma. *Address to the Public; Particularly to the Members of the Legislature of New York, Proposing a Plan for Improving Female Education*. 1819. *Pioneers of Women's Education in the United States*. Goodsell 45–81.

Willis, Gwendolen, ed. *Olympia Brown: An Autobiography*. Racine, WI: n.p., 1960.

Winegarten, Renee. "Women and Politics: Madame Roland." *New Criterion* 18 (1999). *Biography Resource Center*. Farmington Hills, MI: Gale. 27 Nov. 2001 <http://galenet.galegroup.com/servlet/BioRC>.

Winslow, Hubbard. *Woman as She Should Be*. Boston: Carter, 1838.

Woody, Thomas. *A History of Women's Education in the United States*. Vols. 1–2. New York: Science, 1929.

Wu, Hui. "Historical Studies of Rhetorical Women Here and There: Methodological Challenges to Dominant Interpretive Frameworks." *Rhetoric Society Quarterly* 32 (2002): 81–97.

Yellin, Jean. *Women and Sisters: The Antislavery Feminists in American Culture*. New Haven: Yale UP, 1989.

Zaeske, Susan. "The 'Promiscuous Audience' Controversy and the Emergence of the Early Woman's Rights Movement." *Quarterly Journal of Speech* 81 (1995): 191–207.

———. *Signatures of Citizenship: Petitioning, Antislavery, and Women's Political Identity*. Chapel Hill: U of North Carolina P, 2003.

———. "Unveiling Esther as a Pragmatic Radical Rhetoric." *Philosophy and Rhetoric* 33 (2000): 193–219.

Index

Lindal Buchanan is an assistant professor of communications in the Department of Liberal Studies at Kettering University, where she teaches oral and written communications courses. She has published articles on women's rhetoric, Victorian literature, and linguistics in *Rhetoric Society Quarterly*, *Victorian Poetry*, and the *Southern Journal of Linguistics*. Additionally, she received *Rhetoric Society Quarterly*'s Kneupper Award for the best article of 2002 and was a finalist for the Rhetoric Society of America's 2004 Dissertation Award.

Studies in Rhetorics and Feminisms

Studies in Rhetorics and Feminisms seeks to address the interdisciplinarity that rhetorics and feminisms represent. Rhetorical and feminist scholars want to connect rhetorical inquiry with contemporary academic and social concerns, exploring rhetoric's relevance to current issues of opportunity and diversity. This interdisciplinarity has already begun to transform the rhetorical tradition as we have known it (upper:class, agonistic, public, and male) into regendered, inclusionary rhetorics (democratic, dialogic, collaborative, cultural, and private). Our intellectual advancements depend on such ongoing transformation.

Rhetoric, whether ancient, contemporary, or futuristic, always inscribes the relation of language and power at a particular moment, indicating who may speak, who may listen, and what can be said. The only way we can displace the traditional rhetoric of masculine:only, public performance is to replace it with rhetorics that are recognized as being better suited to our present needs. We must understand more fully the rhetorics of the non-Western tradition, of women, of a variety of cultural and ethnic groups. Therefore, Studies in Rhetorics and Feminisms espouses a theoretical position of openness and expansion, a place for rhetorics to grow and thrive in a symbiotic relationship with all that feminisms have to offer, particularly when these two fields intersect with philosophical, sociological, religious, psychological, pedagogical, and literary issues.

The series seeks scholarly works that both examine and extend rhetoric, works that span the sexes, disciplines, cultures, ethnicities, and sociocultural practices as they intersect with the rhetorical tradition. After all, the recent resurgence of rhetorical studies has not so much been a discovery of new rhetorics; it has been more a recognition of existing rhetorical activities and practices, of our newfound ability and willingness to listen to previously untold stories.

The series editors seek both high-quality traditional and cutting-edge scholarly work that extends the significant relationship between rhetoric and feminism within various genres, cultural contexts, historical periods, methodologies, theoretical positions, and methods of delivery (e.g., film and hypertext to elocution and preaching).

Queries and submissions:
Professor Cheryl Glenn, Editor
   E:mail: cjg6@psu.edu
Professor Shirley Wilson Logan, Editor
   E:mail: Shirley_W_Logan@umail.umd.edu

Studies in Rhetorics and Feminisms
Department of English
142 South Burrowes Bldg.
Penn State University
University Park, PA 16802-6200